The South Irish Horse
in the Great War

Cartoon of South Irish Horse Officer dressed circa 1908 by Adrian Wynne-Morgan.

The South Irish Horse in the Great War

Loos, Somme 1916 & 1918, Albert 1916,
St Quentin, Rosières, Avre, Ypres 1918,
Courtrai, France and Flanders 1915–1918

A Brief History

Mark Perry

Pen & Sword
MILITARY

First published in Great Britain in 2018
by Pen & Sword Military
An imprint of Pen & Sword Books Limited
47 Church Street
Barnsley
South Yorkshire
S70 2AS

ISBN 978 1 52673 695 6

Typeset in Ehrhardt
by Mac Style

Printed and bound in the UK
by TJ International Ltd, Padstow, Cornwall

Pen & Sword Books Limited incorporates the imprints of Atlas,
Archaeology, Aviation, Discovery, Family History, Fiction, History,
Maritime, Military, Military Classics, Politics, Select, Transport,
True Crime, Air World, Frontline Publishing, Leo Cooper,
Remember When, Seaforth Publishing, The Praetorian Press,
Wharncliffe Local History, Wharncliffe Transport,
Wharncliffe True Crime and White Owl.

For a complete list of Pen & Sword titles please contact
PEN & SWORD BOOKS LIMITED
47 Church Street, Barnsley, South Yorkshire, S70 2AS, England
E-mail: enquiries@pen-and-sword.co.uk
Website: www. pen-and-sword.co.uk

Contents

List of Illustrations

Acknowledgements

I would like to take this opportunity to thank the many people who have assisted me throughout this project. It would be safe to say that without their assistance this book would never have been completed.

To the Marquis and Marchioness of Waterford for their time, for allowing me to research the 6th Marquis of Waterford's papers and the use of various photos throughout the book, without which I could not have hoped to fill in the many 'blanks' and for kindly agreeing to produce a foreword for the book.

To Julian Walton and Marianna Lorenc for facilitating my research at Curraghmore House.

To the late Patsy Gregan for all his kindness and support during my research.

To Marcus de la Poer Beresford, 7th Baron Decies, for his time and direction relating to the 5th Baron Decies and for agreeing to provide a foreword to this book.

To Mr Billy (William) Good for all his help and assistance and for his kind permission for the use of his father's extensive photographic collection.

To Adrian Wynn-Morgan for the use of the Caricature.

To Mark Ayling for the sketch of the Regimental crest.

To Peter and Patricia Jeffares, who provided the background and memories of Trooper John Honner.

To the Jestin family, who provided me with coffee, biscuits and an insight into the Jestin brothers, and who kindly gave me permission to use their photographs.

To Jack and Barbara O'Connell of Schull Books, who encouraged me to complete this work.

To Jean Prendergast, who has fed me snippets and press cuttings relating to the men of Cork and the South Irish Horse throughout the past three or so years.

To Rosemary Walsh and her family for the introductions, time, information and pictures.

To the Rice Family for their kind provision of a treasured family photograph.

To Tom Burnell for help, assistance and his *War Dead* database.

To Sally Tyas and the Tickhill History Society for their work on my behalf.

To the National Library of Ireland for Trooper Allen's diaries.

To Mr Ken Tucker for allowing me access to his father's service records.

To Mr Bryan Love for his help and assistance with Thomas Fletcher and for the use of family photographs and letters.

To Ms Kathy Davis for the use of the photo of Samuel Leahy's grave.

To the staff at the National Archives, Kew.

To the staff at Carlow Military Museum.

To the staff of Tipperary County Museum for their help in retrieving photos and their permission for me to use them.

To Ms Sally Finn-Kelcey for her help, not only in producing this book, but also her papers relating to George McDonald, her grandfather, sight of which filled in many blanks.

To Henry Wilson and Matt Jones and all the editorial staff at Pen and Sword Books, thank you for taking on this subject.

To my editor, Richard Doherty, for all his time, help and support.

To my great friend Canon Mark Hayden, who accompanied me to France and Flanders, for all his help throughout this project, at times being more proactive than me, for his introductions and contacts and, above all, his support and advice.

To my parents Keith and Judy for their editing and support.

To my wife and family. To Majella for your love and constant encouragement even when I was doubting the project, for giving me the time and support to complete the book and just for being there. To my children, thank you for all your love and patience during this time.

Every effort has been made to ensure that no copyright infringements have occurred, but should anyone feel that they have not been acknowledged they should contact the publisher and future editions will be amended.

Foreword

By the Marquis of Waterford

It has been over 100 years since my great-grandfather, Henry de la Poer Beresford, 6th Marquis of Waterford KP, was asked to raise the South of Ireland Imperial Yeomanry (SIIY) by the then Commander-in-Chief, Ireland, His Royal Highness the Duke of Connaught. A former officer in the Royal Horse Guards, a keen and skilled horseman, the Marquis was the perfect choice to head the first yeomanry regiment to be raised in Ireland since the last yeomanry was disbanded in 1834. Both he and the Marchioness used all their personal influence and persuasion to ensure that this new yeomanry regiment would represent its individuality and true 'Irishness' through both the uniform and the membership. The early years of the SIIY saw them grow from two squadrons in 1903 to four almost fully subscribed squadrons in 1908. When the regiment was reorganized and renamed the South Irish Horse, the Marquis strongly fought for his regiment to retain its individuality and become a special reserve of cavalry regiment, in its own right. His determination to ensure that the South Irish Horse kept its distinctive green uniform, status and Irishness, against the desires of the War Office, is a testament to his commitment to the regiment. The sad and sudden death of the Marquis in December 1911 was a great blow to the regiment and, of course, my family. However, the time he had spent putting in place a strong cadre of officers and non-commissioned officers, together with excellent training of the men, gave the regiment a strong foundation on which to continue to thrive after his passing.

My great-grandfather never saw the regiment in action, but had he survived, I believe he would have made sure they acted with the same selflessness and distinction that they, in fact, did during the Great War. I am pleased to see that a history of the regiment has finally been produced and that its memory will have at last been recognized.

Henry Nicholas de la Poer Beresford
9th Marquis of Waterford
July 2018

Foreword

By the Lord Decies

Dozens of Irish regiments have served the British Crown over the last 500 years, from the mediaeval gallowglass through the regiment of Manus O'Cahan which served Charles I, to those forces raised by James II, William III and their successors in the eighteenth and nineteenth centuries. Many of those regiments have had long and illustrious careers. Others, such as the South Irish Horse (initially the South of Ireland Imperial Yeomanry), existed only briefly, allowing them to prove their mettle in the First World War, before being disbanded as part of the peace process in Ireland in 1922.

The de la Poer Beresford family were intricately involved in the South Irish Horse from its inception in 1902 with John Graham Hope de la Poer Beresford (5th Lord Decies) serving as Lieutenant Colonel of the Regiment, in succession to his cousin (Henry de la Poer) the Marquis of Waterford, from 1912 until 1917. Mark Perry has achieved a notable success in pulling together the history of this largely forgotten Irish regiment with text and photographs of outstanding interest.

Marcus de la Poer Beresford
7th Lord Decies
August 2018

Introduction

My interest in the First World War stems from a picture and the campaign medals of my great grandfather George Edgar Perry. Unfortunately, I know very little about his time in the Army as his service records were destroyed during the blitz in the Second World War. What is more frustrating is that the records of both his older brothers, Frances and Frederick, who also served with the Gloucestershire Regiment and were involved in the First World War, survived. (Frances coincidently also served in the Middle East whilst Frederick was posted to a training battalion and remained in the UK.) As I was leafing through a paperback version of T.E. Lawrence's *Seven Pillars of Wisdom*, there, staring back at me, was a photograph of Sergeant G.E. Perry AVC holding Lawrence's camel and foal. This and another photograph of the event are now held in the Imperial War Museum archives and, along with one or two other items, that is all we have of him. From this very limited information and the census records, I have been able to establish a somewhat sketchy picture of his life.

Born in Bristol, he enlisted at the age of eighteen in the 1st Battalion Gloucestershire Regiment and was a veteran of the Boer War. His first term of service ended in 1901 when he returned from South Africa. He married in the same year and immediately re-enlisted with the 1st Dragoon Guards. He was later posted to India, where my grandfather was born. Following his second discharge, he ran a small successful haulage firm in Marlborough. With the outbreak of the First World War in August 1914 (as with most former soldiers) he was drawn to the colours once more. He joined up first with the Rifle Brigade, was promoted to sergeant and transferred to the Army Veterinary Corps (AVC), serving in Palestine and Egypt. He was Mentioned in Despatches on 5 June 1919.

My interest in the South Irish Horse began when I came across a memorial in the grounds of my local Church of Ireland church. The headstone was dedicated to the remembrance of George Gerald Pasley, aged 19, and to his brother John Vincent Pasley, aged 22. George, a lieutenant in the Royal Flying Corps, had died learning to fly at Upavon on 19 December 1917 and

John, a corporal, South Irish Horse, attached Traffic Control, had died of pneumonia in Cologne on 5 March 1919. They were the only two sons of George and Margaret Pasley, owners of the local bakery.

I had never heard of the South Irish Horse but a brief internet search drew me to www.southirishhorse.com, a website, run by Doug and Hugh Vaugh, which had information on the regiment and its members. This piqued my interest more and I searched, unsuccessfully, for a more detailed regimental history. I did, however, find two articles written for the *Irish Sword*[1] outlining the regiment's involvement in the First World War and also the uniforms pre-1914, but nothing really about the men who served and the relationship of the regiment with Irish society before the war and after its disbandment. Around about the same time, a book called the *Wicklow War Dead* was published. This book listed every man who had died during the war from the county of Wicklow. In it I found not only John Vincent Pasley but also John Gregan, another 'local' member of the South Irish Horse. I therefore decided to see if I could track down any relatives of John Gregan and was very lucky to come across Patsy Gregan, who still lived in Coolboy, John's village. Patsy was able to give me not only photos of John, but his background and story. Sadly, Patsy passed away before I could finish this book. All this led me to decide to continue my research and try and investigate the regiment and its members, in more detail.

Due to the very nature of this research spanning a time period of one hundred years or so ago, sources are somewhat scarce. For instance, personal diaries, letters and first-hand accounts of what it was like to be in the Regiment and, just as importantly, what happened before, during and after the First World War, are either missing or forgotten. I have therefore had to rely heavily on press reports and the incomplete war diaries of the various squadrons as they arrived in theatre. I have also accessed the divisional diaries where possible. I make no excuse for reproducing various press reports throughout this book, where the information contained is detailed and expressive in order to paint this generalized picture of the life and successes of the Regiment.

This book does not purport to be an official history, far from it. It is an outline, or a rough timeline of events relating to the South Irish Horse. It therefore leaves itself open to revision and expansion when and where additional information comes to light. I am not a professional, or even an amateur historian, merely someone who has a great respect for these men and wishes only to tell their story, however poorly. It is my hope that in writing this it will encourage a discussion of the Regiment and hopefully serve as a starting point for those families researching their relatives in the South Irish Horse.

Words to Accompany The Regimental March of The South Irish Horse

Let Erin improve on the days of old,
When her faithful sons shall aid her,
Now her horsemen wear the Shamrock of old,
As they wait for the bold invader,
Waterford with Standard of Erin furl'd,
Leads the Green Clad Knights to danger;
While the rifled lead by his horsemen hurl'd,
Has pierced to the hea(r)t of the stranger.
On the Curragh's plain,
As the South man guards,
When the clear
Cold night's declining,
He sees our hero's and Erin's bard,
As the stars above him shining
Thus shall the SIH in strife to come,
Take part in war, to its glory,
And dying in the fight, for Britain's right
Shall live in Ireland's story.

Samuel Bradford

The South Irish Horse

Come On! Come On!
Gallop along,
With Horses in which we take pride;
We're Off! We're Off!
They may scoff.
But we are the men who can ride.

Don't Tarry! Don't Tarry!
For we can carry
The Gun, that's able to work;
A Spy! A Spy!
Oh, what care I,
We shall banish the German and Turk.

Pauline Mary St Lawrence-Burke

(Part of a series of locally produced poem postcards written by Pauline St Lawrence-Burke to help raise funds for the war effort)

Commanding Officers of the South of Ireland Imperial Yeomanry 1902–1908 and South Irish Horse 1908–1922

Honorary Colonel
Field Marshal HRH Arthur Duke of Connaught and Strathearn KG KT KP GCB GCMG GCIE GCVO, Colonel Grenadier Guards and Army Service Corps and Colonel-in-Chief 6th Dragoon Guards, Highland Light Infantry, Royal Dublin Fusiliers and The Rifle Brigade, Personal ADC to the King.

Lieutenant Colonel
South of Ireland Imperial Yeomanry 1902–1908
South Irish Horse 1908–1911
Lieutenant Colonel Henry de la Poer Beresford, 6th Marquis of Waterford KP.

Lieutenant Colonel 1912–1915
Lieutenant Colonel John Graham Hope de la Poer Beresford 5th Baron Decies DSO.

Lieutenant Colonel 1915–1917
(Temporary) Lieutenant Colonel the Earl of Wicklow

Lieutenant Colonel 1917–1922
Lieutenant Colonel Isaac William Burns-Lindow DSO.

Chapter 1

Beginnings – Pre-War Activity

On 12 June 1922 King George V received the Colours of five of the six disbanded Irish regiments into his care at Windsor Castle. The regiments were the Royal Irish Regiment, Connaught Rangers, Prince of Wales's Leinster Regiment (Royal Canadians), Royal Munster Fusiliers and Royal Dublin Fusiliers. The South Irish Horse, however, did not have Colours and instead presented a plaque to the King.[1]

This presentation marked the end of the southern Irish regiments, following the independence of the Irish Free State in 1922. For the majority of these regiments, the association with the British Army was long and very distinguished with thousands of Irishmen joining the Colours for a variety of reasons, escape from poverty, the law, their families, or just for adventure. However, the South Irish Horse was only in existence for twenty years. As a Special Reserve cavalry regiment, its ranks were not filled with the common peasantry and dregs of society, but with the sons of farmers (both Catholic and Protestant), young bucks out for a bit of adventure for a few weeks in the summer and a spot of hunting, and even a sprinkling of the aristocracy (a marquis, an earl and a lord). This short-lived regiment even had its own Regimental Band, frequently heard at the Royal Horticultural Society of Ireland's annual meeting in Dublin, or at a social tea party in the suburbs of the city, or in the bandstand in Kingstown.[2]

Yet, with all the influential young, and old, gentlemen on the muster list, very little is known, or has been written about the Regiment. Its sister regiment, the North Irish Horse (formed at the same time, with a similar membership), was reformed following the Independence of the Irish Free State and went on to serve with distinction in the Second World War. What happened to this Regiment and why did it 'disappear' from the histories of the Irish regiments?

The South Irish Horse was formed in 1902 as the South of Ireland Imperial Yeomanry, yet it had its roots in the Anglo Boer war of 1899–1902.

As a result of the proposals by Lord Chesham and other Yeomanry officers in October 1899, the existing standing home-based Yeomanry units in Britain (England, Scotland and Wales) were asked to provide service units of approximately 121 men each from their ranks to supplement the British forces in South Africa. The existing Yeomanry units were restricted to serving as part of the home forces. The recruitment of young men extended to Ireland as well. These overseas yeomanry companies (Imperial Yeomanry) were formed around localized areas of recruitment, for instance Belfast, (60th Company) and Dublin (74th Company, 61st Company) and usually sponsored by wealthy landowners and peers.

Although a number of recruits to the Imperial Yeomanry (IY) were 'trained', a great deal of the men were untrained in a military sense and, as a result, not used to the discipline needed for active operations. This led to a number of embarrassing defeats for the IY at the hands of the Boers.[3]

Unlike Britain, there was no Yeomanry in Ireland. Law and order was provided by the Royal Irish Constabulary and the Dublin Metropolitan Police. Only the Royal Irish Constabulary was armed.

In the late 1700s, perceived aggression from revolutionaries in France and at home prompted the formation of an armed (and loyal) Militia to protect the country against invasion, the regular army being deployed to fight the French. The Irish Yeomanry were raised as a number of local units in 1796 to do just that. Local landowners paid for and often commanded this militia. It was during the 1798 Rebellion, that the true brutality of the Yeomanry came to the fore, with catastrophic results on all sides. In the following years, the Yeomanry was called upon to police and put down riots, chase cattle rustlers and any other policing duties required by their sponsors. However, with the introduction of a formal police force in 1814 by then Chief Secretary of Ireland (1812–1818) Robert Peel (the Peace Preservation Force) and later, the Irish Constabulary (Ireland) Act 1836 to form the Irish Constabulary, the need for Yeomanry was reduced. The last Yeomanry unit was disbanded in 1834.[4] 'Yeomanry' and 'Ireland' are two words that would raise the hackles of any independent minded Irishman, whether Catholic or Protestant. With a reputation for brutality and apparent disregard for the law, why on earth would any sane person suggest that a Yeomanry regiment be raised in Ireland?

Sane or not, there had been talk for some time within the Irish Establishment during the late 1890s regarding re-instigating standing Yeomanry regiments on the island of Ireland. A letter dated 22 December 1900 from the (then) Hon. John Graham Beresford, Aide-de-Camp to the Commander in Chief in Ireland, HRH Field Marshal, The Duke of Connaught,[5] broached the subject of raising a yeomanry regiment with the Marquis of Waterford. Beresford discussed the possibility of raising two regiments, one from the south, the other from the north. He highlighted the problems relating specifically to religion in recruiting members, 'Romans might object to joining with Protestants or the Nationalists and Patriots might try and stop recruiting'. He was somewhat cynical as to who should drive the project, not trusting the War Office to be able take into account the 'Irishness' of the situation they would face. He intimated that pay and serving conditions would be the same as the 'English Yeomanry' and that the dress would be khaki. (Little did the Hon. J.G.H.H. de la Poer Beresford know at that time, he was to command the regiment in 1912, as Lieutenant Colonel 5th Baron Decies DSO on the death of his cousin the Marquis of Waterford.) So it was, with some trepidation, that plans were made to form two Yeomanry regiments, one for the southern part of Ireland and another for the more northern (and unionist) part of Ireland (Militia and Yeomanry Act 1901). The King, Edward VII, officially approved the raising of the North of Ireland Imperial Yeomanry (NIIY) and the South of Ireland Imperial Yeomanry (SIIY) on 20 December 1901, the approval being gazetted on 7 January 1902.[6]

On 4 February 1902, HRH The Duke of Connaught called on the Marquis of Waterford (Henry de la Poer Beresford) to form the southern contingent and the Earl of Shaftsbury (Anthony Ashley Cooper) to raise a northern contingent. The Marquis was duly appointed Lieutenant Colonel on 10 February 1902.[7] He was, however, at pains to stress that he would only consider taking the commission if he could see active service. It was left up to the Marquis of Waterford to arrange, recruit and raise the new regiment himself. The regiment was to comprise four squadrons of mounted yeomanry, No. 1 Squadron, in Kildare (the Curragh), No. 2 Squadron-Limerick, No. 3 Squadron-Fermoy and No. 4 Squadron in Athlone.[8] He immediately canvassed his friends and associates for names of prospective members and set about contacting them with a view to joining. He also sought the appointment of an adjutant and was very keen to secure the services of Captain Isaac Burns-Lindow (then of the 8th (King's Royal Irish) Hussars), whose appointment was confirmed on 12 March 1902.[9]

The war in South Africa was still underway and the Marquis of Waterford was offered the command of a squadron of Scottish Horse in the 37th Imperial Yeomanry by the newly-promoted Lieutenant Colonel the Honourable John Graham Beresford on 10 March 1902. He left for South Africa on 27 May 1902. The conditions of surrender between Britain and the Boer nation were signed on 31 May 1902, whilst the Marquis was at sea. He arrived in South Africa and commenced training there, but never saw the active service he was hoping for.[10]

Between the time he was appointed Lieutenant Colonel of the SIIY and his departure to South Africa, the Marquis worked tirelessly recruiting people to help and to join the newly formed Yeomanry. The response was good, but the time that the Marquis had to concentrate on the formation of the regiment was limited. He therefore decided to only raise two squadrons, Limerick and Kildare, not the four he had initially anticipated. The other two were to be formed the following year when he returned from South Africa. When he departed for South Africa, a large amount of this work fell to his wife, Lady Beatrix Frances Beresford. In a letter to Lady Beresford, he wrote

Mind you do all you can about getting the green uniform for the SIIY. They have not given one concession although it is the most difficult Yeomanry to make a success of in the whole Kingdom.[11]

How this new Yeomanry looked was just as important as how it was to be formed. In a letter to the King, Lady Waterford made the point that khaki was definitely not a popular colour in the 'south' and that the green tunic would be far more acceptable. She also highlighted the difficulties in forming a yeomanry unit in Ireland as opposed the rest of the United Kingdom.[12] The establishment and War Office baulked at a Yeomanry regiment having 'fancy' uniforms, Lady Waterford pointed out that the English Yeoman wanted a fancy uniform for smartness, and to look respectable in front of his friends and neighbours. The Irish Yeoman though, would face considerable 'derision on the part of his neighbour' especially if he had to wear the khaki as prescribed by the War Office. It was therefore imperative that his uniform be distinctive and above all 'Irish' in its look.[13] A great deal of thought was put into the style and colour of the uniform by all those involved and the result was the green tunic with light khaki breeches. The green was adopted by both the North and South Yeomanry units, with the NIIY having a white horizontal collar and the SIIY a red one. The persistent pressure by both the Marquis and his wife, using all their family connections and influence over a period of time, was fruitful and the uniform was accepted.[14]

One further obstacle remained in the formation of the NIIY and SIIY, namely, the law. Following the disbandment of the Yeomanry in 1834, it was not permitted to form a home-based Yeomanry unit in Ireland. The Marquis of Waterford was faced with forming a Yeomanry unit without legal backing, writing to his wife:

> Do try and get your father to agitate about the Irish Yeomanry being made legal, it merely wants a short Act of Parliament for this purpose and it seems a thousand pities to risk the success of what I am doing now in an important thing for Irish loyalty, on account of a mere technicality.[15]

Lady Waterford, writing to St John Brodrick, the Secretary of State for War (1901–1903), asked when the new Act was to be presented to Parliament as its delay was causing considerable consternation and disillusionment among the officers and men of the regiment who had already signed up. She also expressed her concern that the Irish Nationalists may use the delay to stir up any potential opposition to the formation of the yeomanry.[16]

Hansard (the official record of all speeches made in the Houses of Parliament) records an exchange between Richard Haldane, the Secretary of State for War (1905–1912), and Mr John Mooney MP (Irish Parliamentary Party):

> Mr Mooney asked the Secretary of State for War if he can state by what authority the body described in the Army List as Special Reserve, Irish Horse, has been raised and maintained; if by statute, what statute; and on what Army Vote are the charges for this body borne?
>
> **Mr Haldane** This body was raised and is maintained under the Militia and Yeomanry Acts, 1901 and 1902, Part III of the Territorial

and Reserve Forces Act, 1907, and the Reserve Forces Act, 1882, and subsequent amending Acts. The charges for it are borne on Vote 3.[17]

Late in 1902 the Marquis of Waterford returned from South Africa, suffering from jaundice and malaria, to convalesce. During this period, he managed to further organize the newly-formed regiment, so that when King Edward VII and Queen Alexandra visited Ireland in July 1903 the Regiment was able to attend in uniform. Field Marshal HRH Prince Arthur, Duke of Connaught and Strathearn KG KT KP GCB GCMG GCIE GCVO, Colonel of the Grenadier Guards and Army Service Corps and Colonel-in-Chief of the 6th Dragoons, Highland Light Infantry, Royal Dublin Fusiliers, and the Rifle Brigade, Personal ADC to the King, was appointed Honorary Colonel of the Regiment. Other officers appointed were Colonel St Leger Moore (second in command), Sir Kildare Borrowes (OC Kildare Squadron), Major Wise (OC Limerick Squadron) and Major Villiers Stuart (OC Cork Squadron). The Marquis of Waterford's wife wrote in her diary:

> On July 21st 1903 King Edward and Queen Alexandra paid their first visit to Ireland.... T's (Tyrone) Yeomanry were on duty for the first time that day and they looked extremely neat, smart in their khaki breeches and gaiters, the much discussed green tunics and green caps. I believe they were the first regiment to have these caps of the staff pattern ... they all had khaki waterproof covers for them, which was an idea of T's both to preserve the cap in bad weather and to make them match when the khaki breeches were worn. T took 10 of his officers in the Levee on the 22nd and I heard that they made a very good impression in the all green uniform worn by officers only.... There was some agitation in Royal circles because the SIY had no full dress headgear....The Northern Yeomanry had a headdress and such an affair it was: a kind of Bersaglieri hat with a nodding plume so that the regiment was described somewhere as 'them of the cocks plumes' and our Southerners called them 'The Barn Doors'! and I regret to say once plucked one of them![18]

With the recruiting area for the Regiment predominantly in the southern part of the country, the Regimental Headquarters was based at the Artillery Barracks in Musgrave Street, Limerick. It was always the intention that the location of the four squadrons reflect the interest of joining the regiment in that particular area. It became clear that the recruitment from Dublin far outweighed the recruitment from the Athlone area and so two Dublin squadrons were formed to replace the Athlone squadron. (See Appendix I for a snapshot of the strength of the Regiment circa 1905).

In August the Regiment had its first annual camp at the Curragh. The Curragh, Kildare, was the principal cavalry training area and barracks for the British Army stationed in Ireland at the time. The Marquis of Waterford was initially only going to field two squadrons for training, Limerick and Kildare squadrons, as he felt that the limited time he had to raise the regiment was insufficient at this time to provide any more men to fill the remaining two squadrons. However, it appears he managed to field three squadrons, the third being the Cork contingent under the command of Captain H Villiers-Stuart. The camp was to run from Friday 31 July to Saturday 15 August 1903, a period of sixteen days.

An article dated Wednesday 19 August 1903 appeared in the *Irish Times* reporting on the camp. After describing the green tunics and general dress of the regiment, the correspondent highlighted the very problem that the Marquis of Waterford had been so conscious of when initially designing the uniforms:

> The appearance in our streets of a regiment of mounted soldiers, clad in green uniforms and wearing on their green caps and tunics large shamrock leaves worked in gold, is an event of more significance in the political relations of Great Britain and Ireland than at first sight might be grasped by the casual observer. For years we have read of punishment being inflicted upon private soldiers in the British Army for the offence of wearing the shamrock on St Patrick's Day, and as to a green uniform and the colour of green generally, it was the emblem of rebellion, or, at least of disloyalty to the British Throne.

He went on to describe the procession of men and horses on their way back to the barracks:

> On Saturday last, they saw the green clad boys of the South of Ireland Imperial Yeomanry ride through the streets of Dublin, while they led the horses of the Limerick, Cork and Waterford squadrons [*there*

was no Waterford squadron, the reporter may have mistaken the Kildare squadron for the 'Waterford' one], which had returned, by train, to their destinations.

Later, he said:

> The officers are representatives of the best families in the South of Ireland. Most of them have already seen service in the cavalry of the line. The NCOs are, in their own way, little less distinguished. For instance, the Sergeant Major is a well-known Government official ... The other sergeants and corporals have earned their positions by long and gallant services in the South African war ... The Yeomanry Trooper is a very different being ... for the most part, gentlemen by birth and education, and apparently the effect of the few who would not come under the definition of gentlemen, of mixing of the many who do, is to level up to that indefinable, but easily recognized, standard ... The names of the different troops at once say where the men have come from. There is the Trinity College Company.... Then there are the Civil Service, the Limerick, the Cork and the Dublin Troops.[19]

Major General Baden Powell, recently appointed Inspector General of Cavalry, was in Ireland and took the opportunity to inspect the SIIY at their camp. He was suitably impressed by their progress in carrying out various cavalry evolutions and riding skill. He said, 'considering that they had only been 13 days in training he thought they had attained to a very considerable standard of efficiency indeed.'[20]

During the period of the camp there were other distinguished visitors who were treated to various exhibition of skills learnt. A sports day was held at the end of the camp with many mounted and dismounted events and games.[21]

One of the many headaches facing the Marquis of Waterford and his permanent staff was the procurement of horses for the training camps. This year, and so eloquently reported by the *Irish Times*, the Dublin (Kildare) squadron was ordered to return the regiment's borrowed remounts to Beggars Bush Barracks in Dublin. For whatever reason the horses were shoeless. Instead of using the railway to transport them, they were marched from the Curragh to Dublin. As a result, they arrived much the worse for wear. Luckily, the correspondent for the *Irish Times* was more concerned about the look of the men than the state of the horses. It would not have boded well for the newest yeomanry regiment to be wrongly accused of having little or no regard for the welfare of the mounts. Through no fault of his own, the Marquis was left with a large bill to pay for the damage suffered by the horses.[22]

With the scarcity of horses, a very welcome visitor to the camp was John Honner, a farmer's son. John, aged 21 at the time and a native of Mountrath, County Laois, had come to the camp with his cousin John Corcoran to sell horses to the Army. They found that if they enlisted, instead of being paid £14 for a 4 or 5-year old, they would be paid £150 per horse by the officers. So, naturally, they both enlisted on the spot. Unfortunately, as John's cousin wasn't quite the minimum required age of 21, his parents successfully managed have his enlistment revoked. John, now No. 224 Trooper, was assigned to B Squadron, Limerick. Throughout this period, up until 1913, both he and his cousin continued to sell horses to the Army.[23]

The raising of a new regiment is costly. As the Marquis of Waterford was given the responsibility of raising the regiment himself, it fell to him and the senior members to help finance the new uniforms, hire of horses, the setting up of the various squadron headquarters and other such items as required but not supplied by the War Office. After much discussion, it was decided that a loan of £2,500 (worth almost £300,000 at date of publication) be secured. For example, the typical cost of an officers' uniform was £44 9s 6d (worth approximately £3,800 at date of publication) and the ORs uniform approximately £6 per recruit (worth approximately £510 at date of publication).[24]

1904 was a full and busy year for the regiment. It started with the dates of the annual camp being announced, 13–30 June, again at the Curragh Camp. The regiment were to field four squadrons A, B C and D, not the three squadrons of the previous year. Dr MacCabe, the regiment's medical officer, started the year by procuring the services of a 'regimental band' under the leadership of Bandmaster C F Allen. Allen had previously served with the Royal Middlesex Yeomanry, Honourable Artillery Company and as Bandmaster for the Harrow Rifles. The cost to the regiment was £150 plus regimental pay (worth approximately £8,600 at date of publication) for the seventeen band members.[25]

In March 1904 the regiment held what would become an annual event throughout the pre-war years and up until the early 1940s – the St Patrick's Day Dinner and Dance. This event was viewed by many as the 'must go to' dinner and pretty much every year the newspapers provided comprehensive coverage on who was there and what was said. Second Lieutenant Lionel Lloyd Hewson (Hon. Captain) was awarded the Royal Victorian Order 5th Class (MVO) on 14 May 1904, following his command of the Royal Escort provided by the SIIY for King Edward VII's visit to Waterford on 2 May.[26] Just prior to the annual camp, a party of eight members of the Limerick Company SIIY competed in a shooting match with the 4th Bn Leinster Regiment. The Limerick Company managed a total of 283; however, the Leinsters finished with 333 points.

The nineteen-day annual camp commenced on 13 June.[27] The two Dublin companies left Beggars Bush Barracks with (the now) Major Burns-Lindow, accompanied by the regimental band. Their total complement stood at 200. It was reported that the regiment now had a total of 430 men with an additional squadron having been raised (from the Trinity College Dublin contingent commanded by Burns-Lindow). The papers also reported that 'there is a great improvement since last year in that moral which distinguishes a crack regiment, and that the South of Ireland Imperial Yeomanry bids fair to earn that name.'

The other two squadrons B (Limerick) and C (Cork) arrived at Kildare station having entrained from their depots. Two and a half weeks of intensive training was undertaken, ending with a series of manoeuvres and inspections by the Commander of the Forces, Lord Grenfell, Major General Morton, commanding 7th Division (Ireland) and Brigadier General Michael Rimington commanding 3 Cavalry Brigade. Following the initial inspection by Lord Grenfell, the regiment was tested in various aspects of Yeomanry drill by squadron and in the afternoon a series of outpost schemes and skirmishes with the 19th Hussars as opponents.[28]

Lady Waterford stated in her diary that:

They had improved a great deal since the last training and were really becoming quite a fine regiment, and although T always lamented the shortness of the Training and the want of compulsion in discipline, he was really very proud of them.

Not only was Dr MacCabe interested in the spiritual (musical) wellbeing of the men, but he was also, naturally, interested in their physical wellbeing. He had noticed that although the men showed a great deal of enthusiasm for physical exercise during the previous two training camps, it was not obvious whether this could be maintained throughout the year. He proposed that this could be met through participation in sports, such as football and hockey. This idea was met with great enthusiasm and plans were put in place to form an official sports club. In order to have a sports club it was necessary to have some sort of permanent base, or club house, and so the idea of the South of Ireland Yeomanry Club was formed. On 8 October 1904, the preliminary meeting of the club was held under the chairmanship of Dr MacCabe. It was agreed that premises be sought in Dublin to house the club and how this would be paid for. Subscriptions and membership rules were also agreed. The club would thereafter be known as 'The South of Ireland Yeomanry Club'. Although premises were to be leased at 22 Harcourt Street Dublin, it appears that this fell through and premises were found and leased at 3 St Stephens Green, Dublin.[29]

The new year of 1905 started with the news of the death of Edward Brownell, 23, from 25 Botanic Road, Glasnevin, a member of the Regiment who worked in the Audit office of III Army Corps as part of the Civil Service. He was a popular member of the regiment and a number of his colleagues attended the funeral.[30]

In early March it was announced that the annual camp would be at No.3 camp, the Curragh. This year they were to be joined for part of the time by the NIIY, who were stationed at No.1 camp. The second annual St Patrick's dinner took place in the Gresham Hotel, Dublin, with over 200 guests. Among these were the Marquis of Waterford, Lieutenant Colonel St Leger Moore CB, The Knight of Glin, Dr F.F. MacCabe and Sir Arthur Vicars KCVO, Ulster King-of-Arms. During the dinner it was noted that a football match had been played between the sister regiments with the SIIY winning the game. Also mentioned was a future point-to-point meeting between the two regiments. A competition to design a headdress for the regiment was launched.[31] A great deal of time and effort was put into designing a new form of headdress for the regiment, but alas, nothing was ever agreed. (When the by then, Lieutenant Colonel Burns-Lindow attended a Levée at Windsor Castle in 1935, he was photographed wearing a shako, not too dissimilar to a design mooted in 1905, but never officially approved.)

The availability of horses for training was again highlighted this year when members of the Dublin squadron bemoaned the lack of horses for mounted training during the year. It became so bad that the attendance at Beggars Bush Barracks for out-of-camp training fell from 100 to a dozen or so in a very short time.[32]

The annual camp began in June for nineteen days, finishing on 15 July. There is no reportage of the camp for this year. Even with the 'Barndoors' (NIIY) in attendance for some of the camp, no events were noted by Lady Waterford, with the exception of the departure of the NIIY. Due to the high turnover of officers and influx of new men, the Marquis of Waterford spent most of his time training with the regiment.

For the following two years, the format remained the same: St Patrick's Day Dinner and Dance followed by nineteen days at camp in June/July. Camp life continued to concentrate on riding, manoeuvres, and close order drills. Each camp was concluded with a day of competition, both mounted and dismounted and field sports.

During this time, the regiment started to build a true *esprit de corps*, with the club's premises at 3 St Stephen's Green, Dublin, encouraging club activities, both sporting and military, having a privately published gazette and various classes of membership subscriptions (maximum of £1 1s per year). The gazette detailed all important events throughout the year, together with articles deemed useful to club members, such as horses and horsemanship. It included detailed descriptions of annual camps, manoeuvres at the Curragh and regimental sports days. Competitions such as shooting, inter troop challenges and inter regiment competitions were reported. The 1906 gazette also carried the names of all members of the regiment and their squadron. One thing the editor of the gazette complained about was the lack of information and articles submitted by the squadrons outside Dublin! Social events appeared to be very much in the fore. There were several sporting events and various teams raised through the club and competing. The regiment's hockey team competed throughout the pre-war years, although not very successfully![33]

Around the same time in London, a major and wide-ranging reform of the Army was being discussed by ministers and government officials. The driving force behind this was the then Secretary of State for War, Sir Richard Haldane. One of these reforms was the reorganization of the Yeomanry and

Militia units into a new Territorial Army and Special Reserve. These reforms were finalized and formed the basis of the Territorial and Reserve Forces Act 1907. In the event of another war, he determined that a minimum of 56,000 men would be required to maintain an efficient fighting force. He proposed to achieve this through the existing Yeomanry and Militia. However, a number of Militia Colonels were not prepared to accept this as they felt that their 'influence' over their own units would be compromised. Haldane therefore formed a 'Special Reserve' comprising semi-professional soldiers totalling 76,166 men and organized in seventy-four battalions of 500–600 men. Each 'Special Reserve' battalion was to support their corresponding two regular battalions. In order to entice the former members of the militia to join the new Special Reserve, a payment of £2 as a 'bounty' for every recruit was proposed. This was very successful with many members taking the bounty and 're-joining'.

How did this affect the two newly-formed regiments in Ireland? Yet again, Ireland was a special case and as such, the reforms did not reflect the rest of the UK. Instead of becoming Reserve regiments supporting a 'parent' regiment, the two Yeomanry regiments were re-assigned as Special Reserve cavalry units in their own right. Discussions between the Marquis of Waterford and representatives in the War Office on the best way of achieving this started as early as August 1907.

In January 1908, the Marquis of Waterford and the Earl of Shaftsbury, the commanding officer of the then North of Ireland Imperial Yeomanry, decided that they should present a combined front in the negotiations with the War Office as to how these new regiments were to be formed and how they functioned. Initially, the War Office were requesting that each regiment provide a Special Contingent comprising two squadrons of men who had received at least six months continuous preliminary training, to act as Army Troops as part of any Expeditionary Force raised. The main problem both regiments had was to provide sufficient men who would qualify for this. As the men were, on the whole, employed (on the farm, running their own estates, in shops etc.), it was a big commitment to ask them to give up six months of their life to train. After discussions with his men, Lord Waterford surmised that even with men prepared to undertake a maximum of two months preliminary training, he could only raise one squadron of approximately 120 men. This would leave over 150 men unable to serve overseas that due to their previous experience, he felt he couldn't lose. Lord Shaftsbury also felt that he would be hard pushed to field one squadron, let alone two.[34]

By July of 1908 the Director of Military Training (War Office) and the two Colonels had agreed the following:

- Both the North and South of Ireland Imperial Yeomanry were to join the Special Reserve and that all members were to be made available for service overseas.
- The annual training was to be increased from nineteen days to twenty-four days, with a further three days required for musketry training (twenty-seven days in total).
- Each man was to complete a minimum of six periods of two-hourly 'drills' (horsemanship, musketry, efficiency) at any time during that year.
- Officers were also required to attend compulsory courses of instruction, including an attachment to a regular cavalry regiment for at least one month within their first two years of service. Further promotion of officers was contingent on successfully completing a course on musketry training for the post of captain and another fourteen days attachment to a regular cavalry regiment for the rank of major.
- Officers and non-commissioned officers were also encouraged to attend voluntary courses in such skills as signalling or Maxim gun handling.
- All men transferring to the new Special Reserve from the Irish Yeomanry were eligible for a £2.00 bonus (worth approximately £230 at date of publication) and retain the same rate of pay of 5s 6d per day in attendance (worth approximately £31.50 at date of publication) they previously enjoyed. Additionally, the successful completion of all yearly training qualified for an annual bounty of £4.00 (worth approximately £460 at date of publication)
- Further concessions were given for the rates for hiring of horses during the annual training camp to take account of the additional days training.[35]

One of the other problems facing both the Marquis of Waterford and the Earl of Shaftsbury was the name change from the South/North of Ireland Imperial Yeomanry as part of the overall reorganisation. Both men were keen to have the name changed to North Irish Horse and South Irish Horse, to reflect the continued public belief of association of the term 'Yeomanry' with previous historical atrocities in Ireland. Although a lot of work had been carried out to promote the good name of both regiments over the last five years, that association still held. These points were put to the King, who disliking their term of 'Horse', changed 'Horse' to 'Yeomanry'. On foot of this, the Army Council went ahead and published the change of name in the *London Gazette* on 10 July 1908 as the North Irish Yeomanry and South Irish Yeomanry.[36] However, after further canvassing by the two commanders (including, it appears, bending the Duke of Connaught's 'ear') approval was given to the more familiar South Irish Horse (and North Irish Horse) and posted in the *London Gazette* on 20 August 1908.[37]

That year's camp at the Curragh was reported in the *Irish Times*, where it was noted that the Regiment was to be disbanded at the end of the camp and reformed as a new Special Reserve unit as part of the Army reforms. It was also noted that the Regiment was to be retained in its existing formation of four squadrons, each commanded and trained by its own officers working within 3 Cavalry Brigade. Over half of the existing members of the Regiment had agreed to sign on to the new unit. (This was a much higher number than in the North Irish Horse!)

The disbandment of the South of Ireland Imperial Yeomanry and formation of the South Irish Horse was officially gazetted in the *London Gazette* on 20 October 1908 *The Irish Times* reported shortly afterwards:

After strenuous efforts the two Irish regiments of irregular horse have been granted the names of the North and South Irish Horse, and the designation 'Yeomanry' has been eliminated altogether. This, for obvious reasons, must have a beneficial effect on the two regiments, which now occupy a unique position in the Army. Both regiments are filling up vacancies caused by the new regulations and by the loss of time-expired men. Younger sons of farmers, men useful with a rifle and used to horses, are the stamp of recruits that are wanted. Under the new scheme the Irish Horse is liable for service overseas when required, and each regiment must have a squadron of 160 men on a war footing, as a reserve for the cavalry of the line, though that squadron will not be split up, and will act as a unit. The annual training in future will extend over some twenty-four days, but there will be facilities in the way of leave in cases of urgency.[38]

Two items of interest are recorded: that of the need for a standing reserve of 160 men on a 'war footing' for overseas duties and that the squadron would not be split up, as in the case of other special reserve regiments in Great Britain. Previously, Yeomanry units were primarily home based for defence of the UK.

On 8 September 1908 Major Henry Charles Windsor Villiers Stuart, the officer commanding C Squadron, Cork, died from paralysis, believed to be as a result of wounds received at Lindley in the Boer War. Major Villiers Stuart, whilst serving in the Yeomanry under Lord Longford, suffered a wound to the heart. Major Stuart enjoyed both sport (sailing) and, of course, hunting. He had joined the SIIY at its conception and was given command of the Cork squadron. A man both liked and respected by the men under his command and by 'men of all classes and creeds' he was afforded a military funeral with full honours. He was laid to rest in Villerstown, Dromana. It was reported that the military escort comprised 400 men representing foot and cavalry regiments, 200 of whom formed the firing party, including a contingent of the South Irish Horse, with the remainder comprising the band of five Irish regiments. The pall bearers comprised officers of the South Irish Horse under the command of Captain Hewson MVO. Major Villiers Stuart was laid to rest with the Last Post and volleys from the South Irish Horse firing party.[39]

1909 followed the same pattern as previous years, with the regimental dinner being held in the Dolphin Hotel on St Patrick's Day. Training outside of the annual camp continued for officers. For example, Captain H.E. Berry carried out training and passed the examination for the use of the Maxim gun in Hythe in April. (Captain Berry was to command C Squadron when they were sent to France with the 16th (Irish) Division as Divisional Cavalry.)

The annual camp was held from 2 to 26 June at the Curragh as usual. Two of the newly-joined officers were to play a part in the later years of the regiment, notably Mr Roche-Kelly and Ralph Francis Howard, the 7th Earl of Wicklow. James Roche-Kelly (a Roman Catholic), from Drumline, County Clare, was the High Sheriff of Clare from 1911 to 1913. He was awarded the Military Cross and became the commanding officer of the 7th Battalion (South Irish Horse) Royal Irish Regiment on 12 April 1918 following the regiment's massive losses during the great German offensive in March. (He died on 30 August 1943, then a captain in Army Service

Corps South Africa.) The Earl of Wicklow was formerly a staff captain in 2nd Life Guards and had served in the Boer War. He was elected as a senator in June 1921 in the newly-formed Irish Free State Seanad and held his seat there until 1928. (His seat was Shelton Abbey in Arklow, County Wicklow, which has since been turned into an open prison.)

Another newly-arrived officer was Major Browne-Clayton, whose family were from Brownshill in Carlow. He was to command the 16th (Service) Battalion Cheshire Regiment in July 1916. This was the last camp that was covered in depth by the press. The main mounted exercise was due to commence on Tuesday (22 June) and finish on Thursday. The four squadrons were divided into two forces: the Red (defending) Force and the Blue (attacking) Force. The Red Force comprised A and B Squadrons, under the command of Major Browne-Clayton and the Blue Force comprising C and D Squadrons, commanded by Major the Earl of Wicklow. The scheme was umpired by Majors Burns-Lindow and Tremayne, with Lord Waterford officiating.

Over the next three days, the two forces travelled from The Curragh southwards to Athy on Tuesday evening, westwards to Maryborough (now Portlaoise) Wednesday and finally north-eastwards to Monastrevin (County Laois) on Thursday before returning to the Curragh. A series of schemes were carried out with each force 'attacking' and 'defending' their positions. What made this particular exercise was that it was carried out in the most atrocious weather. Torrential rain and thunderstorms plagued the men throughout. A brief respite from both the rain and the fighting occurred on the Tuesday night where:

The regimental band, under Mr C.F. Allen, played on the Market Square from 7:30 to 9:30 and a large crowd listened to the excellent programme.

On the Wednesday evening, the weather had become so bad that:

The idea of pitching camp in a flooded field was not pleasant, and it was a great relief to find that Lord Waterford and his staff had secured shelter for the men in Mr Odlum's mill in Meelick [County Laois]. Too much cannot be said for the kindness of the proprietor, especially as the mill had suffered somewhat at the hands of other troops. In return the SIH left the place as they had found it, full of gratitude for shelter that was most acceptable on such a bad night.[40]

Similar conditions would soon be encountered in theatre in France and Flanders but not for a night or two! The detailed reportage of the camp manoeuvres leads me to suspect that the writer was a member of the regiment tasked with detailing the event, for possible recruitment purposes. It also highlights the influence and friends of the Marquis of Waterford in securing alternative accommodation for the squadrons in the appalling weather during the second day of the scheme (Odlum's Mill).

The start of 1910 rumbled with very little difference in the routine of the regiment. The emphasis of that year's annual dinner was to maintain the status quo of the regiment whilst the dust settled around the Army Reforms of the previous year. The camp dates were 9 June–2 July.

Two major events occurred during the year. Firstly, King Edward VII passed away on 6 May 1910 and the regiment sent a wreath as a mark of respect. The wreath was 'One of the handsomest wreaths from this Country … Shamrocks figure largely in the design …'.[41]

Sadly, there was a fatal accident during the annual camp. Nineteen-year-old Trooper Vincent Hogan, from Birr, was knocked down by a horse whilst cheering on a friend in the Troopers' Race. He ran out from behind the line of spectators to cheer on his friend, who was at the time, winning the race. A rider behind Trooper Hogan hit him in the back with his knee and as he tried to get up, he was hit again by another horse. It was a sad culmination of an otherwise pleasant and successful camp.[42]

In August it was announced that the permanent headquarters of the South Irish Horse Club was now at 51 Lower Mount Street, Dublin.[43] A quick look at the 1911 census shows that the residents of 51 Lower Mount Street were the Nelson family, whose head was Archibald Nelson, described as a soldier (Regimental Sergeant Major, South Irish Horse). Facilities such as a miniature rifle range, gymnasium and a billiards room were available, as well as a well-stocked library. The new headquarters was supported through subscription by the members themselves.

In November 1910, Captain D.S. Matthews 17th Lancers completed his appointment as the regiment's adjutant after five years in post. In a final letter to the Marquis of Waterford he outlined the state of the regiment as he saw it and suggested a number of recommendations. One of the many things he reported on was that of the regiment's current strength. It stood at 468 men, only eight short of a full complement. However, he was also worried about quantity over quality and highlighted that standards appeared to have slipped. He advised that the method of recruitment be reassessed. Currently, men were recruited through the office of the permanent staff, rather than from fellow members themselves, where they could stand as a guarantor as to the character of the potential recruit. This led to some 'undesirables' within the rank and file who showed their 'lack of discipline' especially during the last few days of each camp. He also suggested that each potential recruit pay a sum of £1.00 as an entrance fee in order to dissuade the undesirables from attempting to join.

He discussed the continual drain on the regimental funds, with special attention given to kitting out the men, the cost of maintaining the various squadron houses and the inevitable cost of providing or hiring horses for the annual camps. He finished by highlighting the fine work of the permanent staff at 51 Lower Mount Street, namely Regimental Sergeant Major Archibald Nelson, Squadron Sergeant Major W.E. Joice and Squadron Sergeant Major F. Skinner.[44]

The new adjutant was Captain E. Nugent Bankes, 2nd Dragoon Guards. It was during Captain Bankes' tenure as adjutant that there appears to have been a crisis within the headquarters staff. Archibald Nelson, the Regimental Sergeant Major was accused of some 'wrongdoing' sufficiently serious enough to warrant the request for his court martial. His case was sent to Headquarters 3 Cavalry Brigade and after some consideration, it was recommended that he be severely reprimanded by his commanding officer and then discharged. The letter from 3 Cavalry Brigade also contained a report on the conduct of Captain Bankes himself. The report shed doubt on the ability of Bankes to carry out the duties of adjutant and was found to be 'lacking in energy and capacity for organisation of a command.'[45] Captain Bankes was shown the letter containing the charges and responded vociferously in his defence. In his defence, he stated that he had served four years as a staff officer in South Africa with no complaints. Furthermore, he felt that as he had just commenced in post, he needed to rely heavily on his clerk for guidance on how the administrative side of the regiment functioned. His clerk was none other than Regimental Sergeant Major Archibald Nelson who had been in his position for over eight years. Although there is no specific 'wrongdoing', I believe that the problems arose from supressed, missing and neglected important correspondence. Bankes also felt that the Brigadier's comments were grossly unjust and requested that if the charges against him were to be officially known, that he would seek redress from the General Officer Commanding, Ireland in order to clear his name and professional reputation.[46] In the end it seems that the crisis was resolved, with Regimental Sergeant Major Nelson receiving a reprimand from Lieutenant-Colonel G F Milner DSO commanding officer 5th (Royal Irish) Lancers. Captain Edward Nugent Bankes was to leave the position of adjutant replaced by Captain D.H.B. McCalmont, 7th (Queen's Own) Hussars on 28 November 1912. Bankes retired from the Army in December 1912 and joined the reserve battalion of the Royal Dublin Fusiliers. It was with the Royal Dublin Fusiliers that he was killed in action on 26 April 1916. Nelson was discharged with the rank of Acting Regimental Sergeant Major on 25 August 1911. He was to serve with the Reserve Cavalry Regiment at the Curragh during the war, but his actions in 1911 were to follow him when he was refused the promotion to Warrant Officer Class II. He remained as a Squadron Sergeant Major until his death on 18 September 1919 aged fifty-four.

The most serious event that had wide-reaching consequences on the regiment was the death of the Marquis of Waterford. On Friday 1 December 1911, after a successful day with the hounds, the Marquis of Waterford went for a walk in the grounds of Curraghmore House, as was his routine. Taking a short cut back to the house he fell into the river Clodagh and was drowned. His body was not discovered until the following day (Saturday).[47]

The regiment not only lost their Colonel, but also a major driving force behind the formation and running of the regiment. With his family and political connections, he managed to ensure that the regiment was maintained in its existing form during the Haldane reforms. His input into the formation of the regiment gave rise to a distinct *esprit de corps*. Officers and men were proud of the regiment and what it stood for, especially in light of the connotations that surrounded the name of 'yeomanry' in the Irish psyche. With the green uniform and red flash, any member of the regiment was recognizable as 'Irish' as distinct from an Irish soldier in a British regiment.

The Marquis of Waterford's replacement was none other than, Major John Graham Hope de la Poer Beresford, 5th Baron Decies, DSO. An experienced soldier from this established Irish family, he was seen as the obvious choice to drive the regiment forward, whilst maintaining its 'Irishness'. Formerly of the 7th Hussars, spending most of his active service abroad in Africa, he took part in the relief of Matabeleland, the Boer War of 1899–1902 and the Somaliland Campaign in 1903–04. He was promoted and appointed Lieutenant Colonel of the Regiment on 20 January 1912.[48]

With Lord Decies commanding, the administration of the regiment became more centred on Dublin. About this time (1912) the squadron headquarters moved from the Artillery Barracks in Limerick to Beggars Bush Barracks in Dublin. There is no record of an annual dinner being held in March 1912, possibly in deference to the passing of the Marquis of Waterford or that the press coverage of these events was greatly reduced. (I have noticed that following the death of the Marquis of Waterford, reportage on all things South Irish Horse fell dramatically. Long reports on camps, dinners and other events are no longer evident.)

The 1912 annual camp was moved from its traditional place at the Curragh, to Luttrellstown Park, Clonsilla. Lord Decies had moved to Luttrellstown in April in order to take advantage of the nearby Royal Irish Constabulary (RIC) training barracks and facilities in Phoenix Park. The camp started on 22 May and ran until 7 June. At least 420 men attended, including Majors Browne-Clayton, Burns-Lindow, the Earl of Wicklow and Henry Julius Joseph (H.J.J.) Stern – nicknamed as 'Bummy Stern' due to the size of his backside.[49] Major Burns-Lindow was now in command of the Limerick Squadron.[50] The following year the annual dinner was held at the Dolphin Hotel, Dublin, and the annual camp was held at Moore Park in Fermoy.[51]

The New Year opened with domestic and international uncertainty. With the Home Rule Bill due to be signed into law as the Government of Ireland Act and widespread unrest with it in the northern counties, there was a real fear that the predominantly unionist northern counties would resort to arms in order to defeat the Bill. This unrest and opposition to the Bill was also evident within the armed forces. Many unionist Anglo-Irish members of the Army felt torn between their allegiance to the King and their unionist roots should they be called to quell any armed unrest in the north. This came to a head in March 1914, with the 'Curragh Incident' (Mutiny). Internationally, relations between the main European powers were gradually deteriorating.[52] Against the background of this, the regiment under Colonel Lord Decies held its annual camp at the Curragh at the beginning of May to the end of the month (8–31 May). During the camp, a case came before the Curragh Petty sessions involving a Private Giles of the 4th Hussars, who had stolen some kit from a member of the South Irish Horse. He was found guilty and sentenced to six months' imprisonment.[53] Remarkably, the regimental sports day held on 28 May was captured on film and showcased the skills and dexterity of the men both mounted and on foot. The film can still be viewed online via the Imperial War Museum. (www.iwm.org.uk/collections/item/object/1060023376)

However, instead of the three-week camp as usual, the regiment was retained at the Curragh in case it was needed as part of any policing duties arising from unrest in Ulster.[54] This only lasted until the beginning of June and the regiment disbanded as normal. As the men departed the camp, little did they know that they would soon be called to war.

Chapter 2

S (Service) Squadron: Landrécies, The Marne, The Aisne, Ypres, Neuve Chappelle, la Bassée, Aubers Ridge, Loos.

On Tuesday, 4 August 1914, war was declared. The following day the mobilisation of the British Army began. The mobilised contingent was designated the Expeditionary Force (The 'British' or the more commonly known 'British Expeditionary Force', or BEF, was added following the arrival of the Indian Expeditionary Force in Autumn of 1914. The first Indian troops to land in France were the Indian Corps disembarking in Marseilles on 26 September 1914). At Beggars Bush Barracks, following orders issued by the Army Council, Lord Decies was directed to form and mobilize an overseas squadron from the four existing squadrons of the South Irish Horse, namely A, B, C and D. The primary role of the reserve cavalry regiments was to provide a mounted screen and escort to the headquarters train of the BEF. It was decided that only one squadron of the South Irish Horse (SIH) and two squadrons of the North Irish Horse (NIH) would be needed for these duties. A composite regiment was therefore formed, known in the earlier war diaries as the Irish Horse.

George McDonald, at the time a newly promoted corporal in B Squadron, South Irish Horse, was working in his father's fields at the farm in County Wexford when war was declared. He received his call-up papers from the local Royal Irish Constabulary (RIC) sergeant on the Wednesday and, without saying goodbye to his mother, caught the train to Limerick. George McDonald, together with his colleagues including Trooper Louis P. Allen, had been mobilized and ordered to attend Castle Barracks, Limerick. Allen (who kept a diary of this initial period) had departed Dublin via Kingsbridge (now Heuston) Station amid great excitement, arriving at Limerick around 10:00pm. On Thursday morning, the mobilized men assembled and George McDonald recounted:

It was not long before we were called on parade and Major H.J.J. Stern, our CO [B Squadron], informed us that a Service Squadron (S) was to be formed from a troop from each of A, B, C and D squadrons. He added that some men who had been nominated for this Service squadron had not yet reported, due to the fact they were living away from their homes. As the matter was urgent, he asked for volunteers to replace the missing Troopers. Immediately the whole parade moved forward, as one man, he therefore had to select the replacements himself.[1]

Twenty-year-old No. 681 William Harvey, of Bustyhill, Newcastle, County Dublin, was one of the latecomers and had also been working in his father's fields, but only received his mobilization papers four days later on Sunday 9 August.[2] The whole regiment was confined to barracks until the following day, when they all decamped to Richmond Barracks, Inchicore, Dublin.

The composite squadron comprised 184 men as follows (a little over the 160 men prescribed as necessary in 1908): Major Burns-Lindow, Officer Commanding; Captain McCalmont, Adjutant; six officers; squadron sergeant major; squadron quartermaster sergeant; eight sergeants; one lance sergeant; eight corporals; seven lance corporals; 140 privates; two trumpeters; farrier sergeant; corporal shoe smith; four shoe smiths and two saddlers.

The war diaries for the South Irish Horse are somewhat haphazard and a little confusing at times. When S Squadron was sent to France, it was as part of the composite regiment known as the Irish Horse, comprising themselves and A and C Squadrons North Irish Horse. Therefore, for the purposes of their war diary submissions, S Squadron was known as B Squadron, Irish Horse. As the proper B Squadron was not posted to France until 1915, and to avoid confusion, I have taken the step of calling this first squadron to arrive in theatre in August 1914 its original name of S Squadron. B Squadron therefore will only refer to the squadron arriving in theatre in 1915. I feel that my analysis of the war diaries of not only the South Irish Horse, but the divisions to which they belonged, supports this.

Why were the South Irish Horse only allowed one squadron as opposed to the North Irish Horse who had two? Colonel Burns-Lindow intimated after the war that the regiment could have provided two squadrons, if requested, at this early stage:

it may strike old members of the Regiment and others that it is odd that, though a squadron was at Mons and through the retreat, the Marne the Aisne, 1914 and Ypres 1914, none of these honours appears.... The Army Council have been obliged to make a rule that two squadrons of a regiment must be present in any given engagement for which a Battle Honour is claimed.... It is a fortune of war and no one can grumble.

What, however, is to be deplored is the fact that, if the regimental authorities of these days had sent out a second squadron to France in August 1914, as they were asked to, and could have done, the Regiment would now be entitled to have after its name in the *Army List* all those earliest and in some ways most classic, honours of the war. As it is the earliest honour we can claim is Loos.[3]

It may have been assumed that, as the original Expeditionary Force was a reasonably small force of just over 73,000 men, only a limited number of GHQ support troops were required. Or, due to the recent unrest in Ulster over the Home Rule Bill and the Curragh Incident, it was felt that the presence of a larger contingent of the northern raised troops (NIH) guarding the General Officer Commanding (GOC), Lord French would be more palatable to the unionist public? As it was, the NIH provided the escort to Lord French throughout the early days of the war, the SIH provided the escort for Lieutenant General Sir Douglas Haig, the future GOC! Over the next twelve days the regiment mobilized stores, horses, equipment and, of course, men. When they arrived depended on where they lived. The remainder of the regiment, but not including the depot staff and recruits, were transferred to Athlone for garrison duty under the command of Major Browne-Clayton on Monday, 10 August. After S Squadron left for France, it must be assumed that the regiment returned to Dublin (Leopardstown), Limerick and Cork.

S Squadron, now solely based at Richmond Barracks, used their time brushing up on manoeuvres learnt during the annual camps, taking full advantage of the open spaces in and around Phoenix Park. The squadron, comprising six officers and 168 other ranks (ORs) left Dublin, via Alexandra Basin, on Monday, 17 August 1914, en route to le Havre, France. (Captain McCalmont and Lieutenant Stewart arrived a few days later on 21 August together with the remaining eight ORs). They embarked on the steamship

Architect together with the two squadrons of the NIH and, with the exception of a mid-channel challenge by an over-zealous French destroyer captain, had an unremarkable and smooth crossing. No. 870 Trooper George Dixon, assigned to A Troop, recorded the incident in his diary:

> Stopped during night by French warship which fired two shots across our bows and turned searchlights on us. Allows us to pass. We were sleeping on decks and it all looks so picturesque.[4]

Allen, who was on deck and on guard at the time, also noted the French destroyer's challenge at around 0130. He had just been relieved and witnessed the confrontation between the two ships' officers, with both vessels hove-to in the middle of the channel.

Arriving at le Havre at about 8 o'clock in the morning of 19 August, the troops were greeted with the sights and sounds of excited crowds of people lining the quays, bunting, flags and ships' sirens sounding in harbour. Due to the large crowds around the docks, the unloading of the horses and men took considerably longer than anticipated.[5] Eventually men, animals and matériel were unloaded and assembled, ready to march off to a rest camp approximately five miles outside the town, where they remained until Friday.[6] Even then, the march was somewhat impeded by the attention of the local population, especially by the ladies. Surprisingly, it appears that it was only here that the squadron were issued their swords.

As well as preparing their own kit ready for the move to the front line, the men made the best use of their limited time by visiting le Havre. Many a cup of tea and sweet treat was consumed during their brief stay in the town. George Dixon, with two of his friends, decided to explore le Havre: 'Go with Leonard (Pte S. Leonard) and Roe (Kingsley Thomas) to see the town, have tea in a shop on Prom, where we find a lady who speaks English.'[7]

Louis Allen also went into le Havre and described the scene:

> The place is a mass of conscripts greeting us everywhere. We march through the town to a huge camp about 5 miles out. By the time we arrive there our horses, caps etc., are covered with flowers and all kinds of decorations from the ladies. We feel as proud as peacocks. I have never seen anything like the huge white marble-like buildings of the city, also

the buzz and excitement. In France, vehicles pass on the right of the road instead of the left, so I often find myself in trouble with the Gendarmes.[8]

Allen, after being sent back into town by Major Burns-Lindow on an errand, managed to find time to dine at a café and serenade his fellow diners with a few tunes. One lady was so moved that she invited him to come back to stay at her house 'apres la Victoire'. However, at approximately 0130 on Friday 21 August, Allen and the rest of the squadron were off to the front. Assigned as Army Troops for the General Headquarters (GHQ), the squadron entrained at le Havre and journeyed to Busigny. Having ridden to the train station at le Havre, they loaded the horses, kit and themselves onto the awaiting trucks and set off, stopping at Rouen to water the horses and stock up on coffee, chocolate, cigarettes and pastries from the ladies waiting on the platform and then on to Amiens, arriving at 07:30. Once again they were given coffee and sweet treats, bread, and chocolate at the station. Allen, ever the wag, was encouraged to proclaim the men's appreciation at the generosity of the local population in his broken French.

Arriving at Busigny at 0200, the squadron unloaded the waggons, saddled up and started their march towards the I Corps Headquarters (HQ) at Maubeuge. George Dixon continues the story:

August 20th. Leave le Havre at 2am. Entrain at 9am and pass through Amiens

August 21st. Arrive … 2am …. We find it difficult to harness horses. Major (Burns-Lindow) curses like a trooper, finally we move off. I am on a limber

August 22nd. March continued. Find I am responsible as brake man if limber goes down hills too quickly and expected to get off and walk when going uphill. McMillan (D) and Carey on limber [wheeled carriage generally used for carrying ammunition] with me. Spent night by roadside.

August 23rd. March continued. Tired walking. This place all hills, no flat places anywhere. When horses trot, McMillan expects me to double

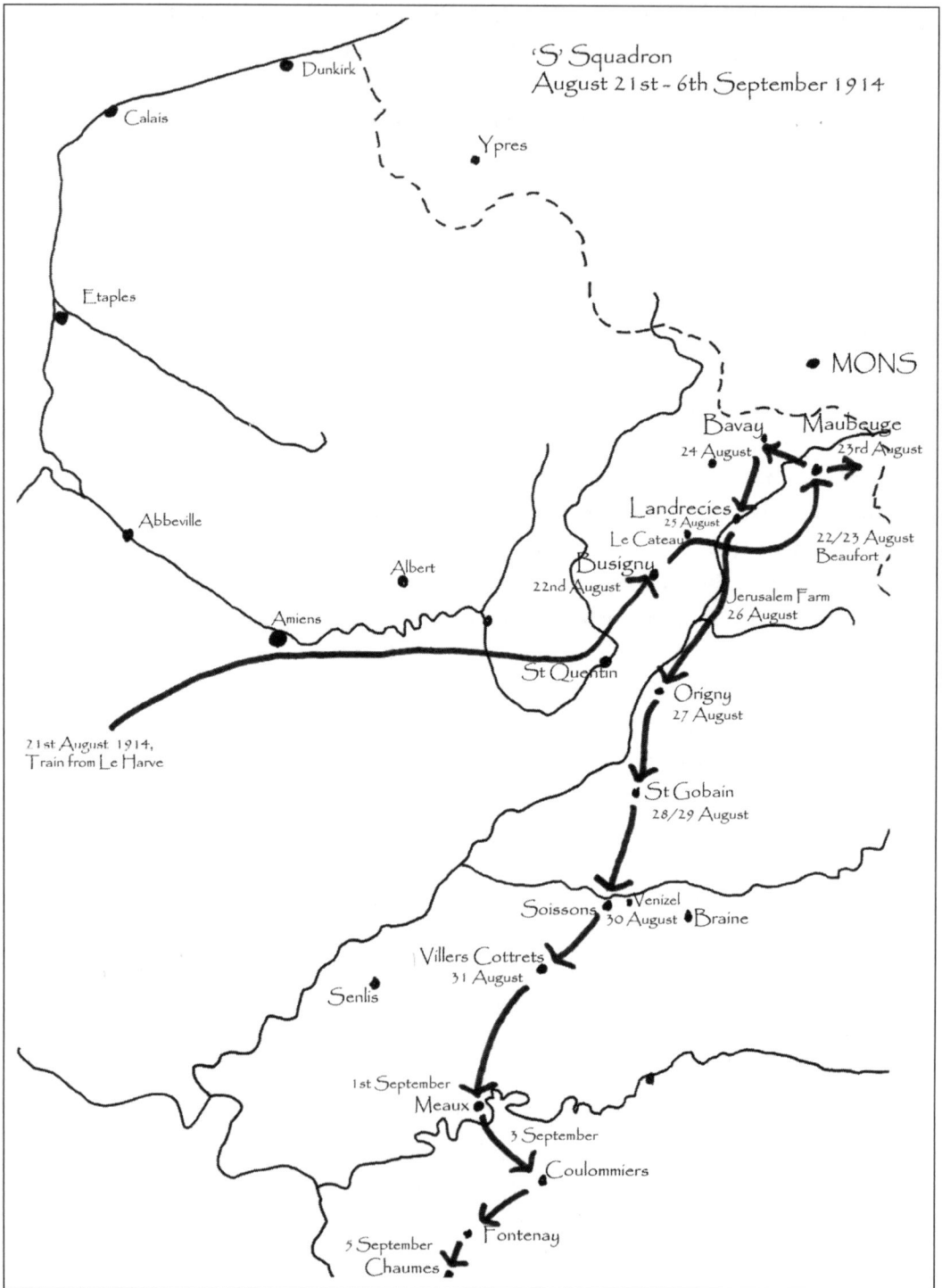

'S' Squadron
August 21st - 6th September 1914

Dunkirk

Calais

Ypres

Etaples

• MONS

Bavay   Maubeuge
24 August   23rd August

Abbeville

Albert   Landrecies
                         25 August
                    Le Cateau   22/23 August
          Busigny   Beaufort
          22nd August
Amiens   Jerusalem Farm
                          26 August
St Quentin

Origny
27 August

21st August 1914,
Train from Le Harve

St Gobain
28/29 August

                    Venizel
Soissons   30 August ●Braine

Villers Cottrets
31 August

Senlis

1st September
        Meaux
                3 September

                Coulommiers

5 September   Fontenay
Chaumes

behind. I told McMillan to go to blazes and got on, every time he went faster, I have to walk. Swear to rejoin Troop at first chance.[9]

As Dixon and Allen were in two different troops, Dixon in A Troop and Allen B Troop, their diary entries enable us to obtain a more complete picture of what was happening to the whole squadron. Allen wrote:

At 2:00am we arrive and dis-entrain at Busigny, and at once the hard work begins. We have orders to join I Army Corps Headquarters (Sir Douglas Haig commanding, and Brig. Gen. Gough). We begin our long march (40 miles to Frontier), draw our ammunition etc. Pass through le Cateau 9:30.[10]

Moving up to the front, the squadron passed other regular infantry units, French regular troops, all headed for Belgium and the ever-advancing German Army. The squadron maintained a steady unremitting pace, not once stopping until they reached Beaufort, just south of Maubeuge, resting briefly at the town hall approximately fifteen hours after they left Busigny. Once again, Allen was called on by Burns-Lindow to use his 'broken' French to locate some liquid 'refreshments'. He succeeded in obtaining six bottles of wine and beer, all gratefully received.

It is here where I suspect the troops became somewhat disjointed. The travelling times of the mounted troops and the wagon-bound troops are, naturally, different. So, when Allen's troop managed to arrive at their destination, Dixon's detachment was either still travelling, or facing sleeping on the roadside, rather than under straw in the more salubrious conditions Allen had to contend with. Allen was travelling with Major Burns-Lindow as his 'interpreter' and would have needed to be at or near the front with the major. After a brief sleep, they saddled up at 0500 and continued to Maubeuge, arriving at Louvroil in the southern outskirts of the city at 0930 on Sunday 23 August. They were met with reports that the Germans were rapidly approaching and I Corps HQ was to be relocated further back in Vieux Mesnil, a few miles to the west of Maubeuge.

The squadron travelled through Maubeuge, where the men stopped to load their rifles, whilst listening to the sounds of artillery and, above them, the buzz of aeroplanes. Everywhere, the French Army was busy, throwing up temporary fortifications and digging trenches in preparation for the inevitable assault on the city. Arriving at General Haig's headquarters (I Corps) at Jeumont (halfway between Maubeuge and Charleroi), they began setting up a temporary bivouac in a local farm. The squadron's primary assignment was to provide a mounted escort for I Corps HQ wagons.[11] One of the troops (B Troop), was ordered to provide a mounted escort to General Haig as and when required. One would have to assume that when General Haig was travelling by motor car, the troop was not required.[12] As well as mounted guard, B Troop were on picquet duty at all entrances to the headquarters at Jeumont. Louis Allen:

> I am posted on a hill and get a view of the Battle of Mons. We halt everybody, Field Officers and all. Once I halted a motor car coming along very hurriedly. The chauffeur swore. I came up to have a look who was inside – two Generals!! – 'Pass Friends' and the raging chauffeur and the Generals had to wait until the said chauffeur got out to start the engine again, – 'smart soldier, but a damn nuisance that SIH fellow'.

With large numbers of refugees, displaced families, men, women and children fleeing the fighting, inevitably accusations of spying by the resident population in relation to 'refugees' would become commonplace. B Troop were to have first-hand experience of this at Jeumont. A local lady approached one of the men and informed him that she had noticed a 'stranger' travelling to and from the village over a 'number of weeks' in suspicious circumstances. The 'fact' that he was half-German fuelled her suspicion and, as a result, the man, and his family, were reported and arrested by members of B Troop in the presence of the Provost Marshal. Later, after the man had been interrogated by the Provost Marshal, he was executed as a spy. Whether he was or not will never be known. However, as he was 'half-German' and not a 'local', his fate was sealed.[13]

On Monday 24 August, following the retreat from Jeumont, the remainder of the squadron finally caught up with the main party bivouacked at the new GHQ, Bavay, about fifteen miles due south of Mons. They could see the results of the intense fighting at Mons, with casualties pouring back from the front, soldiers and civilians alike. B Troop continued to maintain a guard at GHQ, with a section of the party forming an armed escort for General Haig.

We form a body guard to the General [Haig] and march to camp. In the morning, when passing through this town, I was chatting and sympathising with a lady who was dreadfully cut up as her fiancée was at the War. Later, when passing through with the General, before the streams of dead and wounded, she recognised me, and shouted 'N'est pas vie?' (not killed) [sic].[14]

As the result of the fighting at Mons became known, Haig ordered a general retreat of I Corps. Later, around 1600, the squadron moved out of Bavay, once again on the way to Vieux Mesnil, (approximately six miles behind Bavay), this time passing Maubeuge to the east. Such was the speed of the retreat that the squadron could only manage to rest on the side of the road. The long retreat from Mons to the Marne had begun. In his diary Allen recounts a conversation he had with a survivor of the attack at Mons:

An 18th Royal Irish [Regiment] wounded soldier tells me of his experience at Mons, 'terrible slaughter, and yet our retreat was magnificently disciplined and organised'. The Middlesex and Royal Irish were badly cut up. One young officer (about 19, a relation of the Guinness) went right mad and ran all over the place roaring. He ultimately ran right into the enemy. Another poor soldier, with brains protruding, ran amok before expiring.[15]

Moving from Vieux Mesnil, I Corps relocated their HQ at Landrecies, then garrisoned by 4 Guards Brigade. Arriving around midday on Tuesday 25 August, the squadron sent out a patrol of four men to scout around the outskirts of the town. William Harvey, then a trooper, described the result of the scouting mission. Dixon, also part of the patrol of No. 1 Section, recalled finding a German lance and helmet. William Harvey described how, as they travelled along a forest track, they saw Germans. William and the others turned around and raced away, pursued by bullets.[16]

The rest of the squadron prepared their billets and settled down but, at around 1730, the order was given to 'stand to'; Germans had been seen entering the northern outskirts of the town. Louis Allen with his chums had been preparing a new camp, having arrived in Landrécies at 1500:

No sooner there than an alarm comes through 'that the Germans are on top of us'. We 'stand to' with our rifles and fixed bayonets. The Camerons behind and the Guards in front of us. Our officer, [Captain F.H.] Brooke, one leg bare, with sword and revolver ready – but a false alarm. They don't come. About 8 o'clock a cyclist dashed in to say the town was surrounded. No false alarm this time – the beggars had come up like bees, in motor busses. The Irish Horse B Squadron were the first to be on the spot. Like a flash we were galloping to the side of the General, and found him to be in the Market Square with all his staff, revolver in hand.... Our horses being of no use in a tight corner we put them in a yard, and with fixed bayonets take our places in houses facing the market square, ready to let go and fight like the mischief to the last.[17]

Defences were manned and the Germans engaged by the Guards Brigade as they attempted to take the town. William Harvey, watching from a window on the first floor of a house overlooking the advancing Germans, noted that they were pushing forward en masse and even had their regimental bands playing as though on parade. In front of the advancing Germans, Harvey noted that the Irish Guards waited until they were approximately fifty to a hundred yards away before firing on the Germans and then charging them with fixed bayonets.[18]

The battle was fierce; in places hand-to-hand fighting ensued, but by 0230 the Germans had been forced to retire. Although they weren't directly involved in the fighting,

The South Irish Horse were at Landrécies, fighting with the Guards. 'We pegged down our horses,' writes Corporal O'Rourke, 'and had just gone out to get some rations when the alarm sounded 'Germans in town'. We all ran to our horse lines, got our rifles and defended our horses with very slight losses on our side. When we got the enemy back a bit we got saddled up in a minute, and dashed through the town after them. I must say our chaps were very brave under fire.[19]

One of the men present didn't seem to be too worried, namely, a certain trooper George Dixon.

Withdrew into town, barricaded a street, fixed bayonets, go into houses. I fall asleep in basement and awoke in time to get my horse and move off with Troop at 3 am on 26th August.[20]

At dawn the following day, the whole squadron moved south, primarily acting as a rear-guard force and sending out flanking patrols at stages during the day as the artillery and retiring infantry shelled and sniped at the advancing enemy. It was during this march that they suffered their first casualty, one man was wounded from sharp shooters' fire and a number of horses were also hit. They passed through Étreux after a brief but welcome rest in the town, just a few hours before the fateful stand of 2nd Royal Munster Fusiliers.

George Dixon was having a rougher time than most of his fellow troopers. Having been sent back into Landrécies first thing in the morning to give his horse to General Haig, he found that Haig was no longer there. In fact, Haig had moved his headquarters by car some hours earlier at around 2330, to 3 Brigade's headquarters to the east at le Grand Fayt. Collared by an officer of the Coldstream Guards, who requisitioned his horse, he was forced to march on foot at the rear of the Guards' company. Not being used to marching on foot, Dixon soon became detached from the company and was lucky enough to hitch a ride on a wagon, returning him to his Troop (A Troop) still at the side of the road outside Landrécies:

[Corporal G.E.] Evans wondering what to do without horse! when an officer comes up and hands me [Arthur or John] Wallace's horse (which he had had on loan). I mount him and Smythe orders me to go on ahead. Horse tired and will only walk. Wander about for half an hour before I find 'Our Lot'. Hand horse over to Wallace and get a French Spigs [sic] horse, with French saddle etc. Very fast horse.[21]

That night (26/27 August) they bivouacked at (Jerusalem) Iron, a small settlement due south of Étreux. In the immediate aftermath of Landrécies, it appears that a scapegoat was needed and the blame was firmly laid at the feet of a French count working as an interpreter for I Corps general staff. The Assistant Provost Marshal (possibly Lieutenant Colonel Fitzgerald) was called and after a brief interrogation, the count was given two choices: do the 'decent thing', or face a full court martial. He decided on the former and took his own life. The interrogation also led to the arrest of a number of locals who were dealt with by the Camerons, although there is no record of what became of them.

Thursday found the squadron well rested and again forming a rear-guard screen for the retiring troops. Unfortunately, Trooper Harry Costello, 21, from Dublin, was not so lucky. He was called up on 5 August and travelled with the rest of the squadron to France on the 17th. At some stage during the retreat, around Landrécies, his horse was commandeered by an officer and he was issued with a bicycle. He became a despatch rider and 'his bicycle was punctured, and during 26 August, while trying to mend it, some Germans came up in a motor car and captured him.'[22]

Harry spent the rest of the war in a prisoner of war camp at Senne No. II camp (Sennelager) in Germany. He was eventually repatriated at the end of the war and demobbed at Tidworth, Wiltshire. His incarceration was only reported on 25 March 1915, but George Dixon noted in his diary on 27 August: 'Two horses wounded and Costello (cyclist) missing.'

Corporal E.M. Wilkinson, Troopers George Dixon, Richard Brewster, Donald McMillan and James Purcell, all of A Troop, were sent out to the flank of the retreating column and witnessed the retiring artillery in action against the Germans. Whilst they were away, the remainder of the squadron, static at the Iron crossroads, came under fire from the Germans and had to effect an immediate retreat. Allen recorded:

> Sentry on cross roads – when enemy too close get mounted, extend the cross line horses to Nos. 3s – most exciting. We can see the Germans coming along, and their shells are bursting around us. All the line send in heavy fire, this is too warm for us, so the Major commands 'Get Mounted'. We are trotted back in front of Scots Guards, who mistake us for enemy, and send a shower of bullets after us. The only chance is to go full speed ahead, down goes [No. 384 Henry John] McKenna's [who returned to Ireland, 'Time Expired' on 11 November 1915] horse, also [John or Thomas] Connolly's. I let my horse go as hard as he likes, and when field is clear, a ditch and over he goes right into a squad of Highlanders – it was fierce.[23]

After this dramatic flight from the Germans, the squadron regrouped and travelled through Origny to halt in St Gobain for two nights over 28/29 August. Throughout this period mounted patrolling was maintained, sometimes encountering German cavalry, but no real engagement with the enemy occurred.

Although they managed to keep their horses in reasonable condition, one major problem was the inability to re-shoe the horses. As they were continually on the move, the metalled and cobbled roads wore out the shoes faster than normal and there was no time to shoe the mounts. George McDonald recounted the poor condition of the Belgian artillery mounts and noted that they had been worked so hard that they could not move any further. In the end, McDonald's troop was ordered to provide a screen for the Belgians whilst their horses were rested before they continued the retreat. Unlike the French cuirassiers, who were always mounted, the squadron made sure that, when conditions allowed, they dismounted and walked with their mounts for a mile or so. Additionally, they eased the saddle girths at the same time to try and negate saddle and girth galls. They were also under standing orders to dismount approximately a mile outside the rest area or bivouac and walk in.[24]

On Sunday 30 August Louis Allen described the sheer exhaustion the squadron felt during the retreat:

> Falling asleep on horse, and dead saddle weary – it is very long and dreary. Brigade halt for a few hours, at Fermay, Somey. Have a tub bath and sleep – continue – halt for a night at barn in Soissons. At least plenty of rations and rum. We are glad of a drop. A fellow cut my hair bald, with a horse clipper, and I had a bathe in a pond. At Soissons the people were very kind to us. We have been feeding practically on a few biscuits and bully beef up to this.[25]

Having arrived at Soissons, on 30 August, the squadron was sent to Venizel as Contact Squadron. As the French and British armies retreated, communication between them became strained and sometimes impossible. The French Fifth Army had engaged the Germans on 29 August in what was known as the Battle of Guise. As a result of this, the gap between the British I Corps, retreating through Soissons, and the French Fifth Army enabled the German cavalry to cross the Oise river at Bailly and march towards Vauxaillon. This left the French Fifth Army's left flank seriously exposed and could allow the Germans to isolate and ultimately encircle it. Joffre, the French commander, tried to contact Lord French to advise him of this precarious situation and ask him to close the gap between the two armies. Unfortunately, the GHQ was uncontactable. The British liaison officer between the two armies was Lieutenant Edward Spears. In his memoir of the actions of 1914, he records that frantic communications between General Joffre (C.-in-C. French armies), General Lanrezac (Commander Fifth Army) and General Haig of I Corps ensued to try and plug the gap with troops between the two formations. He telephoned the local post offices in I Corps' area to try and find out where they were. It seems strange now, but as the evolution of wireless was still in its infancy, mobile communications on the ground were virtually non-existent. The majority of communications were passed using despatch riders and runners. In this situation, however, the civilian telephone system was still working. Due to this, Lieutenant Spears was able to locate General Haig in Vauxbuin. Even more surprising was the fact that the first soldier he spoke to was Major Burns-Lindow, who was in the vicinity of the post office, presumably providing the mounted escort and protection to General Haig's headquarters party. As with most of these stories, Spears knew Burns-Lindow as he was an 'old 8th Hussar' [The 8th (King's Royal Irish) Hussars]. Having found the whereabouts of General Haig, Spears was able to brief him on the current situation and request the provision of covering troops down by the River Aisne. General Haig sent Burns-Lindow and his detachment to Venizel and ordered them to hold the Chemin des Dames just north of the Aisne. They managed to hold this position under heavy fire until dusk when they were forced to retreat back through the forests around Villers Cotterêts. Spears stated that 'Their timely intervention played a considerable part in saving the [French] Fifth Army and was probably the main factor in blinding the enemy to the open gap behind the left flank of Lanrezac's command.'[26] Thankfully, there were no casualties as a result of this action. It appears that only B and C Troops were assigned this duty as George Dixon makes no mention of the attack, but does mention the nine-mile trek through a long wood before arriving at Villers-Cotterêts. He also mentioned having to do guard duty at Sir John French's house, now at Danmartin-en-Goële:

> To-day I am detailed for Guard on Sir John French's house, nothing exciting, relieved at 6 pm and told to draw a new horse. I got a remount, and it is a rotten horse. [Corporal R.] Hurst sent to base.[27]

He continued:

> [Sergeant William] Jago arrives a little later and orders us to saddle up.
> A and D Troops start out to meet some German prisoners, but after
> about half an hour on road, are recalled as the Camerons have picked
> them up. We spend another night at Coulommiers. Heavy rain all day
> and night. Rum issue before and after our attempt to collect prisoners.[28]

The Camerons referred to by Dixon were 1st Queen's Own Cameron
Highlanders, the infantry arm of the GHQ Army troops, the SIH being the
mounted arm. Together they would share guard and general routine camp
duties as well as the prisoner of war escort and guarding duties with the
SIH.

Having rejoined I Corps, the squadron continued the retreat in a series
of night marches reaching Meaux, on the River Marne, on 2 September
and Signy Signets south of the Marne, on Friday 4 September. Sleeping in
abandoned farmhouses and outbuildings along the way had its advantages,
especially when well-stocked cellars and fruit stores were discovered. The
ability to cook eggs and bacon, or have some fresh fruit and the occasional
drink must have helped the morale of the men tremendously. This was to
be the end of the retreat from Mons and from now on until the solidifying
of the front line at the end of the year, attack and counter-attack continued
from the Marne to the coast of Belgium, as the opposing armies tried to gain
the upper hand.

> We seem to be going towards the enemy at last. Hear they retired about
> 6pm last night. We see the engineers about to blow up bridge, sink boats
> and destroy all means of crossing the River Marne. This is the road to
> Metz. Now see big siege guns.[29]

The squadron set up camp in Chaumes-en-Brie but was called on, once
again, to hunt for German cavalry in the woods around Chaubuisson. The
same Chaubuisson was chosen the following day for Haig's HQ, located
in the Château de Crénille. The squadron billeted a short distance away in
Chaubuisson farm. However, they were only there for a day before orders
were received for the whole of I Corps to advance on the German First
Army in what was known as the Battle of the Marne. Travelling with the HQ

divisional train, the squadron moved up to Choisy-en-Brie, just south of the River Morin, in readiness for the attack. Louis Allen recorded his guard duty with Private Joseph Rankin on Sunday 6 September:

> Guard patrol road for General. His new quarters are at Chateau de Chaubuisson. The [Royal] Flying Corps station is beside us, and they come and go all day – dozens. [There is still a working aerodrome adjacent the Chateau]. Rankin and I are on patrol in wood around château, and we see pheasants rising. The temptation is too strong, so we fix bayonets and get a couple for dinner. The heat is almost unbearable; there is a nice orchard and tomatoes.[30]

From 7 to 9 September the squadron pushed forward through and over the Morin. The advance continued after a short stop at Rebais, through the River Marne itself at Charly-sur-Marne. Guard duties and escort duties were continued together with the general advance and one of the more sobering and sad tasks, collecting the identity discs of the dead. Allen described the scene awaiting them as they travelled over recently fought over ground:

> while scouting watch a German officer being buried by the RAMC men from the hospital. A slow, silent little procession to grave, his only mourner a comrade with a broken arm and very lame. When the clay has quite covered the corpse the British officer (a doctor) in command approaches the German and shakes his hand in sympathy and they return without a word to the shed of Temporary hospital. It is all most touching .... Column advance, we now begin to pass over recent field of bloodshed. First grave to see 'Pte Blood, Irish Guards' a little bed of raised earth, two pieces of stick form of a cross, name written in pencil, and a few flowers. [Michael Blood No. 2925, 1st Bn Irish Guards, died of wounds 6 September 1914. A native of Drogheda, now buried in Nesles-la-Giberde Communal Cemetery.] Dead horses everywhere, helmets, swords, and all kinds of attire. Graves all over the place. Germans have been putting theirs under heaps.[31]

Allen also noted the German tactics when faced with a charge by mounted troops. A corporal of the Royal Scots Greys described attacking the retreating

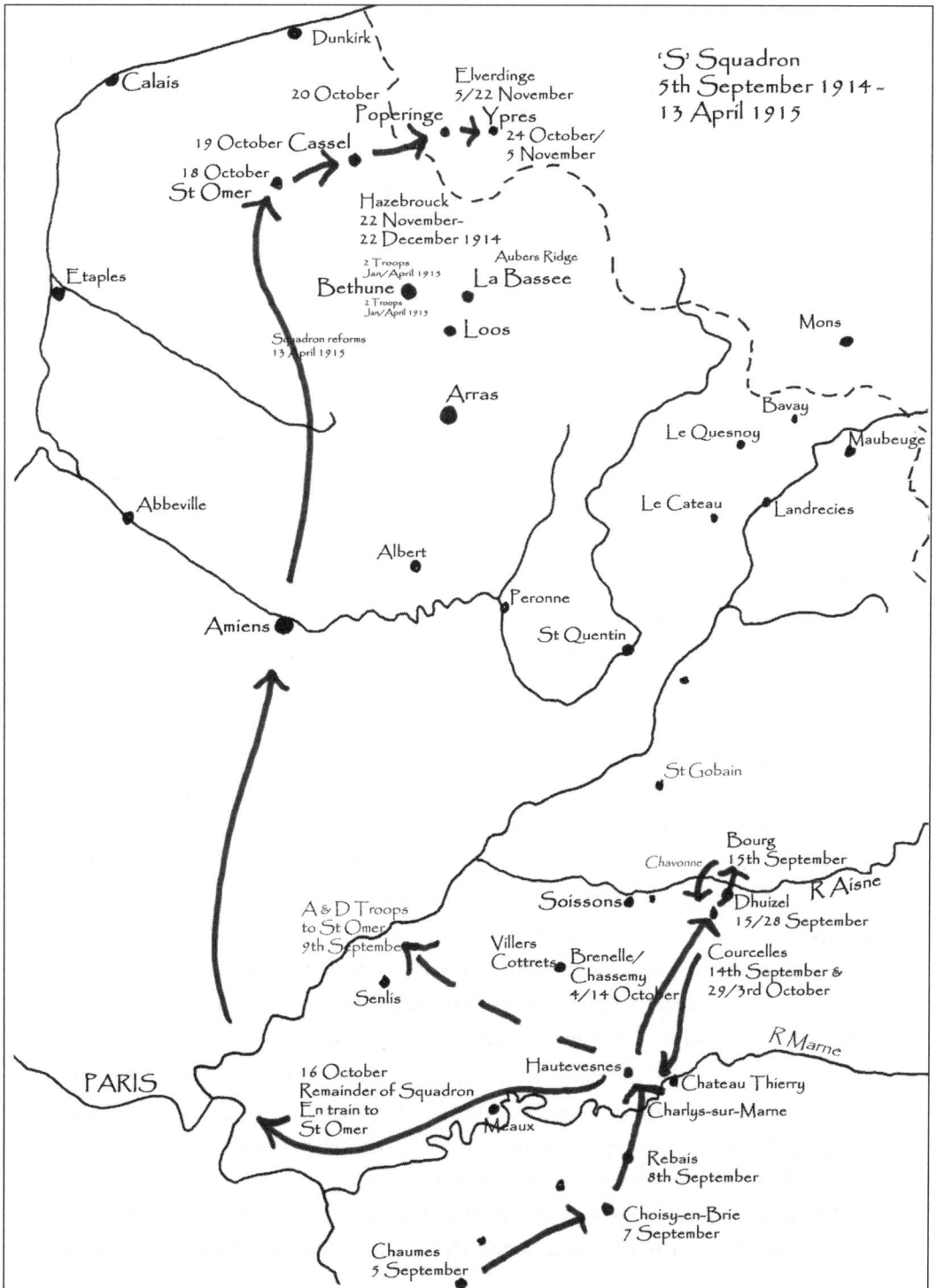

Dunkirk

Calais

20 October
Poperinge

19 October Cassel

18 October
St Omer

Elverdinge
5/22 November
Ypres
24 October/
5 November

Hazebrouck
22 November–
22 December 1914

2 Troops
Jan/April 1915
Bethune
2 Troops
Jan/April 1915

Aubers Ridge
La Bassee

Etaples

Squadron reforms
13 April 1915

Loos

Mons

Arras

Bavay

Le Quesnoy

Maubeuge

Abbeville

Le Cateau

Landrecies

Albert

Peronne

St Quentin

Amiens

St Gobain

'S' Squadron
5th September 1914 –
13 April 1915

Bourg
15th September
Chavonne
Soissons
Dhuizel
15/28 September
R Aisne

A & D Troops
to St Omer
9th September

Villers
Cottrets
Brenelle/
Chassemy
4/14 October

Courcelles
14th September &
29/3rd October

Senlis

R Marne

16 October
Remainder of Squadron
En train to
St Omer

PARIS

Hautevesnes

Chateau Thierry

Charlys-sur-Marne

Meaux

Rebais
8th September

Chaumes
5 September

Choisy-en-Brie
7 September

Germans on horseback. When charged, the Germans 'surrender', but as soon as the horses pass and the swords are raised, the German troops pick up their rifles and fire on them. Naturally, when the enemy was encountered again, the men of the Scots Greys did not make the same mistake.

The Marne was crossed and the following day at Hautevesnes, two of the four troops, A and D (George Dixon's troops) were sent off to IV Corps, joining Field Marshal Sir John French's GHQ at Compiègne.[32] Another troop was assigned to escort prisoners to the railhead at the rear of the advance. (Presumably C Troop as Allen's troop – B Troop – was still with the general.)[33] Again, it must be assumed that once they had completed this task, they returned to the by now, much smaller, squadron. (From this point on, the two parties faced different challenges and in order to simplify their movements, I have split the narrative.)

B and C Troop

Over the next two days they followed I Corps HQ from Hautevesnes to Jouaignes and on to Courcelles. At Courcelles, they were entertained by a very happy Frenchman who had found a lost German soldier wandering around. After despatching him with a blunderbuss, he buried the poor unfortunate soul in his garden and displayed the grave to Allen and his friends.[34] They were then ordered to Dhuziel in order to press on through to Bourg. The whole advance was delayed by a broken bridge over the River Aisne just outside the town of Bourg. It was believed that the bridge had been destroyed by the retreating French forces and now the only way of entering the town was over an aquaduct carrying the canal over the river.[35] They entered Bourg at daybreak on 14 September, ordered to seize Chavonne to the east. They came under heavy shelling from the Germans along the high ground on the Chemin des Dames throughout the day, but were unable to complete their task. In the process three horses were hit. The weather deteriorated over the next two days with heavy rain following their advance. Added to this, the men were travelling light, having had all their extra kit boxed up and returned to base, leaving them continuously soaked to the skin.

Continue march. Another fierce wet day. The major misses the road and we plod along in slush. I am still on foot leading my horse. The major sends me to a passing village for information. I get a jug of coffee and bread from the good lady, badly wanted and off again to rejoin troop. We very nearly get led into a hot corner. Fagged out we reach Hd.Qrs. Jouaignes. Take off all clothes to dry them – sleep in straw.[36]

With the Battle of the Aisne in full swing, 2 Cavalry Brigade was in support of the infantry brigade at Chavonne on 20 September. At around 7:00am, the West Yorks reported that the French troops to their right were retiring, leaving their flank exposed. The French, however, brought up fresh troops (Zouaves)[37] to fill the gap. Part of the cavalry brigade was then sent up to the lines to support the West Yorks in case the French retired again. A further report was received from the West Yorks at around midday, again stating the French were retiring, but was found to be incorrect. Nevertheless, reinforcements were provided by 2 Cavalry Brigade to plug any gaps in the front lines. With all this toing-and-froing, the brigade called on B and C Troops to reinforce them.[38]

As well as providing reinforcements to 2 Cavalry Brigade, escort duties to General Haig and the general staff were continued. Louis Allen wrote:

Escort to General [Haig] (4 of us). Ride with Generals to divisions, then on field of action, over pontoon bridge (bridges have been blown up) many wounded – see 3,000 Algerian troops. The boys have (R.C.) church parade with Munster Fusiliers – I am away with the General. Get back about 8 o'clock. Still at Dhuizel. It is a low lying, unhealthy dirty spot, and we begin to get covered with bugs. The Royal Fusiliers come into our bivuee [sic], trombone player asks to see me. 6th Division coming up."[39]

During the latter part of September, they were based in Dhuizel, but moved to Courcelles-sur-Vesle on 28 September after their billets were shelled by the 'Black Marias' or 'Coalboxes' – large-calibre howitzer shells. The shelling wounded one man and killed two horses.[40] Louis Allen recorded:

We go out early to exercise our horses, one man leading two or three. On our return we are greeted with shells, only yards from us. Our barn has been blown to pieces – one killed, three wounded Highland Light

Infantry – one of our fellows wounded. We cleared away under cover of hills. I go on escort. General has to move back his Headquarters on account of shelling, to near Courcelles. We are fifteen days in Dhuizel. While there we had an outbreak of fever, and were mighty glad to leave it. At Headquarters we killed some chickens in an old farm house. Sleep in a stable.[41]

During the first two weeks of October, the squadron carried out similar duties including searching woods around the billeting troops. C Troop was sent off to Braine, near GHQ on 4 October and was joined by B Troop on the 9th. Stuck in Courcelles, the members of B Troop had to travel daily to Braine to carry out their picqueting duties. A typical entry in Allen's diary records the monotony of guard duty:

Return home from picquet all night, go to Headquarters, return at 12 o'clock, immediately saddle up and go to Braine. Have a hunt for stragglers and spies in woods, they are alleged to be after our heavy guns which are concealed all over the place. Rather a hard and long day marching and crawling through woods. Return to Courcelles for night.[42]

However, on moving to Braine, they had the good fortune to be billeted next to 1st and 2nd Life Guards, whose general conviviality was greatly appreciated by all. On 10 October they were sent to assist in reconnaissance duties in conjunction with patrols from 2nd Munster Fusiliers and 2nd Suffolk Regiment at Chassemy. They were close enough to the front that they were shelled from the high ground around Vailly to the north, the other side of the River Aisne.[43]

On 15 October the Army Troops travelled to the railway station at Fère-en-Tardenois in preparation for their move to Ypres. Entraining at 0200, they travelled via Paris, St Omer, GHQ, Cassel and on to Poperinghe, arriving on 20 October. It was during this train journey that the squadron was to suffer its first fatality during the month of October, 22-year-old Private 861 Joseph Henry Rankin. Joseph was originally from Mountrath, Queen's County, but had moved to Drumcondra in Dublin to work. He was one of the first casualties to be buried in the Boulogne Eastern cemetery, used by the War

Hospitals based in the city. He died on 16 October 1914 and is registered as killed in action. However, during the journey from Paris to Boulogne, Joseph fell out of the truck in his sleep and was immediately killed. He was not the only casualty; a Private Bonham fell out of the same truck and lost his legs in the accident. Joseph had been awarded the 'Recruits' Best Shot 1914' silver cup by Lord Decies at the annual camp in May of that year. (Joseph's father, Joseph Senior, was to be awarded a trophy for his part in the defence of Trinity College during the Easter Rising a year and a half later.)

The squadron briefly met up in St Omer, on 17 October. However, A and D Troops were to remain in the town, whilst B and C Troops continued their trek to Ypres. On that Saturday, whilst exercising their horses, A and D Troops met B and C 'looking delightfully dirty' on their way to Ypres. Their sister regiment, the NIH, was also billeted at St Omer, much to A and D Troops' disgust. Leaving St Omer on 18 October, with a brief overnight stop at Cassel, they continued their trek, arriving at Poperinghe on Tuesday 20 October. At 0300 the following morning reveille greeted the men, with the final march to Ypres that day. They arrived in the town and were billeted at the town hall (the now famous Cloth Hall). Although the billets were good, they had little time to enjoy the delights of the town with the intense fighting to the east of Ypres underway. With no rest in sight for the troops, they were sent as support to 7th Division at Zandvoorde and then moved to support the Connaught Rangers (part of 2nd Division) in the wood on the Menin Road. On that Thursday, 22 October, Arthur Conan Doyle recorded in his history of the campaign in Flanders:

It was touch and go. They [2nd Division] were nearly submerged. It was indeed a vision of joy when the worn and desperate men, looking over their shoulders down the Ypres–Menin road, saw the head of a British column coming swiftly to the rescue. It was the 2nd Highland Light Infantry and the 2nd Worcesters, dispatched from [5] Brigade, and never was reinforcement more needed. Shortly afterwards further help in the shape of a detachment of Munster Fusiliers, two troops of the ever-helpful [South] Irish Horse, and one section of artillery appeared upon the scene.[44]

Allen also noted the action in his diary:

At 3 o'clock we have orders to proceed to the trenches to reinforce the Cavalry who are having a hot time. We march with ammunition limber, leave our horses with a guard behind the railway, and guard a bridge over canal. The artillery are drumming it in. We patrol the roads while the remainder lie in reserve in wood. The order soon comes to go into the trenches. We trot up into a shower of rifle bullets. Hand our horses over and take our places in the trenches all night. During the night up to early morning the rifles are cracking. The 1st Dragoon Guards are beside us. One fellow looses (sic) his head and crawls out of the trenches; he has to be shot dead by his sergeant [Private Cooper or Stewart, 1 DG, both found and buried by the Germans, both wearing spurs.] Four attacks have been made by the enemy tonight, and each driven back. The Household Cavalry are on our left (Hollebeke). We're relieved by the Indians in the morning, tired and weary.[45]

Returning to Ypres and their billets in the, as yet, untouched Cloth Hall on Friday, the men had time to visit the town and cathedral. The town was so crowded with British and French troops along with Belgian refugees that the troops were called on to police the traffic. Later, on 25 October, they entered the trenches for two days in support of 3 Cavalry Brigade at Hollebeke.

On the first day of what was to become known as the First Battle of Ypres (31 October 1914) the squadron, less A and D Troops, was waiting in the grounds of Hooge Château, the HQ of 1st and 2nd Divisions. With the front line under severe pressure, the château became a prime target for the German artillery as it was now a short distance behind the lines. Visible from the higher ground and spotted by air reconnaissance, the collection of cars and horses around the château would have been a fairly obvious target. At around 1330 the first of three shells were fired on the château. The first shell fell on the gardens, the remaining two shells on the château itself. Among the casualties were General Lomax, commanding 1st Division, who was later to die of his injuries and three other senior officers of 1st and 2nd Divisions.[46] Private Thomas Fletcher was wounded whilst running despatches and Private John Johnson had his horse shot from under him. Fletcher was teamed up with Allen riding this despatch, so that messages were duplicated in case one of the runners was hit. Hearing that the news of the push against the British lines by the Germans was serious and that elements of 1st Division were falling back towards Hooge, General Haig rode forward to assess and discuss the situation with his senior staff. Haig, now conscious of the attack on the château at Hooge, went to the front himself to organize and stiffen the lines.[47]

> At Ypres for instance, he [Haig] had at least two narrow escapes. When he had been in France little more than two months he was in the midst of a storm of shrapnel bullets and shells from the enemy, who had broken the British lines. In places parties of the First Corps, overwhelmed by numbers, were retreating, when their commander suddenly appeared on the Menin Road with his escort of the South Irish Horse and made a tour of the lines [31 October 1914].[48]

The *New York Times* in September 1918 reported that he was escorted by a troop of 17th Lancers, but 17th Lancers did not land in France until 7 November 1914.[49]

> On the darkest day, when all seemed lost, down the Menin road galloped Sir Douglas Haig and his smart escort of the 17th Lancers, shells falling thick about them, to encourage the faltering troops – for no other reason, the General's place being behind the line.[50]

A letter from the front dated 16 November 1914 from 'Christy' describes the conditions faced by the squadron at this time:

> We are suffering greatly from the cold and want of clothes. I got neither boots nor uniforms since I came out, but I helped myself to a pair of boots off a dead Frenchman the other night, as it is better to have good boots than bad ones. We lost a good deal of our fellows with sickness, but with regard to wounds not much.
>
> We are in and out of the trenches daily, and always standing to arms. Big guns are going night and day, and the usual list of casualties.
>
> I pity our dear old friends, our horses shivering and starved; but we will bear all to clip the claws of the German eagle…. I am writing this note in an old transport wagon, in the cold and rain. We are moving again shortly, and God knows what of tomorrow.[51]

As well as providing much needed support to 7 Cavalry Brigade[52] as dismounted troops, the main duty of the squadron was to provide communication support for I Corps and cavalry divisions from 31 October. Both mounted and dismounted despatch riders and runners were provided throughout the battle. Robert Brownlow, a journalist for the *Nenagh Guardian* and a trooper in the South Irish Horse, who had been with the squadron since they arrived in August, wrote to his friend and editor of the paper, about his experiences at the front. Of his despatch riding duties, he wrote:

have been through all the fighting round Ypres. In the earlier part of the fight there we had to take to the trenches at a point which was considered weak. However ... we were relieved then put on despatch work. Despatch riding, even though it is a *very dangerous* job, is extremely exciting. I have had shells dropping in twos, threes and even fours round me, and time after time I have been covered with mud and clay thrown up by the bursts. On one occasion a piece of a splinter from a 'coal box' took a piece out of the back of my saddle.... I had a much narrower escape on the morning of the 16th. On that morning at about 6 I had just left the saddle after being in it continuously for twenty-four hours carrying despatches, and was in a small cottage about 300 yards behind the Guards Brigade trenches making a saucepan of tea for myself. There were about twenty other chaps in the same house all preparing breakfast. Just as we were about to do justice to our morning meal a 'Jack Johnson' came on the scene and took out the corner of our 'hotel' and as a result two poor fellows were killed and three wounded....

A despatch rider has to be on the lookout for more than the 'coal boxes'. He must always be on the lookout for 'snipers'. These blooming fellows lurk in the woods to 'pot' despatch riders, scouts, etc. I have had bullets whizzing round me ... but when you lie down on your horse and gallop like h__l you make a very difficult target. Taking a cross country gallop one night from these jokers I got pitched into a drain of water owing to my old nag getting caught in wire.

My God the fighting round Ypres was something terrible ... we were billeted in the Town Hall there for about 16 days [21 October–4 November] when we were shelled out of it as the town was shelled vigorously for weeks. [Three men and three horses were wounded in this shelling].... The whole town is now in ruins.... Even the villages round Ypres are also levelled to the ground. I have ridden through the town several times whilst it was being shelled, and when going through each time I have been nearly suffocated with the smoke from the burning houses.[53]

Squadron Quartermaster Sergeant (SQMS) John Joseph Barber was another regular correspondent, with copies of his letters often being featured in the newspapers. One incident he reported was in relation to the shelling of Ypres.[54] In it he recounted the 'death' of one of the men. It was, in fact, Louis Allen, who was wounded, but did not return to his troop until later and was assumed killed. Allen, in his diary entry for 4 November, gives a more personal account of the shelling:

Get back to Headquarters. It is exciting getting back, as we have to pass through town, and shells coming near. Hd.Qrs. At 11 o'clock. At 4 o'c. Major [Burns Lindow] orders us to change [?] up to General's house. Almost immediately four huge shells come on top of us, but luckily it is a corner house. I am about first at the corner. I heard crashes and smothered with dirt, glass and bits, and knocked right over. I get into the doorway at Hd.Qrs. bleeding rather freely on the head. An RAMC man fixes me up and we get out of the way. (Lt) Colonel Marker DSO (Staff) is lying on the road with his leg hanging off, [Died of wounds 13 November 1914] and Capt [Lt] Banning of the Munsters is cut to pieces. Many others are also killed. Fortunately, Commander-in-Chief and staff are out on rounds. Our Major rallies most of the boys (who haven't been close). They get back and report me amongst the missing, but I managed to get back on foot sometime during the evening. My horse was killed, I think. Never saw him since. Many horses were killed.[55]

Both Fletcher and Cooper Hutchinson were to ride with Allen on despatch duties over the next few days and nights from their billet in a 'garret' beside the trenches now evident around GHQ. (Cooper Hutchinson was to return to Ireland on 8 May 1916 as 'Time Expired'). They needed to be ready at all times of the day and night and it wasn't unusual to be called on to run a message in the middle of the night. Private Robert Ludgate, one of the many men riding despatches during this time, was singled out for special praise for his devotion to duty. On 30 June 1915 Private Ludgate was awarded the Distinguished Conduct Medal for his actions during the preceding November.[56] Robert was to later obtain a commission as a second lieutenant with the Royal Munster Fusiliers in 1918. His citation reads:

> For conspicuous gallantry and good work throughout the campaign as a Despatch Rider, particularly during October and November 1914, at Ypres. During this period he was constantly employed day and night, frequently under fire, and gave a fine example of devotion to duty.[57]

With GHQ now moved about a mile behind the town of Ypres, the Troops were re-billeted on 11 November in a farmhouse a further mile away at Elverdinge, approximately two miles from the front and Ypres. This meant that they could rest and, more importantly, eat proper food – milk, eggs and butter. This was fortunate as the weather suddenly turned from rain to snow on 19 November and continued in this vein. Prisoner of war escort duties to Poperinghe and despatch riding continued as well as guard duties at GHQ. Allen also recorded his duties in great detail and on 14 November, he experienced the following:

> Despatch riding at 3rd Division. Rode down behind Ypres. The houses are blown to atoms. The roads full of pit holes caused by shells. A poor beggar lying on the road outside Ypres with his head completely severed from his body, also a field officer lying dead. Each time as I passed through here (for 5 days) I have seen these poor chaps, not removed. Despatch to Lord Cavan. He is in a dug out under the ground. I am sniped at on my gallop up to him, but get through. At 3rd Division there are some engineers – Irishmen – one fellow is a Dublin man. They treat us to a grilled steak, spuds and everything. We are in a hot spot now (5 of us) [one of whom is Private Brownlow] and sleep in a dug out under the ground, which we prepare. Heavy shelling all night. MacCarthy [852 Private P MacCarthy MiD 5 April 1915 Trans 662 (HS) Labour Corps 7/7/17] is shot by sniper today [in shoulder].[58]

Brownlow continued to report his experiences at the front:

> We are in a rest camp for a few weeks as we are to be fitted out with
> new clothing, boots, etc. It is now hard to get a new rig out as our old
> ones are in rags. Nearly all my spare time has been taken up putting on
> patches, so you can see I am a jack of all trades.... .
>
> Whilst waiting for despatches in a stable at a village called Hooge,
> about three miles north of Ypres, a big bronzed faced Turco (an Algerian
> soldier) came in and made signals to us to give him some bread. As he
> had a very bulky haversack we were very slow in complying with his
> request. When one of lads pointed to the haversack the Turco quickly
> pulled it to the front and, opening, proudly exhibited the mutilated
> head of a German. We got a bit of a shock, but still we could not help
> laughing.... . Our horses are very much the worse of the hardships they
> have undergone but with this rest they will pull up again. We have had
> some great days hunting lately. We go out with sticks and a few dogs
> and generally manage to pot a few hares or rabbits. Of course we often
> miss a hare and hit a hen 'accidentally'. A duck too often falls a victim
> to one of these 'mistakes'.[59]

Sadly, after this long and very informative letter to the editor, on 4 December
1914, Robert Brownlow died as a result of cardiac syncope following asthma,
aged just 24. He was found at 0600 dead, in his billet, at the Chemin de
Cinque Rues, to the north-east of Hazebrouck, becoming the second casualty
of the regiment.[60] Living and working in Nenagh, he was a member of B
Squadron, Limerick, and had volunteered to serve overseas at the outbreak
of war.

The two Troops were withdrawn from the front line on 21 November
together with I Corps, to rest at Hazebrouck, moving to Hinges on 22
December. Christopher Doyle from Mill Street, Baltinglass, wrote home to
his brother on 18 November 1914:

> Just a line to say I am still on the lands of the living, still fighting and
> marching. Since I last wrote you my old chum [Thomas] McDonald,
> of Barn Hill, Castledermot, has left me, and I feel a trifle lonely
> over his departure as we were great chums: perhaps I will not see

him again. [Thomas McDonald survived, and was released (Time
expired) 4 May 1916]. I met a good lot of Baltinglass boys out here at
commencement of the war, but I think they must be all dead by this
time. It is a terrible war, all the whole place devastated by Germans.
I pity all the poor Belgian people, they are lying all around their
ruined villages and looking on sorrowfully at their once happy homes,
with a despairing look on their resigned features. The scenes which
surround me, while writing this note to you, are perfectly sickening:
snow falling fast, and dead bodies of German soldiers, horses, guns,
wagons, lying around. We cannot look at these scenes with pity, as the
Germans killed a lot of our fine men. It is our turn now; there is a lot
of heavy siege guns after joining our force, and with their assistance
we are doing good work. We have sometimes to meet the Germans
10 to 1. When we get at them with the bayonet, the English speaking
Germans hold up their hands and say, 'comrade, comrade, do not kill'
but we show no mercy. I was in a couple of tight corners but pulled
through safely. The officers in my corps are all fine fellows, roughing
it like ourselves. This week will tell a lot, as I write now, our wagons
are again loaded with ammunition for the firing line. I saw Sergeant
L. Cummins about a month ago, he was then well. Better news next
time–your fond brother

PS Love to all

PS The South African War was only a side show compared to this, as
thousands are falling weekly. When we arrived out here we got a great
reception from the French and Belgian people, nothing too good for us.
We are doing our best to clear the country of the hated Germans, but
we want plenty more men from home to help us.[61]

No. 119 Sergeant Laurence Cummins proceeded home to Plunketstown,
Castledermot, on five days' leave on 28 November 1914. His trip home
was reported in the *Nationalist and Leinster Times* on 5 December 1914. In
it they reported his impressions of the war at the front and his 'exploits',
including the background to one of his souvenirs, a German *pickelhaube*
retrieved from a German who 'fell a victim to Sergeant Cummins'
bayonet'.

A and D Troops

A and D Troops left for Field Marshal Sir John French's HQ on 9 September, marching through Coulommiers and bivouacking in Romeny-sur-Marne, through to Bezu-Saint-Germain, finally arriving at Fère-en-Tardenois in the afternoon of Monday 14 September. Fère-en-Tardenois was at this time the French General Headquarters as well as the main railhead for the British forces in the area. Here they met with A Squadron NIH, who had been billeted in the town since 11 September. Here, once again, together with A Squadron NIH, they came under the umbrella of the 'Irish Horse' and as such found themselves working with and, at times, for the NIH. Fatigues, such as cleaning tack, equipment, men and matériel, was undertaken with a vengeance, as the weather during their stay was atrocious. In all instances, whether it was raining or not, the horses needed exercising, leading to further kit cleaning. George Dixon and his colleagues were called out regularly to run messages or to search for spies. One such night, the 16th, Dixon recalled:

> A Troop sent out to search for German stragglers. My horse no good. Borrowed [James or Stephen] Sullivan's. Those left behind kept busy in clearing up the ground round about. We return about 5 pm with a few German prisoners. [M.J.] Foley and [John, to be A/QMS]Pollard [MSM] have found themselves some girl friends in our absence.[62]

The routine over the next few days was similar; either they were out hunting for any German cavalry, or stuck in camp, cleaning kit, all in the unending rain. As expected, living in conditions not conducive to their health and soon, cases of enteric fever (typhoid fever) started to appear within the troop with several of the men reporting sick. With this in mind, on Tuesday 22 September, the two troops moved camp away from Fère-en-Tardenois to a small hamlet called Seringes-et-Nesles, approximately a mile to the east. When the move had been completed the majority of the troops were, once again, off hunting for German cavalry, leaving Corporal George Evans to supervise the camp clean up with George Dixon, Foley and John Pollard. Camp routine was sometimes interspersed with small inter-section competitions, football matches or other sporting events. After the two troops had moved to Seringes, a series of shooting and tent-pegging competitions was held; however, the shooting competitions were hastily abandoned due to 'safety' concerns. Tent pegging was one of a series of 'Skill-at-Arms' tests beloved of the cavalry. A competitor would, whilst mounted, charge at a small tent peg fixed in the ground and try and dislodge it using either a lance or sabre. Whilst watching this event at the annual camp in 1903, Lady McCabe (Surgeon Major F. McCabe's mother), piped up in a very distinctive Irish brogue, 'Tell me now, son. Do they do that in real warfare?' 'Well no, mother', replied Dr McCabe, 'not exactly, but sometimes they charge …'.

As a result of the earlier outbreak of enteric fever, both Troops were inoculated, but this inevitably lead to a series of reactions to the vaccine, meaning that most of the men were laid low for a couple of days. The beginning of October found them still in Seringes-et-Nesles and still hunting the elusive German cavalry. Dixon recalls a specific hunt undertaken on the night of 3 October, within the deeply-wooded area between Beuvardes and Mont St Pere, approximately seven miles south of Fère-en-Tardenois:

A Troop leave camp at 6 pm for some more Uhlan [sic] hunting. We get a rum issue at a farm which is used as a base, this is situated between Beuvardes and Mont St Pere, where we left our horses. Capt Smyth said that our objective was a large farmhouse, surrounded by many trees. Jago, Wilkinson and myself are detailed off as scouts and our job was to look the place over and report back with any signs of people or their movements. We set off and reach the trees which appear to be an orchard. We creep through the trees to the edge of the clearing in front of the house. We creep all round the house but see no sign of life or movement anywhere. After going round it about three or four times, we decided that they were all asleep or no one was there, so returned to the farm to report back to Capt Smyth, arriving back there just after 10 pm. At 3 am Capt Smyth decided to take all the Troop and search the house. All were ordered to fix bayonets and not to make any sound whatsoever. The distance to the house was a little over 300 yards. Jago and [Corporal E.M.] Wilkinson were sent on ahead as scouts while we creep up behind in single file. When about 100 yards from the house and still in orchard, we stop and wait for scouts to return. It was quite laughable as every now and then someone would step on to a twig or a small broken off branch. The noise would echo in the still quietness of the morning like a pistol shot, also I had to wake [Stephen] Sullivan, whose snoring could be heard far and wide. The scouts return and report all clear, we creep up to the house and surround it. Capt Smyth went in with a few men and searched it, but the birds had flown, if they had ever been there. We went back to the farm, collected our horses and after a few hours returned to camp at 10 am tired, sleepy and wishing all Uhlans [sic] in Hell.[63]

Thursday 6 October saw the men finally packing up and cleaning all their kit in readiness to move. After loading the transport wagons and stores on the trains, they left Fère-en-Tardenois at about 1800 for Abbeville, arriving late the next day. The arduous task of unloading all the limbers, wagons and horses off the train took the men most of the evening and then on to new billets in an existing barrack block. Unfortunately for the horses, their stabling comprised lines in a field, something they had avoided in the more salubrious surroundings in Seringes. Staying in Abbeville until Tuesday 13 October, normal camp duties resumed, this time with the added advantages of a large town, including cafes, sightseeing and the obligatory group photographs. However, the stay was short and they were once again loading the transports, limbers and horses on the train for a move to St Omer.

Wakened about 4.30 am and ordered to saddle up. Quite a surprise. Luckily Joe [Foley] had not undressed so he was ready, if not quite sober. [Dixon had had to bring Joe Foley back from Abbeville after he had drunk too much.] We move off and meet A Troop at Station, who we find had been up since 3 am getting ready. So we No. 1 Section congratulate ourselves on not having been with them though we had to supply night guards and line guards while we were with them. Entrain at 8 am and pass through Boulogne and Calais, eventually arrive at St Omer at 10 pm, where we billet in private houses in town.[64]

Once again, the unloading of all their kit had to be carried out. This time the stabling allotted to them was of such poor quality and dirty that it took them the whole of the following day to clean them out. Normal camp routine resumed: exercising the horses, cleaning tack and equipment, kit inspections and guard duties. Once again they were billeted with the NIH and inspections were not only carried out by their own officers (Captain Smythe) but also Major (Viscount John Henry Michael) Cole, NIH. This could not have been easy for the men to accept. Since the beginning of September, the two Troops had been effectively confined to barracks and unlike B and C Troops had not been in any form of action. This inactivity started to tell with both the officers and men becoming frustrated which, in turn, led to a distinct lowering of morale. Added to this, on Saturday 17 October, whilst exercising their horses, they met B and C Troops 'looking delightfully dirty' on their way to Ypres. Dixon summed up the general feeling throughout the men succinctly: 'This is a war, not the Royal Barracks, Dublin. Begin to wish I was in the trenches.' At last, A and D Troop left St Omer at 0900 on 23 October, travelling to Steenvoorde, where they stayed for the night before passing through Poperinghe, arriving at Ypres on the evening of the 24th. They were billeted with C Troop at what was a former gymnasium, leaving the horses in lines outside. Now the squadron was, once again (albeit temporarily), complete. It appears that A and D Troops were destined not to go to the front like B and C Troops, but to resume guard duties in the town itself and around the GHQ at the Cloth Hall. Additionally, they were tasked with guarding German prisoners of war in the town until taken to the rear by whichever infantry unit was available. Moving billets again, they settled into the cavalry barracks close to the Cloth Hall, but two days later on 30 October, were moved to the rear and had to return to Steenvorde. Whilst on guard duty at the Cloth Hall in Ypres, George Dixon was to see many important people, one such man being the mayor of Ypres. The mayor was arrested later and shot as a spy. This was even mentioned in the *New York Tribune*, making the headlines on 23 November 1914.

Rumour has it that we are for the trenches, McCombe seems to have the wind up about this – I don't give a damn, but later when McCombe says he is delighted – Well, I wonder! On fatigues this morning drawing rations from near the Railway Station. We are attacked by German aeroplane, who dropped a bomb about 20 yards from one wagon. No casualties. On return ordered to get ready to move. Horses inspected by a Flag Lance and Staff QMS. We open fire on enemy aeroplanes and artillery join in, good practice for them. Soon we are ready to move. As we leave we see a large observation balloon go up in the sky. The din then was terrific. We move back to Steenvorde, where we spend the night in a barn, the horses pegged out in some fields. All are downhearted at having to go back. Rum issue.[65]

William Joseph Pogue McCombe was always winding George Dixon up and was the bane of his life. He was noted by his colleagues as being a bit of a 'boss' and was continually haranguing his chums. He was usually put in charge of his section and seemed, at times, to throw his weight about a little too much. He was sent home in March of 1915 and Dixon recorded 'sent home with skin disease, after all his baths and boasting that he would be immune from such troubles' much to the amusement of his colleagues. William was commissioned later that year on 19 July 1915, into the Sherwood Foresters (Notts and Derby Regiment). He was to be killed in action with the 10th Battalion, trying to take Bayonet Trench, Arras, on 23 April 1917.

From the day they had arrived at the front on 23 August until 22 November, the squadron had been in the frontline. Mons, Landrécies, the retreat to the Marne, the ensuing battles of the Marne and Aisne, the race to the sea and the First Battle of Ypres, all with the loss of two lives, is a remarkable achievement. (Some wag in the Guards Brigade was overheard to say they thought that they had had it 'cushy').[66]

After being pulled out of the front line at Ypres and rested, the squadron was once again split up with two troops attached as Army Troops to IV Corps and the remainder (B Troop and C Troop) staying with I Corps, moving to the Béthune area, and billeted in Hinges. The detachment with IV Corps comprised A and D Troops and was under the command of Captain Ralph Blackett. Blackett was the son of the late Colonel Edward William Blackett, 7th Baronet Blackett and a veteran of the Anglo-Boer War. He served in 14th (The King's) Hussars and was on the staff of General French's cavalry division as a captain. He was appointed captain in the Royal Irish Fusiliers in 1905 and was on the retired pay reserve list of officers, before being appointed lieutenant with the South Irish Horse in 1912. The war diaries for this detachment are scant to say the least, but the indomitable George Dixon was still with A Troop and had recorded their activity in his diaries (see Appendix II).

Briefly, however, the usual police duties, escort duties and orderly duties were undertaken by the detachment, an average of seventy-seven men and three officers at this stage. The (rather brief) diary for the detachment records that fourteen men joined from the base, one man was sent to prison, one man transferred to Squadron HQ (presumably at Hinges) and three men sent to hospital. Over this period, a recorded fourteen men arrived in France on 17 December 1914, with another sixteen men arriving on 20 January 1915.[67]

George Dixon recorded a number of incidents that are of great interest, although some not directly involving the South Irish Horse. Whilst performing guard duties in Béthune on 9 February 1915, Dixon was called on to assist with two prisoners who had previously escaped custody. As a result, they were ordered to handcuff the prisoners. Unfortunately, the keys to the handcuffs had gone missing and the two men were left shackled for the whole night. Although this seems a rather unremarkable incident, it transpired that later on in the month at least one of these prisoners was shot at dawn. There are only three men who were recorded as shot at dawn in the same time period, namely, George Collins (1st Lincolnshire Regiment), shot at Locre on 15 February 1915 for desertion, and William Price and Richard Morgan (2nd Welsh Regiment), both for murdering their CSM, Hughie Hayes, in Béthune on 20 January 1915. They were executed on the same day as Collins, 15 February 1915, at Béthune. The circumstances surrounding these executions would point towards the two men referred to by Dixon as being Price and Morgan. Collins' regiment was based at Locre and his court martial was also at Locre on 7 February. It is highly unlikely that he would have been transferred to Béthune before being returned to Locre for his execution. Also, Dixon mentioned two people, so it is likely that he was referring to Morgan and Price who were court-martialled at Béthune and subsequently executed in the town.

Dixon also highlighted the trials and tribulations of being in barracks for a considerable time without front-line action. Frayed tempers, light-fingered colleagues and drunkenness seemed to be at the forefront of his mind. Interspersed with monotonous guard and orderly duties, exercising the horses in horrid weather and fatigues, all this inactivity had a deleterious effect on the morale of the troops. Two of his friends, Donald McMillan and Thomas McClean, were arrested for drunkenness at the beginning of

February, and McClean, this time in the company of Stephen Sullivan, was court martialled by the camp commandant for drunkenness and sentenced to a month's detention. One of the worst crimes to be committed in the barrack block was that of theft from your comrades. There appears to have been a thief within Dixon's barracks and although they had their suspicions, no one was ever caught.

Two of Dixon's colleagues were so dispirited with their inactivity that they decided to apply for a transfer to the Grenadier Guards: they were Benjamin Hall Todd and Cecil Vere Wilson. Todd, aged 24 was killed in action on 10 March 1915, during the Battle of Neuve Chapelle. With no known grave he is remembered on the le Touret Memorial. Wilson, aged 32, initially serving in the Grenadier Guards, was then commissioned and transferred to the Royal Berkshires with the rank of second lieutenant. He died of wounds received during the fighting at Delville Wood and was buried in the St Sever Cemetery, Rouen, on 31 July 1916. They were not the only ones to consider transferring. McMillan transferred to the Royal Engineers Signals Service, Joseph Hubbard transferred to the Army Ordnance Corps in 1916. Dixon himself was commissioned into the East Yorkshire Regiment and was in turn awarded the Military Cross.

It was around this time that 19-year-old Shoeing Smith (S/S) Albert Lyons was sent to Rouen's No. 10 General Hospital after contracting measles in the field. Albert (Bertie) from Oughterard, County Galway, was one of the four shoeing smiths who had been sent out with the squadron at the outbreak of the war. (According to the medal rolls, he arrived in theatre on 21 August 1914, a couple of days later than the rest of the squadron.) He was never to recover from the bout of the measles and died on 13 March 1915. He is now buried in St Sever cemetery, St Sever, Rouen.

There is no official record of B and C Troop's activities during the beginning of 1915. What is known, however, is that they were with I Corps and present during the Battle of Neuve Chapelle, primarily running despatches at and around Festubert. A small article in the *Irish Times* dated 14 April 1915 reported that J Allardyce, L[ouis] Allen, Thomas Jestin and R. Lougheed had been wounded on or before 9 April 1915 (28 March). It is quite conceivable that these men were wounded during the Battle of Neuve Chapelle. Luckily, all four survived the war. With no breakthrough on this front, the detachment reverted to more typical duties, providing labour for improving breastworks, defences, moving supplies up and down the front, and mounted and dismounted training.

Sergeant Joseph Spittal, 23, was with B and C Troop and recounted his experiences in a number of published diary entries contained in the *Nationalist and Leinster Times* dated 12 February 1916. Having been with the regiment since 4 April 1910, he departed for the front line as part of a small detachment of seventeen replacements on 14 April 1915. Arriving in France, he was faced with the realities of the war after passing through Merville on the way to their billets at Estaires (between Hazebrouck and Neuve Chapelle) on 17 April. He recounted seeing the graves of fallen soldiers in isolated pockets all around the countryside, marked with simple wooden crosses in between the ruins of heavily shelled buildings. His billets were situated approximately three miles from the front line and taking a walk with James Kilroy (No. 933, who had arrived a few days earlier) noticed:

> endless trenches and rows of barbed-wire entanglements, saw graves of soldiers hurriedly buried and house and bridges in ruins. The roar of guns in increasing volume broke on our ears as well as the distinctive noise of bursting of shells .... We approached within 1½ miles of the firing line, and as it grew dusk, the whole place seemed alight with huge searchlights playing across the trenches, with here and there, the glare of the maxim guns. This was the night the English captured Hill No. 60 and hence the terrific bombardment.[68]

On Tuesday, 13 April 1915, B Troop and C Troop, previously at Corps HQ and under the command of Captain Watt, joined 2nd Division based at Béthune, taking over from B Squadron 15th Hussars as the Divisional Mounted Troops.[69] It can be assumed that the detachment at IV Corps rejoined the rest of the squadron around this time. They comprised five officers and 129 other ranks and were based in the l'Horlogerie area to the south-east of Béthune. They moved closer to the front line with the divisional HQ to le Hamel during the division's operations against la Bassée.[70] One troop was detached to provide support at Richebourg, St Vaast. A further troop had been assigned to I Corps HQ, comprising an officer with forty other ranks. On 20 May, whilst in the rear lines, the squadron came under heavy enemy artillery bombardment, wounding Captain R. Smythe.[71]

Apart from the detachment at I Corps HQ and C Troop at Mazingarbe, the rest of the squadron remained on standby during operations around la Bassée. Throughout June and July, the situation remained unchanged. The majority of July was taken up by working on second-line trench defences. The squadron had become, effectively, pioneers. A move from Béthune to le Quesnoy in August, still on the Béthune-Loos-Neuve Chapelle-la Bassée front, did not mean mounted duties. Far from it. Working parties for cable-laying and general works for the Royal Engineers (RE) continued approximately 1,500 yards behind the lines at le Pantin and were interspersed with equipment inspections and policing the roads during Lord Kitchener's visit to the British and French lines. Captain Blackett, who had been in command of the detachment sent to assist IV Corps in December and January of 1914–15, left the squadron to take up duties in charge of the Depot in Ireland (at that time in Carlow).

Sergeant Spittal appeared to have been part of the detachment operating with I Corps. He described running despatches on 30 April:

Ride to Bac St Menir and Rue de Calais [Rue Bac St Maur NE of Estaires to Rue de Calais, Hazebrouck] in the afternoon, and go to Armentiers [sic] with despatch. We could not spare our horses on some parts of the journey. It was very open country, and at parts looks right into the enemy's lines. Anyway, we got through safely.[72]

After writing about the build-up to the Battle of Aubers Ridge, he then went on to describe the opening bombardment on Sunday 9 May.

Bombardment commenced at 3:30am. Precisely at the half hour, every gun let go, with a shock which simply shook the earth. Not many minutes elapsed until the Huns replied. Myself and four men were sent on duty at a point (Croix Blanche) [approx. 2,000yds south of Fleurbaix] not far from the trenches, to take prisoners, stragglers, etc. About 6:00am the first batch of wounded came past and continued all day in dimensions which reminded one of a crowd coming from a football match. They were from the RI Rifles, Royal Berkshires, Lancashire Fusiliers and Rifle Brigade. [Probably on their way to la Trou Aid Post behind the Croix Blanche post]. We were told when the guns started the Germans evacuated their first line of trenches. The English advanced and gained the trench, and were immediately flooded out. Anyone who escaped from this inferno was lucky. Maxims and rifles literally mowed men down. Shells blew men and trenches to bits. The RI Rifles advanced with fixed bayonets and now the fight commenced in earnest. Briton and German died propping each other up, having met with bayonets and stabbed together. Heaps of dead piled up. This continued all day, the English gaining trenches and leaving them again. Shells were flying everywhere thicker than crows in springtime. You could, with difficulty, hear the man next you shout. At night it seemed to get worse. Everywhere seemed alight with the glare of maxims, rifles and bursting shrapnel shells. All night long this went on. The stream of wounded kept passing and we heard of men being bayoneted by those savages when they lay helpless on the ground, and now longer able to fight. It would be hard indeed to describe one's feelings.[73]

Later, on Friday 15 May, having been sent to join No. 416 Private William Peters on duty, he had a narrow escape from a 'Jack Johnson' shell. He managed to avoid the shell, but was hit by some spent shrapnel in the back, although not injuring him. His horse, in his words 'seemed to know the danger and would actually jump anything'. He was then on duty in Fleurbaix for the week of 16 to 22 May. During this time he was stationed in the trenches. He recalls an incident whilst in the trenches:

A Saxon put his head over enemy trenches and shouted – 'Me no shoot. Have you got paper? Are anti-German riots over in London? Have two children there.' One of our fellows, an Irishman by his accent, shouted back – If you remain there a second longer your children in London will be orphans.' A hint was never taken in quicker time.[74]

On 12 June, he described an action that may well have resulted in his Mention in Despatches:

Fray starts at 2:00pm. Two fellows get killed by grenade, and at 3 o'clock we get it from every side. From every side shells are literally rained on us. We get the order to stand to our horses, not a nice job when high explosives are falling around, but there is no alternative. We got what was left of the horses safely away, with what was left of ourselves. Such a scene! Bits of horses and men flying all round. Not many of us will ever forget it. And who could run away and leave a wounded comrade? So you chance it and carry him out of the shelled area. Many got hit, but I escaped – the fortunes of war I suppose. We are shelled for half an hour, and afterwards we bury the dead where they fell – men and horses. Fancy, we sleep tonight within a hundred yards of this place.[75]

Captain Smythe returned from sick leave together with Private David Jenkins, who had been attending cadet school. Jenkins, who was to be promoted corporal, was eventually commissioned in the Indian Army Reserve on 24 September 1918.

With the preparations for the upcoming 'push' on the Loos front, the squadron, as Divisional Mounted Troops, trained with the mounted machine-gun section (MMG) to provide rapid mounted support and reconnaissance in the event of a 'breakthrough'. The training lasted over six days, culminating with the squadron at readiness on 25 September, attached to 2nd Divisional HQ in the woods adjacent the canal at le Quesnoy (le Quesnoy Keep)

Second Division were concentrated to the north of Loos opposite la Bassée. As the Battle of Loos developed throughout the 25th, the division were ordered to assemble a brigade comprising three battalions (Carter's Detachment) in support of 7th Division. One of these battalions, the 1st/5th King's (Liverpool Regiment), was recalled at 2235, from their assigned duties as prisoner of war (PoW) escorts and depot guards, control post duties etc. The Divisional Mounted Troops were re-assigned to cover these, resulting in the squadron taking over the I Corps PoW cages at Beuvry at approximately 0100 on 26 September. They were to remain on duty there until 5 October.[76]

Billeted at le Quesnoy for the next three months, work on winter billets, second-line trenches and squadron training was the order of the day. An inspection of the Division was carried out by His Majesty at the end of October, as part of his visit to the combined British and French forces. (The King also inspected a contingent of A Squadron as part of the II Corps visit on 27 October.) As the October weather turned for the worse, squadron training had to be abandoned on numerous occasions, sometimes being so bad that exercising the horses became difficult and occasionally impossible. The billets started in October were continually improved and upgraded with thatched roofs, metalled roads with shale cutting timber for lumber and general building. Captain Watts, having taken over the squadron when he and the three troops arrived in March 1915, handed over the squadron to Captain Smythe and returned to England on 12 December 1915.

Thirty-third Division took over from 2nd Division at Béthune on 27 December. The squadron vacated their quarters in Beuvry on the 29th and marched to the billets prepared by the 33rd Divisional mounted troops (their sister regiment, F Squadron NIH)[77] at the Chemin de Beau Repaire, Caintrainne, on the outskirts of Lillers. With the billets cleaned over the next few days, general squadron routine and training recommenced. Four officers were sent to the divisional grenade school for a week's instruction on 3 January. At the beginning of January, the squadron strength stood at six officers and 159 ORs. (It should be noted that the hay ration was reduced from 10lb to 6lb per horse by the HQ QMS on the 11th. In winter, when there is not enough grazing for horses, to reduce the hay ration is not going to be good for the general wellbeing and upkeep of the horses, cavalry or otherwise, bearing in mind the majority of transport was horse drawn.)

Having just settled into the billets at Beau Repaire, the squadron was on the move again with 2nd Division, back to Béthune, to relieve 12th Division in the Festubert-Givenchy area, and marched out on 19 January to le Cauroy (Corroy), west of Hinges. After cleaning up the recently vacated billets (again) they were attached to 2nd Division Royal Engineers repairing the le Touret Line support points around le Touret and Loisne until the middle of February (16 February). As one can imagine, working parties, digging and repairing trenches, escort duties, military police duties and despatch riding, weren't on the bucket list for aspiring young cavalry officers and the young bucks in the ranks. From the great retreat of Mons and the actions throughout October and November the previous year, the relative inactivity must have preyed on the minds of these normally active young men. Transfers to line regiments and commissions were often sought and given.

As the division went into corps reserve on 20 February, they were, in effect, resting, so the squadron could continue its training after spending almost a month digging and repairing works. Second Division relieved the French 18th Division over the period 27–29 February and the squadron moved from le Cauroy to Hersin, Sains-en-Gohelle, a move south of their original position. The month of March proved to be wet and snowy. Unfortunately, as spring was close by, damage to the trenches was exacerbated due to the thawing mud and had to be continually repaired.

I could find no record of what the squadron was doing from this date onwards until the squadron formed 1st South Irish Horse with C and E Squadrons. I have, however, managed to piece the following information together from various war diaries.[78] The squadron was based in Sains-en-Gohelle for the first half of March, together with Divisional HQ and Bruay for the second half. It would be assumed that general training, escort duties, APM duties were the order of the day. The average strength of the squadron was six officers and 150 other ranks. Out of these generally there would be one officer and approximately twelve to fifteen other ranks away at Divisional HQ or attached to the signals office, divisional signalling HQ, as runners/despatch riders.

The division was resting from 27 March, but on 1 April the squadron, together with the divisional cyclist company, were sent off to Samer to train with 1st Cavalry Division at their mounted troops training school, for a fortnight. They appear to have been billeted at Hesdigneul-les-Boulogne and trained around Hesdin-l'Abbé. They participated in a field day against 9 Cavalry Brigade on 14 April; there is no record of how they performed, though. The training was completed on the 17th and the squadron returned to 2nd Division arriving on the 19th at Sains-en-Gohelle where they remained until the order for Divisional Mounted Troops to cease was given and left the division on 10 May, to form IV Corps Cavalry with C and E Squadron SIH. The new unit was known as 1st South Irish Horse (1 SIH).

The following table shows the 186[79] men entitled to the 1914 Mons Star, (i.e. men who had been in France and Flanders between 5 August and 22 November 1914), in other words, those men who had been with S Squadron and what happened to them after that first year at war:

Officers entitled to 1914 Mons Star	8
Men entitled to 1914 Mons Star	178
Of those :	
Commissioned	39
Time Expired (TE)	31
Transferred	17
Left TE and rejoined	4
No Longer Fit	7
Died	4

Chapter 3

A Squadron – Dublin – 21st Division, Loos, Armentières, Ribemont.

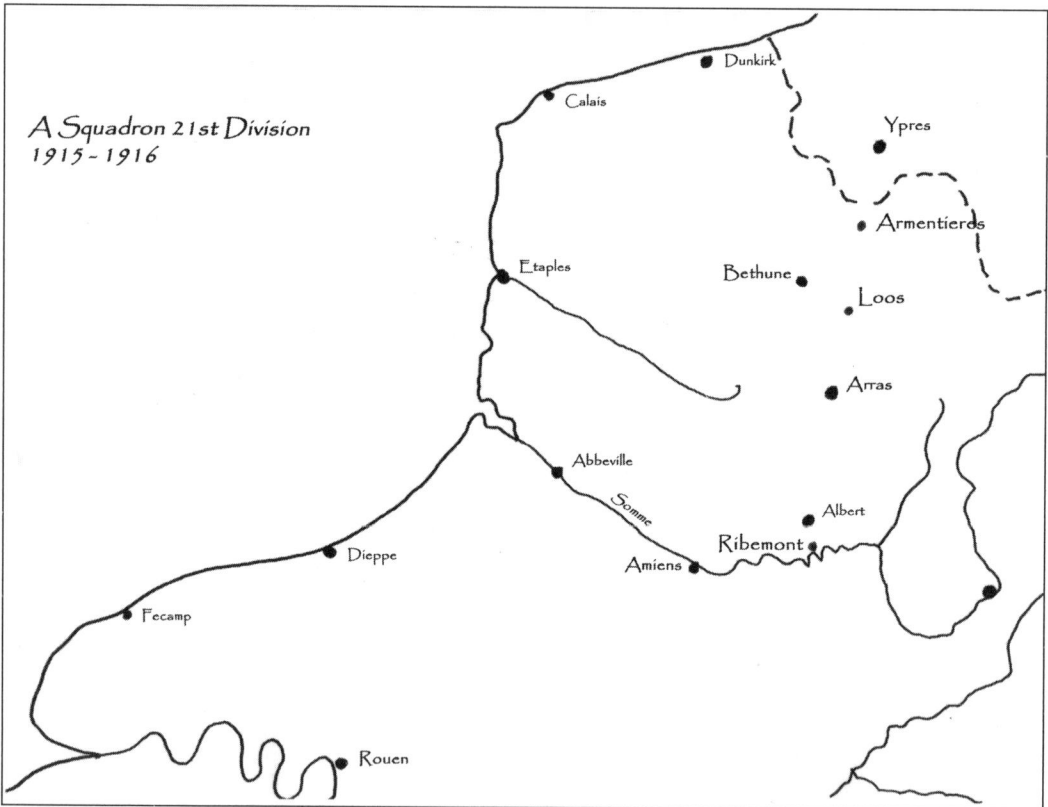

A Squadron 21st Division 1915-1916

A Squadron, under the command of Captain Noel Furlong, had been mobilized since August 1914. Having left Dublin for Doncaster on 11 December 1914, initially as part of the home defence forces, they joined 21st Division from Tickhill, Yorkshire, where they had been stationed for two months previously.[1]

The squadron suffered their first tragic episode whilst stationed at Tickhill. Patrick Charles Mitchell, a member of 2 Troop and originally from

Roscommon, had returned home from South America where he was working as an engineer to answer the call to arms. During his stay at Tickhill, he fell ill with meningitis. He had previously suffered from malaria during the course of his work, and was therefore not strong enough to be able to recover from the bout of meningitis and died in St George's Nursing Home, Doncaster, aged 28. His funeral was well attended by both soldiers and townspeople, with members of his troop forming a guard of honour escorting his coffin on a gun carriage provided by the Royal Artillery to the cemetery, where he was buried.[2]

The squadron trained with the division in and around Aldershot, Hampshire. On 11 September they departed Farnham in two sections and travelled to Southampton to await embarkation on the SS *Anglo Canadian*. The troop manifest records the squadron as being six officers and 141 ORs in strength, but the war diary records that only 135 officers and men departed Southampton. (Even more confusing, allowing for early arrivals and stragglers, the medal roll would indicate only 127 officers and men.)[3]

Arriving at le Havre the following day, the squadron disembarked and proceeded to St Omer by train. The division headquartered at Watten, France, where further training was to take place. Routine drills were interspersed with bomb throwing and gas drills. In a letter to his father, Sergeant W.R. Martin wrote:

we have had one or two experimental tests in bomb throwing; an operation more dangerous to the attacker than the attacked. The bombs are somewhat like unto a tennis ball with a fuse, which strikes on a band fastened to the left arm. The fuse is timed for 4 secs! and it takes one all the time from striking to the throw, as on the very tick of time off goes the beastly thing and anything within a 50 yard radius goes 'west'.[4]

After four days' training, the whole division departed the Watten area for the Loos front. A series of night marches over the next five nights had the squadron arriving at Bruay-la Buissiere, approximately five and a half miles behind the front lines.

On Saturday 25 September 1915 the Battle of Loos commenced. Initial successes led to General Haig calling on his reserves to exploit the situation. Unfortunately, Lord French had the reserves so far back from the front lines that deployment took too long and was ineffective. Having received orders to move at 1030 that day, the division reached Mazingarbe during the afternoon. The divisional HQ troops left at 1500 and arrived at la Philosophe around 2100. The divisions reached their allocated positions along the front line during the night, and were ordered to continue the attack along the line of Hulloch and Hill 70 to regain the objectives lost overnight as a result of successive German counter-attacks. The attack on Hill 70 commenced at 0900 on Sunday.

Arriving at dusk on Saturday, the squadron bivouacked behind the staff HQ and were ordered to stand-to at 0300. During the morning, as the attacks commenced, some of the squadron's officers were given traffic control duties around la Philosophe. It soon became clear that the attacks along the front line weren't going according to plan and, around noon, Major General Forestier-Walker called on an escort of two SIH officers (Second Lieutenant Norman Anderson and Lieutenant Cyril Gage Kirk) to accompany him to the front lines. Due to a further deterioration in the progress of the attack, divisional headquarters tasked three of the remaining squadron's officers to carry out a reconnaissance of roads to the rear of the lines around 2000.

Still awaiting orders to advance, the squadron was now standing about 300 yards away from two heavy artillery positions. These positions were subjected to return artillery fire from the Germans. Some of this return fire fell close to the squadron and two shrapnel bursts, either side of the horses approximately fifty yards away, convinced Captain Furlong and the HQ staff, to relocate the whole squadron half a mile to the west towards Sailly Labourse. Further shelling by the enemy forced the squadron to move even farther back towards Sailly Labourse in the early afternoon. Watching the Germans counter-attack the division in the evening of the 26th, Sergeant Martin saw

A most awful sight. The lines of trenches were lit up by fire-balls and these, combined with the rattle of musketry and the big guns, reminded one very much of a huge firework display.... The noise simply beggars description – big guns, rockets, rattle of musketry, and the roll of maxims were too terrible for words.[5]

After a fruitless and costly attack, the divisions were relieved during the morning of 27 September and began moving to the rear around Vermelles and

Sailly Labourse to join the squadron. The squadron carried out policing duties to ensure the retiring divisional troops arrived safely. So ended 21st and 24th Divisions' part in the Battle of Loos. Approximate casualties for both divisions over the two days amounted to 4,300 men killed, wounded and missing.[6]

Sergeant Martin again described the chaos of the roads to the rear of the front line as the troops of 21st Division retired, being 'blocked by all sorts of traffic – horses, motors and men moving along; ambulance wagons hooting their horns just like at home, and all under fire from the Jack Johnsons'.[7]

The 21st Division, as a whole, was ordered to retire in order to refit and retrain. Over the next five days, and in very wet weather, the squadron endured a hard march back from Loos, travelling north-west through Béthune, Aire, Morbecque, Hazebrouck and onto Strazeele. Located between St Omer, Steenvorde and Lilliers, Strazeele became the squadron's winter billet. The squadron soon fell into camp routine with horse and stable management, exercising, kit inspections and small-arms training. A small contingent of one officer and thirty ORs took part in an inspection of II Corps by the King at the RFC airfield in Bailleul on 27 October 1915.[8]

Regular training in small-arms, bombing, sword drill, mounted drill and scouting exercises was also maintained. As required, personnel were seconded to the Assistant Provost Marshal (APM) to undertake traffic control duties, policing and PoW guard duties in and around Armentières. To fulfil this necessary requirement, a permanent presence of one officer and thirty men to be located in Armentières were assigned by divisional headquarters.

With winter closing in, bad weather made the upkeep of the billets and horse lines a continual struggle. More than once the existing billeting arrangements were discussed and other potential farms inspected, but none matched the existing facilities. In early November, divisional headquarters decided to keep the squadron in their existing billets rather than move them closer to the Division's current lines outside Armentières. It was essential that work to improve and upgrade the existing lines be undertaken, so timber shelters for the horses were constructed and a new cookhouse and latrine lines installed. A second farm was also commandeered and housed a further thirty-two men and horses.

Towards the end of November, the divisional cyclists were ordered to form a trench grenadier battery, utilising rifle grenades, spring grenades and trench-catapult grenades. It was decided that the battery should also include a detachment from the divisional mounted troops. Accordingly, sixteen volunteers under Lieutenant Anderson were sent to join the grenadiers to form the trench-catapult platoon. Each platoon was then divided into two smaller sections comprising eight men. Intensive training in the use of the catapult was carried out in Armentières.[9] Trench catapults were known as Leach-Gamage trench catapults after their manufacturer, Gamages of London. They were Y-shaped devices designed to throw a 2-pound projectile over the trench parapet. Constructed from timber, with rubber straps to 'throw' the bomb, the straps were put under tension with a rack-and-pinion mechanism which, when released, fired the bomb.[10] Similar bombs to that described by Sergeant Martin earlier in the year were still being used.

Special grenade stations were being constructed at three different locations on the front line held by the division. A trench system known as the 'Mushroom' just in front of la Chapelle d'Armentières was chosen, as it extended into no man's land in the shape of the head of a mushroom and was considered just close enough for this type of weapon. The grenade stations were completed by the middle of December and were operational with the first shots fired on the 21st. Further activity during the following few nights to cover working parties in no man's land commenced but drew retaliatory fire from the Germans. On the night of the 22nd the Germans shelled the catapult station position with high explosive (HE) shells.[11] Some of these exploded on the position, killing three members of the section, 1068 Private Francis Larkin, 1073 Private Leopold Le Bas and 1144 Private William A. Sadlier. Leopold, the youngest casualty at 19 years of age, was a native of Rathmines in Dublin.[12] Francis, twenty-two, educated at Blackrock College, had joined the South Irish Horse at the beginning of the war and was a versatile sportsman, playing football, rowing and cricket.[13] William, also of Rathmines, was a former insurance clerk.[14] His younger brother Gerald was to lose his life in May 1917 fighting with 54th Australian Battalion. Mr and Mrs Sadlier lost both of their sons to the war.

The catapult battery continued to be a nuisance to the German lines over the rest of December. A further three men were sent to replace the casualties on the 27th. One of the three, 977 Private R. Sheppard, was wounded by shrapnel before he even made it to the station. On 11 January 1916, the section suffered another fatality, that of 844 Private Daniel Shanahan. Aged only 22, he was fatally wounded when a rifle (Newton Pippin) grenade misfired. Private Shanahan was a native of Cork, living in Upper John Street, Cork, and was working for Cork Corporation in the waterworks department before volunteering in Mallow.

Captain Noel Furlong wrote to Daniel's mother:

I deeply regret having to inform you of the sad news of your son [Daniel's] death. He was killed in action at Armentières on January 11th, in the front line trench, while throwing bombs with our catapult battery. Words fail me to tell you how much I myself and the whole squadron sympathise with you in your bereavement and I mourn the loss of a most promising soldier who, had he lived, would, I feel sure, have gained distinction for himself and the regiment – Yours truly,
Noel Furlong, Capt. 16th January, 1916[15]

Also, Lieutenant A.V. FitzHerbert, Daniel's troop commander, wrote to Mrs Shanahan:

Dear Madam – I have just returned from leave, or would have written sooner to say how very sorry I am that your son Dan has been killed. Since he joined the squadron he has been in my troop – he was such a smart soldierly looking fellow, sat a horse so well – it may be some small compensation to your grief to know this, and that he died nobly doing his duty in the front line. He was one of the many who stepped forward and volunteered for the work – fine fellows all of them, and we want more to finish the war quickly. My sincerest sympathy in your loss….[16]

Over the next couple of months, the grenade station was used to varying degrees of success. Smoke grenades were occasionally used to confuse the enemy and make them think that an attack was imminent. One particular incident was recorded in the war diary of 21st Divisional Cyclists:

12 February 1915: Two officers with parties to work 8 rifle stands + 4 spring guns with a catapult party of SIH in 79/80 trench for bombardment of German trenches at dusk (5:15pm) by smoke bombs

to make enemy expect an attack and man their trenches. Very effective shooting by S(pring) Guns. The bombs had the desired effect of leading enemy to expect and attack + gas signals + red rockets for reinforcements were noticed immediately we opened fire.[17]

Back at the billets, camp routine continued. The sheer monotony of this routine, in poor weather, sometimes without even the ability to properly exercise the horses, must have been difficult. In addition to this, the squadron's strength was being continually undermined with more and more men seconded to other duties, leaving the remainder to pick up the slack. In February Captain Furlong complained:

> During this month I had 30 men and 1 officer attached to the APM for police work and 16 men and 1 officer forming a catapult battery. This left me with three sometimes four horses per man and I could do nothing but stables and keep them in exercise.[18]

It must have been with great relief that the squadron returned to full strength after St Patrick's Day with the return of all the seconded men, prior to the squadron being transferred to XIII Corps on 30 March 1915.

The squadron moved out of Strazeele and entrained, bound for Ribemont and XIII Corps once again. Over April the squadron settled into general camp routine. This time, instead of training some of the men for trench-catapult duties, twelve men under Lieutenant Fitzherbert were chosen to train as divisional snipers.

The usual police duties were required, with again thirty men and an officer seconded to the APM. Now trained, the divisional snipers went to the trenches. Towards the end of April another sixty men were required for unloading duties lasting three days.

At the beginning of May, the squadron moved out of their billets to prepared horse lines in the woods around Ribemont as a precursor to becoming part of XV Corps Cavalry. Divisional cavalry had been discontinued by the Army Council and replaced by corps cavalry, comprising, in the case of SIH squadrons, three squadrons of cavalry and a headquarters section. The decision to change from smaller Divisional cavalry units to the larger corps cavalry unit was, in part, due to the stagnation along the front line and differing interpretations of cavalry doctrine within the Army Council. (Professor Stephen Badsey in his book *Doctrine and Reform in the British Cavalry 1880–1918* explains this change in thinking in a far more detailed manner than I could ever hope to do and it is outside the remit of this work.)

Chapter 4

B Squadron – Limerick – 32nd Division
Flesselles, Behencourt, Contay

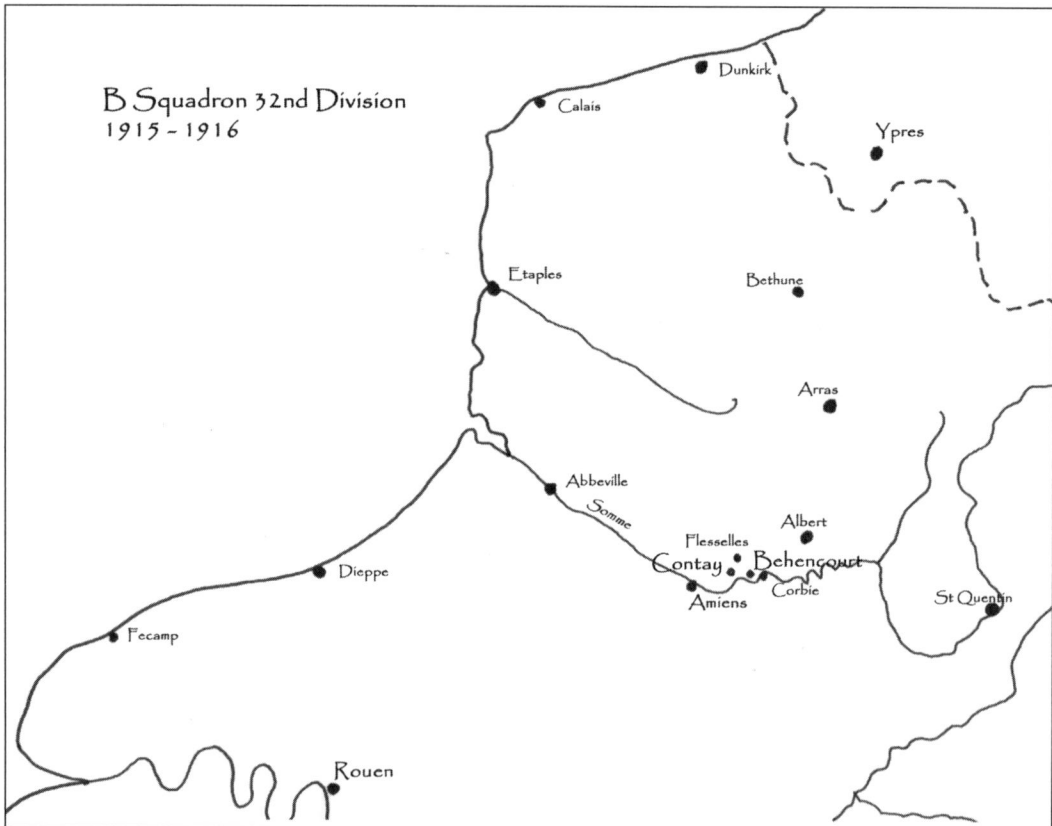

B Squadron 32nd Division
1915 - 1916

Dunkirk

Calais

Ypres

Etaples

Bethune

Arras

Abbeville

Somme

Albert

Flesselles

Contay · Behencourt

Corbie

Dieppe

St Quentin

Amiens

Fecamp

Rouen

On Thursday 25 November 1915 B Squadron arrived in France having travelled from their camp on the edge of Salisbury Plain at Codford, Wiltshire. The squadron under the command of Major Henry Stern had been training with 32nd Division as Divisional Cavalry.[1] Comprising 121 officers and men, they disembarked SS *African Prince* at le Havre and proceeded to the first bivouacking point at Famechon. Over the next two days, they travelled to Flesselles to join the division, via Ailly le Clocher and Olincourt. Flesselles is located north of Amiens in the Somme region of France.[2]

Arriving at the beginning of the winter, the men were immediately employed on wood-cutting duties and improving the existing billets under the supervision of the Royal Engineers. This continued throughout the months of November and December, even when the squadron moved from Flesselles to Behencourt. The division was relieving 51st (Highland) Division and the squadron moved into billets previously prepared by D Squadron North Irish Horse, much to the NIH's annoyance.[3] Prior to leaving Flesselles, 1025 Private Joseph O'Callaghan was called before a field general court martial (FGCM), charged with 'Striking a Senior Officer' on 16 December 1915. He was found guilty and sentenced to one year's hard labour.[4] (He was to re-join the squadron and later transferred to the 7th (South Irish Horse) Battalion Royal Irish Regiment.) With the squadron at Behencourt, 21-year-old Lieutenant Colvill's troop remained behind at divisional HQ. Born in Artane, County Dublin, George Chaigneau Colvill was the second son of the governor of the Bank of Ireland and one of the young up-and-coming officers of the regiment, having been commissioned in August 1914.

For the remainder of the squadron, forestry work was again the order of the day with Captain Edgar Lecky Phelps JP, (46) from Roo, Cloghera, County Clare, in charge, based at Fréchencourt. Captain, later Major, Phelps would return to Cahir in October 1916.

At the beginning of January, divisional headquarters moved from Flesselles to Senlis, with the squadron remaining at Behencourt. Lieutenant Colvill's troop returned to the squadron and was replaced at Senlis by Lieutenant Bence-Jones' troop. Twenty-one-year-old Lieutenant Campbell W.W. Bence-Jones was another of the young up-and-coming officers of the squadron. Although born in London, his parents, Reginald (Justice of the Peace and High Sheriff of County Cork) and Ethel, lived in Lissalan, County Cork. (His brother Philip was to earn the Military Cross). The divisional headquarters moved again in February, this time to Henencourt, with the duty headquarters troop following. A fire broke out under mysterious circumstances in the stables of the château being used as Divisional HQ; thankfully no men or horses of the troop were injured (or implicated).

The squadron would have been continually training when not cutting wood and maintaining their billets, and throughout January, February and March, the routine remained the same: woodcutting, HQ troops, training and threshing; not what the men were expecting when they signed up for the cavalry. Occasionally, men would be sent out to the Assistant Provost Marshal (APM) for duties and also to the Mounted Military Police (MMP). Some of the young 'gentlemen' would, to pass the time, arrange race meetings, go poaching for hares and shoot partridge.[5] April saw the squadron relocating to Contay, where they remained until leaving 32nd Division as a result of the re-organization and removal of divisional mounted troops on 13 May. This saw the end of B Squadron acting as divisional cavalry and what amounted to pioneering duties for the squadron. It would not be long until some of the squadron was to see action and to suffer their first casualty in the ensuing fighting around the Somme. In the meantime, the squadron joined A Squadron and, together with C Squadron Surrey Yeomanry, formed XV Corps Cavalry Regiment on 14 May 1916.

Chapter 5

C Squadron – Cork – 16th (Irish) Division, Westrehem, Hurionville, Vaudricourt and E Squadron (newly formed – Cahir) – 39th Division, Hazebrouck

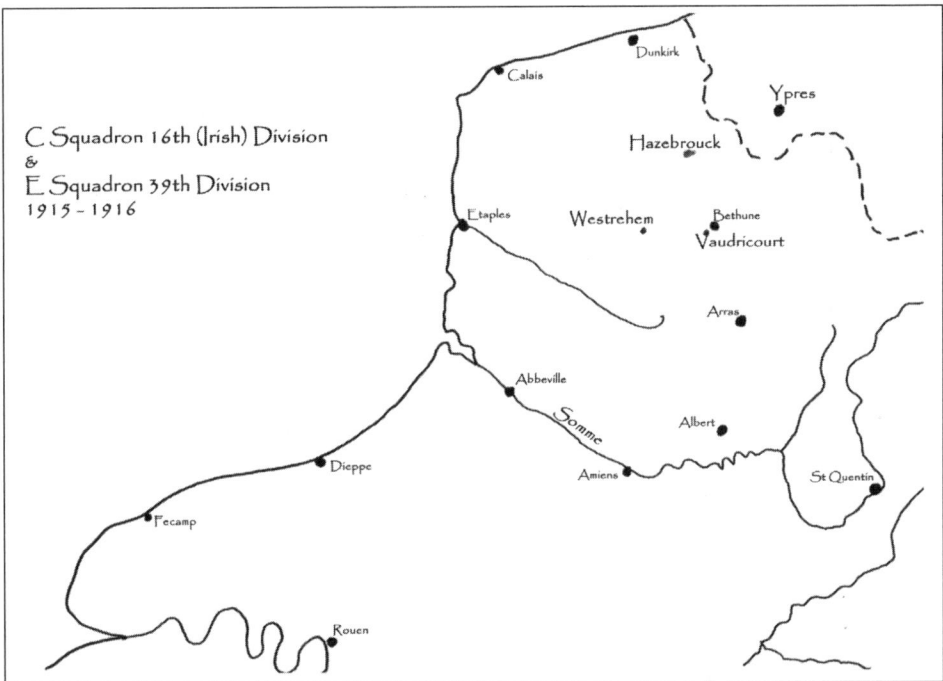

C Squadron, as part of 16th (Irish) Division, had, from September 1915, been training with the division in and around Aldershot prior to their embarkation for France. The other Irish division, the Tenth (Irish) Division, also had a squadron of SIH assigned as Divisional Mounted Troops. However, the Divisional Mounted Troops (SIH) were removed from the 10th Divisional strength just before the division embarked for the Dardanelles.[1] As 16th (Irish) Division was also in England at the time,

I believe that C Squadron (originally assigned to the 10th Division) was re-assigned to the 16th Division as their Divisional Mounted Troops (The 53rd (Welsh) Division briefly had a squadron of SIH assigned to them, on paper at least, before heading off to Suvla Bay). They appear to have made many friends in Camberley as a farewell dance and concert put on by the Catholic Schools for some members of the division, including members of C Squadron, was very well attended.

> Trooper William May, of the South Irish Horse, said he esteemed it a privilege to second the vote of thanks to Father Twomey and the ladies of his congregation. The Irish soldiers had never before in any other place been so well received as in Camberley district, and especially at the Soldiers' Club at the Catholic School … he wished to express the gratitude of the South Irish Horse. Speaking as an Irish Protestant, he knew that all the Protestants of the South Irish Horse had a great admiration for Father Twomey, because he made no distinction of creed whenever he had any hospitality to dispense. On the other hand, they noticed that he was very attentive to the spiritual needs of the Catholic soldiers. The fearless bravery of the Catholic chaplains at the front made a deep impression on all the non-Catholic soldiers. He desired to support a vote of thanks to Father Twomey and all his helpers, and asked them to accept the everlasting gratitude of the South Irish Horse.[2]

Entraining at Farnborough, Hampshire, the squadron arrived at Southampton to board and sail on the SS *Maiden*, arriving in le Havre on 19 December 1915. The squadron, comprising six officers and 141 men, travelled to Fouquereuil by train, then marched to their billets at la Buissière, west of Béthune, arriving late on the 20th. As there were no existing horse lines, the horses were picqueted in a field, whereas the men bedded down in barns. The ensuing bad weather, combined with the temporary horse lines led to the field being badly poached. Added to that, the poor condition of the horses, and lack of proper billeting facilities for the men, contributed to the decision to relocate the squadron. They were ordered to leave on the 28th and arrived at their new billets in Westrehem the next day. On 1 January 1916 the divisional headquarters also moved from Drouvin to a château at Bomy and then on to Amettes.[3]

Aside from normal duties, training and cleaning billets, forty-four men were employed on police duty for 15th (Scottish) Division whilst they carried out manoeuvres in the divisional area. When General Joffre arrived to inspect the division, another eighty men were employed on police duty along his route. Moving into I Corps reserve area on 28 February, the squadron relocated to Cantrainne. The weather at the end of February and beginning of March was typical: cold, frosty and snowy. As a consequence, roads became very dangerous and slippery for horses to traverse. The war diary shows that, on 4 March, a reconnaissance of routes for assembly areas could not be carried out due to the snowy weather. (The reconnaissance was completed the following day.) A further move four days later found the squadron billeting at Hurionville. Further policing duties occupied most of the squadron as well as digging duties for the Royal Engineers and general trench repairs. A further section of ten men and one NCO were assigned to escort duties for General Gough. All in all, as the war diary continually states, 'nothing unusual occurred today'.

A move from Hurionville to Vaudricourt, as the division went into the line, occurred on 27 March and the general 'pioneering' duties continued. From March into April, and then on to May, saw the same routine and 'nothing unusual occurred today'. However, on 10 May, a section of twenty-five men was called on to man 'straggler posts' in connection with an attack carried out in the evening. A straggler post was a location along a pre-determined line behind the attacking troops to catch 'stragglers' – wounded soldiers, soldiers who have 'lost their way'/company/regiment etc., malingerers or deserters – and then sort them accordingly. This would have been carried out in conjunction with the regimental and military police. For the men attending these posts, it must have been very demoralizing for them to catch the stragglers when they themselves were retained at the rear for 'the great breakthrough'.

As with the other squadrons, the middle of May brought the dissolution of divisional mounted troops and the formation of corps mounted troops. C Squadron joined S and E Squadrons to form IV Corps Cavalry Regiment.

E Squadron

Commanded by Captain Gilmore O'Grady, E Squadron arrived in theatre on 16 March 1916 and was assigned to 39th Division as Divisional Mounted troops. However, they did not train with the division in England but instead joined at Hazebrouk, having travelled directly from Ireland and disembarked at le Havre. A small advance party was with the division at Witley prior to their departure for France but it was of great concern to Major General N.W. Barnardiston MVO that 'the Divisional Squadron was not with the Division during its training'.[4]

Having set up billets at Hazebrouk and commenced training with the division, the squadron moved to new billets at la Haye on the 24th in heavy falling snow. Divisional training continued unabated throughout March and April and until the middle of May.[5] Then, as with A, B, C and S Squadrons, E left to become IV Corps Cavalry, joining S and C Squadrons. A last word on the re-organization of the Divisional Mounted troops was recorded by the GOC 39th Division:

The loss of the Divisional Cavalry and cyclists has been much felt. During trench warfare these units were able to furnish considerable assistance in Divisional duties, such as Road Control and so avoid the depletion of the fighting strength of infantry brigades.[6]

There has been some speculation that two squadrons of the South Irish Horse were sent to Palestine and remained there throughout. The regimental memorial to those who served and fell during the war in St Patrick's Cathedral, Dublin, has France, Flanders, Egypt and Palestine inscribed at each corner, but the regimental honours list does not mention anything other than battles in France and Flanders. I have, however, found reference to some members of the regiment serving with other regiments and being posted to the Middle Eastern theatre following the re-organization of the front-line squadrons in July. Also, smaller parties of men were sometimes attached to divisions as required and remained with them throughout the war. For instance, three men were attached to the HQ of 53rd (Welsh) Division in 1915 prior to the division departing for Gallipoli. Two of these men were Privates 1222 Henry Hudson and 1163 G. Blakemore. The three soldiers went to Gallipoli with the division and came ashore at Suvla Bay. Split up at A Beach, the trio went about their duties attached to their assigned headquarters, presumably for despatch and signals duties. Hudson was slightly wounded during this campaign and was evacuated to Malta to convalesce. When he was better,

Lieutenant Colonel Henry de la Poer Beresford, 6th Marquis of Waterford, Commanding Officer, South of Ireland Imperial Yeomanry (1902–1908) and the South Irish Horse (1908–1911). (*Courtesy Lord and Lady Waterford personal collection*)

Other Rank's uniform, original design 1902. (*Courtesy Lord and Lady Waterford personal collection*)

Officer's uniform, original design 1902. (*Courtesy Lord and Lady Waterford personal collection*)

Officers of the South of Ireland Imperial Yeomanry 1906:
Back Row L. to R.: 2/Lt E.L. Phelps, 2/Lt G. O'Grady, 2/Lt Sir Richard Leveinge, Maj. I. Burns-Lindow, 2/Lt W.H. Ball, Capt. F.M.J. Jennings, 8th Hussars (Adj), 2/Lt Sir J.L. Cotter, J.W. Bayliss (Quartermaster), 2/Lt R. Gethin, Capt. J.H. Tremayne *Front Row L. to R.*: Lt D. Fitzgerald, Knight of Glin, Capt. J. O'Grady Delmage, Maj. L.O. Williams, Maj. F. Wise, Lt Col The Marquis of Waterford, Maj. St Leger Moore, Maj. Sir Kildare Borrowes, Capt. D.S. Matthews, 17th Lancers (Adj) *Seated*: 2/Lt L.L. Hewson MVO, Capt. A Somerville, Surg-Lt F. MacCabe, 2/Lt W. Goulding. (*Courtesy Lord and Lady Waterford personal collection*)

On manoeuvres at the Curragh: Captain Stern, General Gough and the Marquis of Waterford. (*Courtesy Lord and Lady Waterford personal collection*)

Limerick Squadron watering horses at the annual camp, circa 1903. (*Courtesy Lord and Lady Waterford personal collection*)

Some of Limerick Squadron, the parade square, Artillery Barracks, Limerick, circa 1903. (*Courtesy the Mitchell family*)

James O'Brien (left), Trooper William Good, C Squadron (centre) and John T. Shorten (right) with friends at the annual camp, the Curragh. (*Courtesy Mr William Good*)

Troop of SIIY ready to embark at the railway station. The troopers still carry the Lee Enfield Mk 1 rifle and Boer War era ammunition pouches. (*Courtesy Jack and Barbara McConnell*)

Group of sergeants in various states of undress at the annual camp, circa 1912. (*Author's collection*)

A C Squadron troop photograph in Riverstown, Glanmire, County Cork, with William Good, aged 16 (front row, middle), 1911/1912, now as the South Irish Horse and with the Mk III short magazine Lee Enfield (SMLE) rifle and 90-round pouches. (*Courtesy Mr William Good*)

Camp life for C Squadron at the Curragh, May 1914. In just two months' time many of these men would join the Expeditionary Force in France in time for the retreat from Mons. (*Courtesy Mr William Good*)

Squadron commanders and NCOs of the regiment at the Curragh, 1914. (*Courtesy Mr William Good*)

The obligatory 'Formal' Troop photograph, with their furry mascot, on home service. (*Author's collection*)

A trip to A Squadron's farriers at Tickhill, Yorkshire, 1914–15. (*With permission, copyright Tickhill Historical Society*)

Troop photograph, A Squadron, at Tickhill, Yorkshire. (*With permission, copyright Tickhill Historical Society*)

B Troop, S Squadron, France 1915. (*Courtesy the Jestin Family*)

Group of NCOs 'in the field' somewhere in France, circa 1915. (*Courtesy Mr William Good*)

Group photo of Sergeant William Good and 'pals', France 1915. (*Courtesy Mr William Good*)

Sergeant Good with friends, France 1915. (*Courtesy Mr William Good*)

An informal snapshot again 'in the field, France' 1916. (*Courtesy Mr William Good*)

The larger than life figure of Sergeant Ashleigh Cooper, training sergeant, mounted, outside the stable block, Cahir Barracks. (*Author's collection*)

As a corporal with his friends of the training cadre, Cahir Barracks, 1916–17. (*Author's collection*)

Kildare Squadron, 1904. (*Courtesy the Mitchell family*)

Group of officers including, I believe, Captain Ralph Blackett SIH, location unknown, circa 1917. (*Author's collection*)

No. 2239 (25823) Pte Albert Swifte, killed as he returned to his billets from the front line, Ste Emilie, on 12 December 1917. (*Authors own Collection*)

Pte Thomas Jestin. Thomas was to lose two of his brothers, Martin, formerly of the South Irish Horse, and John, with the Canadian Infantry. (*Courtesy Jestin Family*)

Group photograph of the Regimental NCOs, home front, circa 1915. (*Courtesy Walsh Family*)

Training Troop, Cahir Barracks 1916–17. (*Author's collection*)

'Stables somewhere in France'. (*Courtesy Mr William Good*)

No. 1261 Pte John Gregan was shot in the head and subsequently died of his wounds on 21 June 1917. (*Courtesy Mr Patsy Gregan*)

Group photo with William Roe, taken at Cahir Barracks, 1918. (*Courtesy Walsh Family*)

Sergeant Major Thomas Fletcher, aged 23, with his family whilst on leave in 1917. Thomas was to die of wounds at the American base hospital in Rouen, on 11 April 1918 following the German offensive of 21 March 1918. (*Courtesy Bryan Love*)

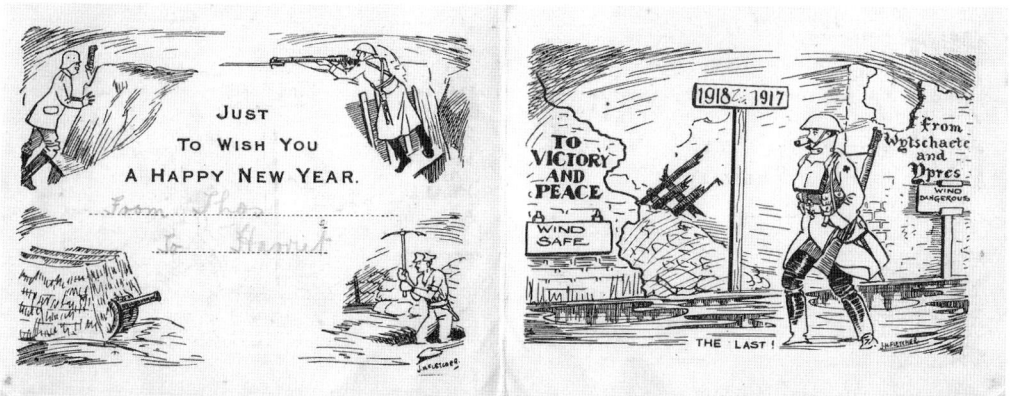

JUST
TO WISH YOU
A HAPPY NEW YEAR.

1918 1917

TO
VICTORY
AND
PEACE

WIND
SAFE.

From
Wytschaete
and
Ypres

WIND
DANGEROUS

THE LAST!

A Christmas card sent by Thomas Fletcher in 1917. (*Courtesy Byran Love*)

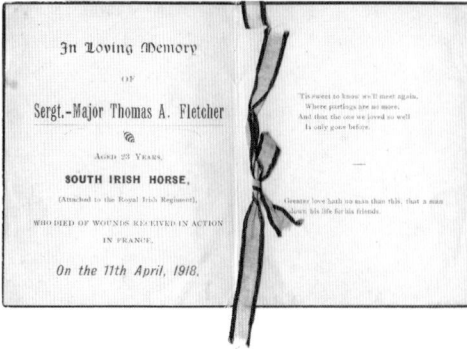

Thomas's 'In Memoriam' card. (*Courtesy Bryan Love*)

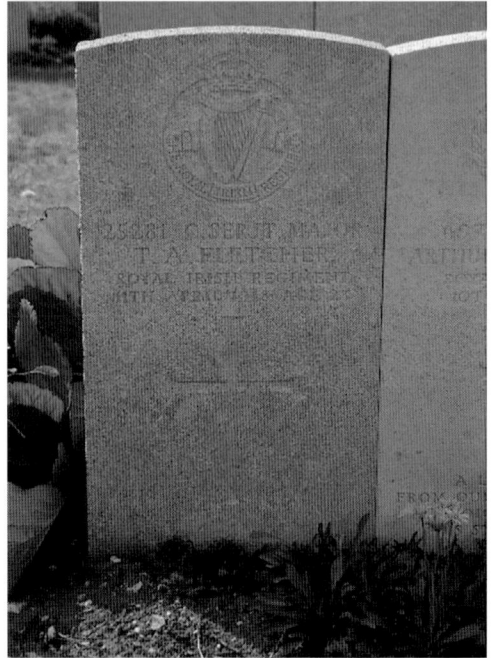

Thomas's grave in St Sever Cemetery, Rouen. (*Author's collection*)

22-year old Samuel Leahy who, only after a few weeks at the front, was shot by a sniper whilst in the trenches for the first time. (*Courtesy Ms Kathy Davies*)

Buried at Philosophe British Cemetery, the original wooden grave marker was replaced by the more permanent stone headstone. (*Author's collection*)

he had a little trouble as the SIH weren't in that theatre of war and there was doubt cast as to why he was there at all. Luckily for him, he managed to return to Gallipoli and to his attachment. He remained at Gallipoli and was amongst the last troops to be withdrawn. The fate of the other two men at that time is not known but, later, they were all re-united in the Sinai Desert. Both Hudson and Blakemore had by then been transferred to the Military Mounted Police (MMP). Following the advance of 53rd Division, the men were assigned many duties, one of which was guarding gold coins to be used as currency in Gaza. The division did not succeed in capturing the town in the initial assault, so the gold had to be returned. The men ended up in Jerusalem and were billeted in the Victoria Augusta building.[7]

Other men who were fighting in the campaign arrived later, having been transferred to the Dorset Yeomanry as part of the re-organization of the mounted units in France. Needless to say, there were casualties, including two fatal. Private George Gray, a former member of B Squadron, having served in France, was transferred to the (Queen's Own) Dorset Yeomanry. He died from influenza on 10 October 1918 and is buried in Haifa War Cemetery. Private Joseph Loughlin was also transferred and also died from influenza three days earlier on the 7th.

Chapter 6

1st South Irish Horse (1 SIH) – C, E and S Squadrons – I Corps Cavalry Regiment, Vaudricourt, Drouvin

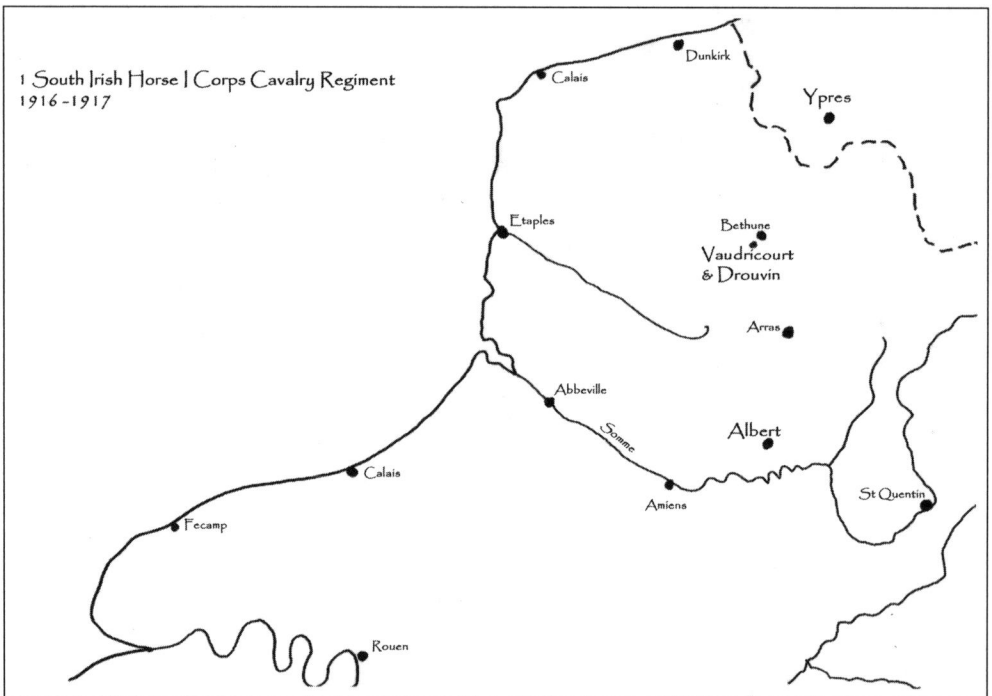

1 South Irish Horse I Corps Cavalry Regiment
1916-1917

On 17 May 1916 1st South Irish Horse (1 SIH) was formed, comprising S, C and E Squadrons. Now attached to IV Corps and stationed at the château in Fresnicourt-le-Dolmen and Vaudricourt, the regiment was briefly spilt up again with C and E Squadrons travelling to the 1st Cavalry Divisional training area at Hesdin l'Abbaye for a fortnight, following the footsteps of S Squadron a few weeks before.[1]

Returning to their respective billets on 21 June 1916, both squadrons continued their routine training and duties. The regiment was based in the

Loos area of the front line; the ensuing actions at the Somme farther south had little effect on the duties and general training.

As with every sector of the front not engaged in offensive action, maintenance was the order of the day and, as such, working parties were continuously needed both in the trenches and behind the lines. A good source of labour for these tasks was the mounted contingent, in other words, 1 SIH and the Corps' cyclists. July meant undertaking carrying duties for their fellow countrymen of 16th (Irish) Division and, when they moved to the reserve, 15th (Scottish) Division. So, when 8th Division arrived from the Somme earlier in the month, working parties were also attached to it. John Honner recounted that during their time at the front in 1916, the French refused to feed the 'Irish' for seven days. A Scottish 'Regiment' brought them enough supplies to make up for the missing food. It must be assumed that this incident would relate to the time when 1 SIH were working alongside 16th (Irish) Division and 15th (Scottish) Division. I am not sure why the French would be responsible for food and supplies, unless this was a local arrangement. As a result of the Scots' generosity, John had a tattoo made of a Scottish Highlander on one arm when he was eventually demobbed![2]

Throughout the latter part of 1916 and until the middle of 1917, the regiment remained in Drouvin and operated behind the Loos sector. Without exception, work comprised working parties in and out of the trenches, traffic control duties throughout the I Corps area, prisoner of war escort and guard duties and divisional dump duties. ('Dump' in this context means the area where stores, ammunition and other material required to serve the front-line troops were maintained and kept.) It must have been incredibly frustrating for the men and officers alike, to spend their days as pioneers and policemen. The odd regimental sports' day or Sunday parade were the only variations to the monotony of life behind the front line.

Very occasionally there would be a 'scheme' arranged for a day or, if they were lucky, combined training with the Corps Cyclists. One such 'scheme' was arranged for 12 September when the whole regiment (less the 105 men on traffic control duties and essential working parties) travelled to the First Army training area for a combined exercise with the Corps Cyclists and No. 2 Mounted Machine Gun Battery.

For the regimental snipers, trips to the trenches were frequent, as the skill was continually in demand. As well as snipers, a few men were detailed for OP (observation post) duties in the front line. However, it seems that opportunities to 'hit back at the Hun' were few and far between. Casualties were inevitable during these forays to the front line, with two men wounded on working parties on 2 September and Captain Edward Loxley Firth wounded as a result of shelling on the night of 28/29 August whilst in the reserve area. Lieutenant Brodie was injured on 4 September and was evacuated to England to recover.

Christmas 1916 brought some relief for the regiment as S Squadron was ordered to attend two weeks of training with a company of the Corps Cyclists at the First Army training grounds. C Squadron was sent there also on S Squadron's return and E Squadron replaced S. The remainder were stuck with the drudgery of working parties, traffic control, PoW escorts and guards and observation duties, all in the cold and wet winter weather of 1916–17. So, throughout January, February, March and April, the duties remained the same, but with added unseasonably cold and snowy weather.

It is not unsurprising, however, that casualties including fatalities slowly started to mount. One man was killed in action at the end of March, another in April and two more in May. On 31 March 1917 1401 Private John Jordan, aged 23, was the first man to be killed. Formerly a painter living in Ranelagh, John was the eldest son of seven children. His father died the following year. It can be assumed he was in the front line, either as a sniper or on a working party. Twenty-year-old No. 2089 Private Joseph Kerrigan was killed on 13 April. Joseph, from Drumcondra, who had only been in France for a few weeks, was fatally wounded whilst manning an observation or 'battle' post.

'I regret to inform you,' [writes Captain Wardell], 'that your son, Trooper Kerrigan, was killed in action on the 12th inst. He was hit by a piece of a shell when on duty at a "Battle Post", and only lived a few hours after being hit. During the short time he was with my squadron he made himself most popular with all, and was a most promising soldier. It was indeed sad his being knocked out so early in his career. Please accept my sincere sympathy.' (Lieutenant Walter Purcell, the Troop commander) – 'As your son's troop officer'… I wish to convey my deepest sympathy to you and your wife. Although your son was with us [only] a few weeks, in that time I found him to be a keen soldier – always cheerful under any circumstances, and very much liked by his comrades. I am enclosing a photograph which was taken a short time ago; I am sending it because I don't know if he had time to send you one.'[3]

No. 1742 Private James E. Bentley from Dolphin's Barn, Dublin, a mechanical dentist before the war, was 22 years old when he was killed in action on 14 May. Two weeks later, No. 1668 Private Samuel Leahey from Howth was to suffer the same fate. Samuel, aged 22 and one of ten children, was attached to 2nd Battalion York and Lancaster Regiment when he was killed. Based in the Hulluch Right sector of the Loos front on 27 May, he was, as his sister recalled, keen to get 'into the fray', poked his head over the parapet to have a shot and was killed.[4] Both men are buried in the la Philosophe Cemetery in Mazingarbe.

At the beginning of June, a number of brigade-sized raids were carried out by 46th (North Midland) Division around the Riaumont district of Loos in front of Hill 65. This was to consolidate the area in preparation for a large-scale attack towards the Souchez river by the division and 4th Canadian Division. The planned date of the attack was the morning of 28 June. In order to facilitate the attack, new assembly trenches were required from sections of the recently-captured German trench (Absalom), northwards to Crocodile Trench. Four hundred men from 138 Brigade were to dig the southern section of the new trenches, and 340 men from 1 SIH and I Corps Cyclists (170 men each) the northern half. The work was to commence on the night of the 15th and continue until complete (before the 28th). For the next fourteen nights the men from 1 SIH left their billets at Aix Noulette, passing through Whizz Bang corner and Absalom trench to the new assembly lines, aptly known as Cavalry and Cyclist Trenches. The threat of enemy shelling or raiding was ever present and, over a number of nights, unfortunately, resulted in some fatal casualties.[5]

One of the digging party was No. 1261 Private John Gregan. John, aged 24, was a native of Coolboy, County Wicklow and had been working on the Fitzwilliam Estate in Shillelagh as a labourer, joining up at the start of hostilities. A few weeks before, in May 1917, he had overstayed his leave and had come to the attention of the local RIC, who arrested him and escorted him to the local railway station in Tinahely. He was caught unawares and, unfortunately, didn't have time to say goodbye to his mother, who was away from the house at the time. On hearing of his arrest and subsequent transfer back to the front, she was distraught, as she had a premonition that she would never see her son again.[6] She was proved correct; he was to become one of seven fatalities out of a total of thirty-five casualties over the next few nights digging those assembly trenches. This became the highest casualty rate suffered at one time by all squadrons of the SIH whilst mounted.

Alfred Corrigan and William King were the first two fatalities, killed by shellfire on the night of the 19th. Alfred, 22 years old, formerly of C Squadron and from Garretstown, Rathvilly, County Carlow, was the brother of John Henry Corrigan, of B Squadron, commissioned in 3rd Royal Irish Regiment on 30 July 1917.[7] The second casualty of the night was No. 1951 Private William King aged 20, a native of County Kildare and the son of a farmer. No. 1497 Private Charles Willoughby was killed the following night. Charles, then 22 years old, was another Carlow native. John Gregan was shot in the head the following night, dying at the casualty clearing station in Noeux-les-Mines on the 21st.[8] Three more fatalities occurred on the night of the 22nd; Privates 1825 Patrick Murphy, 445 Joseph O'Sullivan and 1579 Thomas Pierce. Patrick Murphy, aged 21 and from Tipperary, would have enlisted at Cahir. Twenty-six-year-old Joseph O'Sullivan from Friendly Cove, Durrus, County Cork had been out with the regiment from the beginning of the war. Thomas Pierce was a van driver before the war, working and living in Islandbridge, Dublin. His mother had already lost a husband and now was to lose one of her four sons to conflict.[9]

Corporal David Jenkins, one of the many wounded on the night of 25 June, was diagnosed with shellshock, but apparently only for three days, as he was back with the regiment on the 28th. He survived both this and the retreat in 1918 and went on to receive a commission in the Indian Army Reserve on 29 September 1918. Corporals William Larkin (E Squadron) and William O'Hara were wounded at the same time (shellshock), O'Hara returning to duty on 18 July, Larkin the following day. The war diary for the end of June recorded:

> The following wire was received from Corps Headquarters with reference to the above working party: GOC 46th Division has asked I Corps to convey his appreciation of the good work done by the South Irish Horse, whilst attached to the Division.[10]

Small comfort to friends and relatives of the men who died and were wounded, given that they were not 'in action' at the time, but rather 'digging' trenches. Joseph Clynch, at home on leave during this period, returned to find a great many of his pals and colleagues from his squadron either killed or wounded. In a letter home, he recorded that there were over seventy casualties. (Joseph was to be killed in action a few months later.)[11]

About this time, and with increased pressure from the Government and the Army Council, a re-organization of front-line cavalry units had begun to take place. The need for more horses for the Middle East front meant that Haig was left with no choice but to reduce and dismount some of the cavalry regiments in France and Flanders. It was decided that the majority of these units would come from Yeomanry regiments, which meant that both the South and North Irish Horse, as Special Reserve cavalry regiments, would be included.[12]

Notice arrived on 13 July and by the 20th, all 448 horses had been inspected and a decision made as to how and where they would be re-assigned. By 25 July, to all intents and purposes, the horses were gone. The regiment entrained at Achiet-les-Grand for Beaurainville for re-organization and training, joining 2nd South Irish Horse on 27 August to transfer to the newly-raised 7th (South Irish Horse) Battalion Royal Irish Regiment.

Chapter 7

A Squadron South Irish Horse, B Squadron South Irish Horse and D Squadron Royal Wiltshire Yeomanry, (later Hertfordshire Yeomanry), F Squadron South Irish Horse, XV Corps Cavalry Regiment, IX Corps Cavalry Regiment, XVIII Corps Cavalry Regiment – 2nd South Irish Horse (2SIH), Ribemont, the Somme, Vimy, Arras, Ypres

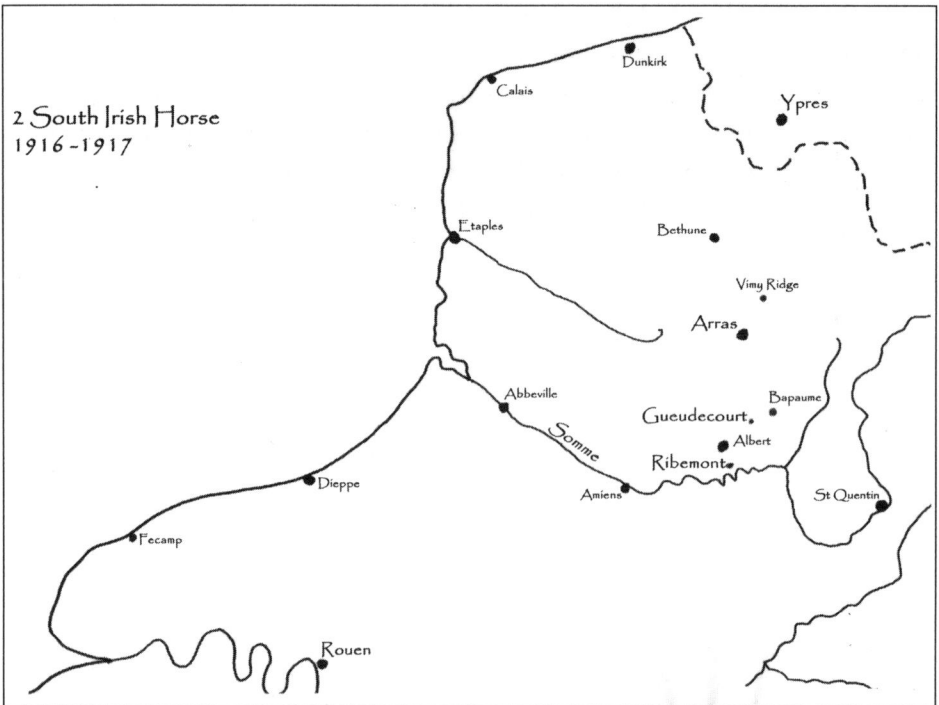

A Squadron started to settle in to their billets between Ribemont and Heilly when C Squadron Surrey Yeomanry arrived on the 10 May and B Squadron SIH arrived on Sunday the 14th to form XV Corps Cavalry

Regiment. As Major Stern was the most senior officer, he took temporary command of the regiment until a permanent CO could be appointed. On the 21st, C Squadron Surrey Yeomanry were replaced with D Squadron, Royal Wiltshire Yeomanry, together with their HQ section, all under the command of Lieutenant Colonel Ulric Thynne. Command of the regiment was therefore passed to Lieutenant Colonel Thynne, relieving Major Stern to return to B Squadron. Forty-five-year-old Lieutenant Colonel Ulric Thynne, formerly of the King's Royal Rifle Corps and now the commanding officer Royal Wiltshire Yeomanry, was a veteran of operations in Chitral, India and action during the Boer War in South Africa, and was well used to command. Instead of commanding the Royal Wiltshire Yeomanry, he would be faced with commanding a predominantly Irish regiment, with all their little quirks and foibles![1]

Now that the regiment had a semblance of permanency in their make-up, general routines and duties returned with a vengeance. As mentioned before, the largest part of squadron duties was the provision of working parties for anyone who needed labour (or so it appears). Instead of carrying out the old 'divisional' fatigues and APM, MMP and escort duties, the squadrons were now undertaking corps duties – little change, therefore, for the mounted troops. For instance, one day, 15 June 1916, the dispersal of men was as follows:

A Squadron	B Squadron
1 NCO and 8 men escort XV Corps Commander 1 Officer 1 NCO and 20 men attached to XV Corps APM	1 Sgt and 22 men proceeded to Mericourt to be attached to XV Corps as mounted police 2 horses evacuated to 12th Mobile Vet Section
1 officer 1 NCO and 30 men attached to 21st Division APM Remainder exercise and camp routine 12 men digging party at Bray	
Remainder either on fatigues, unloading at Heilly Station or digging gun emplacements at Bray	

Looking at the squadron strengths prior to the amalgamation of the squadrons, A Squadron had six officers and 112 men, B Squadron had six officers and 115 men, in total twelve officers and 227 men. One troop (approximately twenty-eight men and one officer) was at corps HQ. Taking both squadrons together, over half their strength was away on fatigues, digging duties, MMP etc., leaving 104 men to look after all stable duties, exercising and grooming and general camp routine. I do not have any figures for the Royal Wiltshire Yeomanry, but I can only assume they would be similar. The war diary for XV Corps Cavalry Regiment stated at the end of the month: 'two teams per squadron were trained in handling the Hotchkiss Guns. No other training was possible owing to numbers furnished for Police, working parties etc.'[2]

As the build-up to the 'Great Push' (Battle of the Somme) continued, A and B Squadrons were employed carrying out the usual camp duties, exercising the horses and general fatigues. A number of men were attached to the Assistant Provost Marshal (APM) for XV Corps and 21st Division. One NCO and eight ORs were acting as escort for the XV Corps commander, Lieutenant General Sir Henry Horne. Another section was also saddled with digging gunpits around Bray in preparation for the artillery bombardment.

XV Corps was part of Rawlinson's Fourth Army and comprised 7th Division, 17th (Northern) Division, 33rd Division and 38th (Welsh) Division. On 1 July 1916, the corps was to attack the German front line along the la Boiselle-Fricourt-Mametz line, adjacent the French Sixth Army, achieving most of their objectives on Z Day or Z Day +1 capturing Montauban and Mametz villages. However, to the north of these villages, the attacks failed.[3]

That momentous Saturday found the regiment at Ribemont-sur-Ancre, having paraded in full marching order at 2315 the previous night before moving to their pre-attack billets. The regiment stood to at 0600 on 1 July, in readiness to advance at half an hour's notice. Waiting for the order to move up the line to take advantage of a 'breakthrough, the regiment did not move from that place all day'. As it became clear that a major breakthrough was not going to happen in the immediate future, the regiment was put at two hours' readiness from 2 July onwards. Camp routine and exercise close to the camp were recommenced and two bomb-carrying parties of men were sent to Mametz Wood. The 2nd turned to the 3rd and so on, with no orders to move, aside from the two hours' readiness. Camp routine continued, replacements arrived from Ireland and the bomb parties at Mametz Wood continued. The 12th saw the first fatalities in action since January 1915. No. 901 Private M. Farrell had been part of the bomb-carrying party when he was killed by shellfire in Mametz Wood. Twenty-four-year-old Matthew, originally from Killian, a small townland between Roscommon and Mountbellew, in County Galway, was a pupil of the state agricultural school at Athenry, County Galway. He enlisted in Galway and came out to France with A Squadron on 11 September 1915.[4] As his body was never recovered, he is commemorated on the Thiepval Memorial. He was not the only casualty of that day; three other men were wounded, all from B Squadron: Privates 1658 William Walshe, 1201 Paul Lacy and 976 Thomas Murtagh, the last-named dying from his wounds the following day. Thomas, 18 years old, with three sisters, was the only son of the family, living at Talbot Street, Dublin. Enlisting in Dublin, he was a member of B Squadron and had been with them since they arrived on 23 November 1915.[5]

On the night of the 13th, the regiment moved to Citadel Valley, just south of Fricourt, to bivouac there in preparation for the attack on Bazentin Ridge the following day. Kept in reserve for the next three days at half an hour's notice to move again, it was as part of this action that 2nd Indian Cavalry Division took part in the cavalry charge at High Wood on the 14th.[6] The regiment paraded at 0700 on 16 July and returned to their billets at Ribemont. With no more operational duties, the regiment continued with digging for and laying cables, repairs to roads and carrying parties. Very little training was possible with all the working parties out, but an effort was made to train the dismounted men signalling and advance and rearguard action procedures. The usual drain of men and NCOs required for duties with the APM continued. Previously, one troop from B Squadron, under Lieutenant Bence-Jones, had been attached to 7th Division as a tactical troop on 14 June, but returned prior to the attack on 1 July. On 28 July 1916 Lieutenant Bence-Jones was sent to take charge of XV Corps' prisoner cages at Meaulte, but was relieved by Lieutenant C.G. Colvill on 23 August and returned to the squadron at Ribemont. The whole of August was taken up with working parties in and around Mametz and Montauban and what limited training could be undertaken with so few troops at regimental HQ. The war diary stated:

Regiment still in camp training.... Owing to the number of men on detachment and the regiment being under orders to move at 2 hours' notice, no mounted training was possible. Training in signalling, rifle and bayonet exercises continued.[7]

August rolled into September and still no request for the regiment to go into action. Instead, working parties and camp routine was the norm. Elsewhere, preparations were underway for a new advance, this time at Flers-Courcelette, within XV Corps area. A push on this front was due to commence on 15 September and, in order to prepare for any advantageous breakthrough, three troops, Lieutenant Anderson's troop of A Squadron, Lieutenant Bence-Jones' troop of B Squadron and Lieutenant Davy's troop of D Squadron Royal Wiltshire Yeomanry were to be attached as tactical troops to the New Zealand Division, 14th Division and 41st Division, respectively. These troops detached from their respective squadrons over 12 and 13 September. The remainder of the regiment marched and bivouacked in the southern outskirts of Bécourt-Becordel village on the 15th and, again, were to be at two hours' notice to move. The Battle of Flers-Courcelette was the first battle in which tanks were used. (Major H.J.J. Stern's brother, Sir Albert Gerald Stern, was the Chairman of the Tank Supply Committee, later the Tank Supply Department, and was intimately involved in the development and delivery of tanks to the Western Front.)[8]

> That day [17 September 1916] I motored to Amiens for lunch with Major Wood and went to Bray-en-Somme, where the tanks were parked at a place called 'The Loop' – new Tanks and battered Tanks together. I met my brother, Major Stern, and Colonel Thynne, in command of a composite regiment of the South Irish Horse and Royal Wiltshire Yeomanry, and took them over to see the Tanks, which created an immense sensation. We met the cavalry returning from the battle front. They had not been used.[9]

One of the many duties undertaken by the men was that of document searchers for corps Intelligence. The men would be tasked with searching through abandoned dug-outs and the bodies of Germans to find and retrieve any intelligence material, such as letters, documents and maps, and return these to corps or divisional headquarters for analysis. Whilst not immediately in the front line, the searchers would have to follow the advancing troops and would be exposed to hostile machine-gun, rifle and artillery fire. On this occasion, A Squadron provided two men for this duty on the 14th to work with XV Corps Intelligence, the other squadrons providing another four men. During this period, of the six men on such duty, one died of wounds and two others received wounds. One of the men was slightly wounded in action, the other two men whilst at rest in Longueval.[10]

Another important and dangerous assignment for both men and officers was corps forward observation duty, reporting on movement of troops, progress and any counter-attacks. The officers would have been assigned for reportage, the men as runners and messengers. Captain A. Fitzherbert and Second Lieutenant E. Hamilton were in charge of eighteen ORs assigned to these duties. No. 950 Private Harry Wilkes was one of these men. On 17 September Harry and two others were wounded by shellfire but he died of his wounds the following day. Another member who had arrived with A Squadron in September the previous year, Harry Edward (Rahkal) Wilkes was 21 when he died. Born in Exeter, and living in Drumcondra, Dublin, Harry's father was an SQMS for the Army Pay Corps. Harry was a stockbroker's clerk in Dublin and had signed up on the declaration of war in August 1914.[11]

With the attacks continuing on the 18th a re-organization of the tactical troops meant that Lieutenant Bence-Jones' troop was transferred to 21st Division and Lieutenant Davy's troop to 55th (West Lancashire) Division. This was going to be a very dramatic move for Lieutenant Bence-Jones and his troop a few days later.

The Battle of Flers-Courcelette drew to a close on 22 September without the regiment or any of the tactical troops seeing action. Another attack due to start on the 25th September, known as the Battle of Morval, was meant to push the Germans back towards le Transloy and the high ground behind Gueudecourt. The attack commenced on the 25th but became bogged down around Gird Trench. A resumption of the attack on Gird trench by 21st Division commenced the following day. At 0715, a tank tracking up Pilgrims Way commenced its run along Gird Trench, moving south-eastwards to the Guards Divisional boundary at the end of Gird Support Trench, following behind, 7th Leicesters' bombing parties clearing the trenches as they went. By 0945 the Leicesters had the trench cleared and joined up with the Guards Division. With only five ORs wounded, the attack was very successful and they captured eight officers and 362 other ranks.

With Gird Trench secured, 6th Leicesters sent patrols out to see whether Gueudecourt was occupied. Finding it unoccupied at 1500, they sent a further two companies to secure the village.[12]

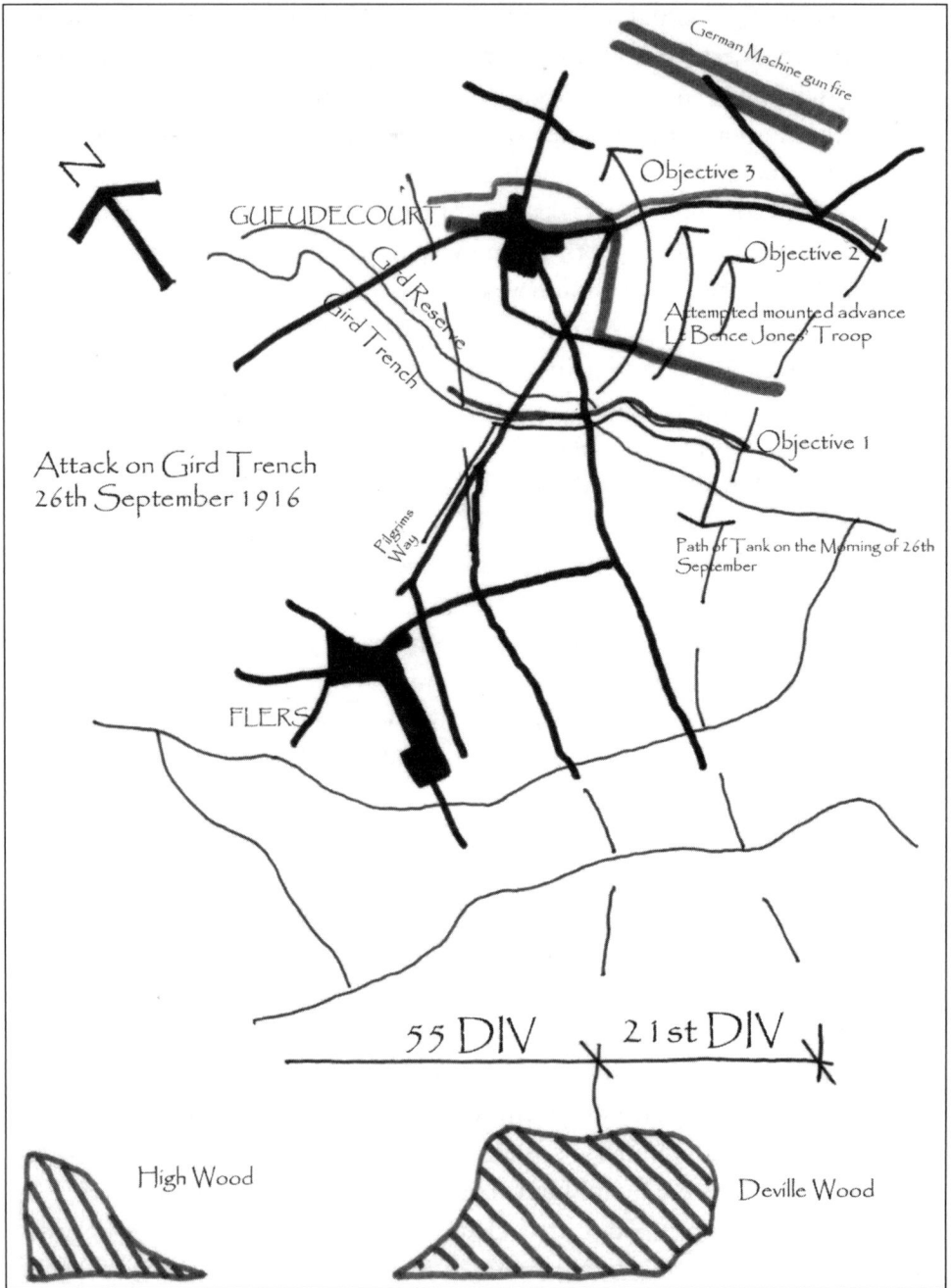

Attack on Gueudecourt (Map based on 21st Divisional Diaries).

Lieutenant Bence-Jones' troop was at the time attached to D Squadron 19th Lancers (Fane's Horse), under the command of Captain Fitzgerald, then standing to around Carnoy as duty squadron.[13] At around 1130 they were instructed to reconnoitre the high ground between Flers and Gueudecourt towards le Transloy as it was believed that Gueudecourt had been abandoned by the enemy. The lancers proceeded to the sunken road to the west of Gueudecourt.

Around 1230 reports were received at 5 Guards Brigade and Division HQ that large numbers of German troops were counter-attacking from the Transloy heights towards Gueudecourt. A counter barrage from the 7th Divisional artillery was called in and reports followed that, as a result of this, large numbers of the enemy were seen retreating in disarray to the north of Gueudecourt towards le Transloy.[14]

Meanwhile, 19th Lancers had tried to advance to the north from their location at the sunken road, and had already come under shell and machine-gun fire, suffering casualties just in reaching the sunken road. Further mounted patrols were sent out from the sunken road, but were again heavily shelled and returned unsuccessful. The whole squadron then proceeded into the village and set up a defensive line from the sunken road through the village.

At 1200 Lieutenant Bence-Jones received orders from the GOC 21st Division to scout the high ground to the east of the village.[15] His troop saddled up and proceeded to the sunken road directly south of the village. They arrived at 1400 and commenced to try to secure the high ground. Bence-Jones sent out two mounted patrols in an attempt to secure his objectives and then went himself but was met by substantial, well-aimed machine-gun fire, wounding his horse. The troop dismounted and, on the orders of Captain Fitzgerald, retired to the north-west part of the village. With the Germans visible on the high ground in considerable numbers, the troop opened fire in conjunction with the dismounted lancers. It was during this firefight that No. 970 Private Matthew Allen was shot and killed. Using their Hotchkiss guns and rifle fire, they kept the enemy at bay until relieved by 6th Leicesters at around 1800, when they retired.

The lancers' losses amounted to three ORs killed, seven wounded and thirty-five horses killed and twenty-four wounded. The majority of these were as a result of artillery fire during the advance to Gueudecourt and on their retirement from the village. Lieutenant Bence-Jones' casualties were, on the other hand, relatively light with only one man killed and four horses wounded, including Bence-Jones' own horse. Twenty-one-year-old Matthew Allen was the only casualty. A Dubliner, born in Donnybrook on 3 March 1895 to Patrick and Mary Allen, at 16 years old he was working as a messenger and then for Pim Brothers, Georges Street, Dublin. He joined up with the South Irish Horse when war was declared in August 1914.[16] He was a member of B Squadron and travelled to France with them in 1916. He has no known grave and is commemorated on the Thiepval Memorial. Campell Bence-Jones, together with his friend Second Lieutenant Walter Joyce, was to transfer to the Irish Guards a month and a half after this action.

This mounted action should be seen as one of the more successful uses of cavalry during the France and Flanders campaign. A swift use of mounted resources when the opportunity arises combined with scouting, reconnaissance in force, active mounted and dismounted patrols, holding actions until the main infantry force arrives are classic cavalry tactics.

For the rest of the regiment, the routine remained the same with working parties, APM duties and various non-combatant detachments. Over two thirds of the regiment were on detachment during September with ten officers and 237 ORs away.

October began with the death of Corporal Victor MacMullen, A Squadron, from wounds received the previous day. He had been with the squadron since its arrival. Victor, 28 years old, born in St Finbar's, Cork in 1887, the son of the Cork City Engineer, was also an engineer, but on the G.S. and W. Railway, Buenos Aires.

> (he) had done a good day's work of a dangerous kind. Late in the same day he received a shell wound, and died in hospital next day. 'He was a splendid chap,' wrote the captain commanding A Squadron, 'and the whole Squadron mourns his loss.'[17]

As with the end of September, the beginning of October saw the majority of the regiment out on detachment and other duties, leaving training and general camp routines very difficult for the remaining troops. B Squadron veteran Private Thomas Byrne, whilst attached to corps Intelligence was reported missing on 12 October, presumed dead. Thomas, 20 and from

Ballinasloe in County Galway, was the son of the local asylum attendant and had six siblings. His body was never found and he is remembered on the Thiepval Memorial. His brother, Michael, also in the South Irish Horse, was killed on 21 March 1918; he is remembered on the Pozières Memorial.

With action on the Somme front slowly coming to an end, there was no need for the regiment to be on continuous standby at two hours' notice, so it was placed in corps reserve at the beginning of October. A steady relief and change of corps responsibility started with elements of the regiment proceeding to X Corps area, replacing the existing mounted units there. The tactical troops on detachment were recalled, their responsibilities being taken over by Australian mounted troops. Camp routine and training, where possible, was maintained. An accident caused Lieutenant Colonel Thynne to be sent back England with a sprained ankle on 8 October and Major Stern assumed temporary command, as well as continuing to supervise the transfer of various elements of the regiment to X Corps at Fréchencourt. Due to the number of men on other detachments and corps duties, A Squadron SIH and D Squadron Royal Wiltshire Yeomanry had to form a composite HQ squadron under Captain Furlong to provide temporary cover for a squadron of X Corps carrying out police duties etc. A snapshot of the way a squadron was spread out is given in A Squadron's diary:

> 24th October – 1 troop and HQ sqn at Fréchencourt, 1 troop Corbie, 1 troop Behencourt, 1 troop Ville – All on traffic control.[18]

On 30 October the complete regiment, less the composite squadron remaining at Fréchencourt, arrived at Flesselles under XV Corps area control. Essentially B Squadron was with XV Corps, A and D Squadron (composite) was servicing X Corps requirements and the remainder were on Corps detachment. On 15 November, the rotation of squadrons changed yet again with A Squadron, now no longer a composite squadron, being relieved by D Squadron Royal Wiltshire Yeomanry at Fréchencourt, to proceed to IX Corps area at le Schaexhen under the overall control of Plumer's Second Army. The RWY who were stationed with IX Corps proceeded to join their other squadrons to form 1st/1st RWY, XV Corps Cavalry. B Squadron SIH was sent to join A Squadron on the 21st, joining the Hampshire Carabiniers to form IX Corps Cavalry Regiment under the command of Lieutenant Colonel Walters. They were to remain with IX Corps until 16 January 1917.[19]

Although under a new corps, the duties, unremarkably, remained the same, with both squadrons farming out their men on the same duties. Below is a typical list of attachments for November and December for both squadrons:

18 men attached IX Corps camp commandant
9 men attached to IX Corps APM
14 men and 1 officer and 2 Hotchkiss guns anti-aircraft at Caëstre
4 men and 1 officer observers on Hill 63
17 men and 1 officer attached APM 36th Division
2 Signallers to Kemmel
1 man batman Jewish chaplain
1 man attached musketry training camp IX Corps
4 men and 1 officer Training Brigade 1st Cavalry Division
1 man cookery school
1 officer 1 man sniping school
7 men signalling course IX Corps
12 men and 3 Hotchkiss guns to Caëstre
18 Men to Bailleul for duty under camp commandant
1 officer and 17 men attached 25th Division for traffic duty at Nieppe

On 21 December a parade was held to award the Military Medal to the following men for outstanding bravery in connection with the catapult bomb station in Mushroom Trench earlier in the year:

239 Sergeant Richard Kingston Jago
1049 Corporal Ralph E. West
1109 Corporal William S. Smyth
1293 Private Henry Eustace Rutherford

Of these four, Ralph West transferred to the Corps of Hussars and was subsequently commissioned in 2nd Reserve Cavalry Regiment on 22 June 1918; William Smyth was to receive a commission in the South Wales Borderers on 20 April 1918; Henry (Harry) Rutherford, who had already received a Mention in Despatches (MiD) on 13 June 1916, and was to receive a further MiD on 15 May 1917, was not to survive the war. He was, at the age of 21, now a corporal in 7th (SIH) Battalion Royal Irish Regiment, and died of wounds received on 24 April 1918. Richard Jago was to receive a commission in the South Irish Horse on 16 April 1917.[20]

The end of 1916 and the beginning of 1917 saw A and B Squadrons still encamped at le Schaexhen until receiving orders to transfer to XVIII Corps on 16 January. Digging and wiring parties were still the order of the day, with limited squadron training when and where possible with the remaining men. A march to Framecourt, via Morbecque (A Squadron) and Nuncq (B Squadron) over the next couple of days saw the squadrons settling into their new billets approximately one and a half miles apart under XVIII Corps. With wintry weather and heavy snow falls, the march was made very difficult for both horses and men. This bad weather continued throughout January, limiting squadron training and exercises to prepared tracks. Both squadrons had to resort to simple ground training as any mounted training would have been far too dangerous. Whilst the squadrons were at Morbecque and Nuncq, a party of eighty men and two officers proceeded to Pas to construct an over-winter camp there. Police duties were still mounted and thirty men from the two squadrons were sent off to 46th and 49th (West Riding) Divisions for such work.

With the construction of the new billets at Pas-en-Artois coming along, both squadrons decamped and arrived at Pas. It appears, however, that the billets had not been completed and it was all hands on deck to finish the work; both squadrons (less men on detachment) were put on construction duty. The work took until the beginning of March to complete.

Camp routine was quickly established and the usual round of horse exercise, mounted and dismounted drill, signalling, gas drills and general fatigues continued. Two troops of A Squadron were detached for APM duties around the divisions, smaller detachments being released for APM duties at corps level. Breaks in this routine were scarce; a visit to the baths, a regimental parade, or church parade seem to be the only changes the men experienced. Small highlights, such as the presentation of Good Conduct badges to sixty-eight other ranks of A Squadron on 18 March would have been celebrated with some gusto. However, the following day news was received of the death of No. 2061 Private F. O'Connell, B Squadron, blown up by a mine, whilst on traffic control duty at Ransart. Twenty-year-old Francis was the son of a farmer from Rathvin, Peppardstown, County Tipperary, and a former pupil of Knockbeg College, Carlow. He had enlisted in Dublin shortly after the outbreak of war.[21]

At the end of March the overall strength of the regiment (including 1st Hertfordshire Yeomanry) was twenty-three officers and 362 other ranks, approximately 130 men per squadron.

The bad weather continued through to the beginning of April with squadron training curtailed to dismounted duties, due to poor ground conditions from the snow and rain. Camp fatigues and woodcutting was the order of the day for those not training and, of course, divisional APM traffic control duties throughout the corps area.

On 9 April the Arras offensive, including the Battle of Vimy Ridge and the First Battle of the Scarpe, commenced. Both First and Third Armies were involved, First Army at Vimy and Third Army to the south at the Scarpe. The boundary between the two armies was approximately three miles north of Arras in front of the ridge at Vimy. A small detachment of one officer and nine men had been sent to the Third Army Traffic Control Section two days earlier on the 7th. John Honner was one of these. He recalled the area around Vimy just prior to the major offensive by the Canadians on 9 April:

> A 10-square-mile valley of trees before the battle, from Sunday to Thursday there was dreadful slaughter and such an enormous loss of life. There lay a 4–deep layer of dead bodies … looking over the valley where once the trees grew looking like a field of kale where cows had been let out to feed, completely levelled with the occasional stalk standing here and there and covered in dead bodies.[22]

Whilst there, one of his chums, from Dublin, happened to look at his mount, a mare, and commented that she didn't look well. John immediately inspected her and realized the mare was in trouble and he helped her deliver a healthy foal. Naturally there was great excitement all round and this helped alleviate the cavalrymen's spirits. Both the mare and foal survived. There is a Canadian official war photograph entitled 'Vimy the Foal' of a mare and foal born during the battle at Vimy. Whether this is John Honner's mare and filly is highly unlikely, but it would be nice if it were.[23]

For the rest of the men, little changed until the 26th when the regiment moved to Fosseux, approximately nine miles west of Arras. The new camp was cleaned over the next two weeks. Most of B Squadron was assigned traffic duties around the Fosseux area, from Saulty in the south to Wanquetin in the north. On 3 May Captain Ralph Blackett returned as second in command B Squadron. He was to remain with the regiment until the end of the war. Apart from the obvious and by now monotonous routine of the men, the month of May saw small detachments sent away for training and a detachment of officers and NCOs was sent to the front lines for training in observation duties. There seems to have been a slight problem with the regiment's trumpeters as they were called to parade 'dismounted' twice a day for four days running and then again, after the weekend, on the following Monday. One wonders whether their kit was up to scratch, or whether they had become somewhat lackadaisical in their general routines for the commanding officer to order this? The Hotchkiss gunners were also paraded for a week, but I suspect this was for practical reasons and drill, rather than a kit deficiency.

Monday 21 May saw a welcome trip to the baths for the men, a chance to clean up after all the cleaning and camp routine. The following day saw the Hertfordshire Yeomanry squadron train with the regiment for the last time after returning from detached duties. At the end of the week the Hertfordshire Yeomanry squadron handed over their horses and transport to F Squadron, SIH. F Squadron had arrived from Ireland on 19 May and had made their way to Fosseux to join A and B Squadrons. F Squadron was the final operational squadron to transfer to France and Flanders and, as they were incorporated directly into 2nd South Irish Horse, there does not appear to be any record of a war diary or subsequent paperwork. With the arrival of F Squadron, the total number of men was now twenty-eight officers and 503 other ranks.

With the majority of B Squadron on traffic control duties throughout May, A and F Squadrons were 'Training under squadron arrangements', to include equitation, musketry, map reading, foot drill and Hotchkiss-gun training. The general shortage of men seems to have affected the regiment as with the rest of the army, since there is now specific mention of dismounted drill for backward men under the watchful gaze of Regimental Sergeant Major Smith in the war diary for May 1917.

With preparations underway for the major summer offensive in the Ypres area the regiment with XVIII Corps moved up towards the Ypres salient, decamping from Fosseux on 9 June and travelling to Herzeele via Saint Pol-sur-Ternoise, Auchel and Steenbecque. They arrived at Herzeele on 13 June.

With that in mind, 2nd South Irish Horse was never to see action as a cavalry unit. The move to Herzeele and, briefly, for a day to Poperinghe was the closest the regiment came to the front lines in the salient. A series of moves to the rear of the lines and towards the coast ensued over the next two weeks. Leaving XVIII Corps as their Corps Cavalry Regiment, they moved westwards from Herzeele to Zegerscappel for five days, then to Condette, just south of Boulogne via Bonningues-lès-Calais until 11 July. A regimental training programme was drawn up and instigated throughout their stay at Condette. One can only surmise as to what this entailed. They would have been concentrating on musketry drill, physical fitness, equitation, map reading, Hotchkiss gunnery and foot drill. The final move as a mounted cavalry regiment came on 12 July 1917 when the regiment relocated to Maresquel-Ecquemicourt, the GHQ troops' area. Haig's GHQ was approximately eight and a half miles to the north-west at Montrieul-sur-Mer. Amidst all this uncertainty the horses still needed to be stabled, fed and looked after.

In July, as part of the re-organization of mounted Yeomanry regiments by the Army Council, notice was received that the regiment, along with 1st South Irish Horse, was to be dismounted and reformed as an infantry battalion. For F Squadron, that would mean only two months in the saddle before becoming 'infantry'. It can only be assumed that, as notification of the withdrawal of all horses came to 1st South Irish Horse on 13 July, this notification would have arrived with 2nd South Irish Horse about the same time. As a result, 325 riding horses out of the 489 horses on strength were sent to Marseilles for onward despatch to the Middle East on 19 July. All saddlery was cleaned, dubbined, inspected and packed for the same reason and sent on 21 July. On the same day, Saturday, dismounted training commenced in earnest for all squadrons. Although the horses had been transported to Marseilles on the 19th, two officers and seventy men were despatched to help with the loading and transport to the Middle East as a 'horse conducting party' on Saturday 4 August. With that, the dismounted training continued until Monday the 27th when the regiment was joined by its sister regiment, 1st South Irish Horse, and formed the new 7th (South Irish Horse) Battalion Royal Irish Regiment.[24]

2nd September 1917

My Lady

I know you will forgive my troubling you with a letter just now but I wanted to let you know that our Regiment are dismounted to become an Infantry Battalion, now we have to start all over again to learn trench warfare the conditions of which we are too well acquainted with already. However, My Lady, as we say 'Duty is Duty'.

I was home on leave in July at Colmondely and found Barbara and the children looking very well, but the leave was too short.

We have two Curraghmore boys here, Kelly and Walsh, joined us last week, both are looking very well and strong. I was sorry about Frank Strudwick [Footman at Curraghmore]. I saw him twice at the Somme going into action and again on the way out, but have not seen him since. I believe he went up at Messines. [Frank, aged 30, was killed in action on 7 June 1917, whilst serving with 6th Royal Irish Regiment. He has no known grave and is commemorated on the Menin Gate.][25] My Lady I trust all is well with you at Curraghmore. We look forward to the time when all can be home again.

There is a long way to go yet. Was promoted to Sergeant 4th August 1917. We are now hurt by the loss of our horses.

I beg to remain, My Lady, ever your obedient and faithful servant,

A. Goodchild (Sgt), A Squadron SIH[26]

Chapter 8

The Home Front (D/G Squadron – Leopardstown, Carlow and Cahir)

Although it appears that all the attention was on the formation and preparation of the composite squadron for overseas duty, this was not quite the case. All squadrons were mobilizing and those that were not assigned to S Squadron, were still required to respond to their call-up papers. One such member was No. 784 Bandsman Donald William Duncan, C Squadron, Cork. Joining the Cork squadron as a bandsman in 1913, Donald served two years of his six-year short service commitment and, in June 1914 following the annual camp, left for the Isle of Man. At the outbreak of war he contacted the regiment's adjutant, Captain McCalmont, by telegram, and was advised to look out for his 'Army Form D 463B' call-up papers. Duncan was 40 years old. During the next few weeks he contacted the squadron twice and, receiving no reply, assumed that he was deemed too old to be called up. He was therefore deemed 'absent from mobilization 5-8-1914' and officially recorded as a deserter. He remained free from attention throughout the war, his status only coming to light in 1936 when Duncan sought out his formal discharge papers.[1]

With the Service Squadron off to the front, a re-organization of the standing squadrons was carried out in preparation for overseas duty. There is no record of where each squadron was prior to their embarkation, so I can only assume the following: A Squadron to Athlone, before being sent to Yorkshire in November 1914; D Squadron relocated to Leopardstown Racecourse (approximately six troops – 180 men) from Beggars Bush Barracks, C remaining at Riverstown House, Cork, for the time being.[2] B Squadron remained in Limerick until at least the beginning of March 1915 before being sent to Codford to join 32nd Division in England. Vivian Shannon remembers

when I was taken to the (Ennis) Showgrounds where what must have been a complete Squadron had assembled and then later I stood with my parents and a lot of family friends and watched the Squadron ride through Ennis and along the road to the railway station and then my father took me to the railway yards where they were loading the horses, to say goodbye to Maeve and McClusky (Vivian's family's horses), who were off to war. I think this Squadron joined the remainder of the unit in Dublin or the Curragh before going overseas. I can remember the great applause and the cheers the Squadron got as it rode through Ennis and there was a huge crowd at the railway station to see the trains pull out, one with the horses and one with the personnel.[3]

The Regimental Headquarters (RHQ) was at this early stage still based at Beggars Bush Barracks with Colonel the Lord Decies as Commanding Officer. Major, the Earl of Wicklow, was second in command, Captain O'Grady, officer commanding the contingent at Leopardstown, Captain Furlong, Limerick, and Captain Watt at Cork.

The main priority for the regiment was to ensure a steady supply of men to maintain it at full war readiness. As with other Irish regiments, the South Irish Horse went all out with a recruiting campaign, advertisements appearing in all the national and local papers. A typical advertisement posted in the *Irish Times* on Saturday 15 August explained:

Men wishing to enlist in the South Irish Horse should apply to the Headquarters of the Regiment at Richmond Barracks between the hours of 10am and 1pm. Signed Decies. Lieutenant Colonel South Irish Horse. Dublin 1914.

On 1 September 1914 the *Irish Times* carried the following:

THE SOUTH IRISH HORSE
Volunteers Wanted

TO THE EDITOR OF THE IRISH TIMES

SIR – Would you very kindly, through your paper let it be known that volunteers are required for the South Irish Horse? The South Irish Horse – the only volunteer mounted corps in the South of Ireland – has already had the distinction of one squadron being selected for service, which is now doing its share to uphold the best traditions of Ireland at the front. May I appeal to all young, active Irishmen who can ride and shoot to come forward at once and give a helping hand? May I also ask the heads of our large business firms, banks and employers of labour in general throughout Ireland, if they cannot come themselves, to do all in their power to help in this national crisis? The headquarters of the South Irish Horse are at Beggars Bush Barracks.

Yours, etc. DECIES,

Lieutenant Colonel, commanding South Irish Horse.

Dublin August 31st 1914.

Needless to say, the response was good, with young men from all walks of life, civil servants, bank clerks, workers from the larger firms such as Guinness, men from the Royal Irish Constabulary (RIC), shop assistants and labourers, to name but a few, responding to the call. Not all, however, were suited to the cavalry. These men, although enlisted with the South Irish Horse, were soon reposted to the main infantry units, such as the Royal Irish Regiment, the Leinsters, the Royal Munster Fusiliers, the Royal Dublin Fusiliers, depending on where they initially enlisted. Others would find themselves discharged unfit for service after a few weeks of training.[4]

The regiment had its fair share of underage applicants. John Bond from Cappamore, Limerick, was one such recruit. A farm labourer, he enlisted in Limerick on 14 April 1917, stating his age as 19 but, after it was discovered he was in fact underage, he was discharged. Another type of 'recruit' was Eugene Hickey, a 20-year-old from Port Abbeyfeale, County Limerick. Eugene had previously enlisted in the 4th Battalion Royal Irish Regiment as Eugene McCarthy, and having, presumably, found this not quite to his taste, deserted the Royal Irish Regiment. Instead of returning home, he then re-enlisted, this time fraudulently, in the South Irish Horse, in Tralee, where he would not be recognized. When it came to light that all might not be well with his enlistment, he was confronted whilst training in Cahir and confessed. The result was Eugene being returned to his original unit. For all his machinations it appears he survived the war.[5]

Tragedy was never far away, with the death of one recruit, a man named as 28-year-old Edward Ryan of 3 North Summer Street, who was admitted to the Meath Hospital on 28 August 1914 with poisoning. He died two hours after admission. He was dressed in the uniform of the South Irish Horse, but sadly no record exists of his enlistment, so we cannot say for certain that he was a recent recruit, or that he had been recalled to duty at the outbreak of the war.[6]

Life in barracks at this early stage of the war would have been frenetic, with pre-war reservists being called up and sent as replacements to the squadrons out in France, returnees from the front, time expired, home on leave or to be sent out to the officer training corps prior to commission. As well as the regiment, other arms of the army (infantry, cavalry, artillery, Army Service Corps etc.) would be in part or wholly based in and around Dublin at this time. Barrack space was therefore at a premium. Being mounted, the regiment required not only accommodation for the men, but accommodation and ground for exercising their horses. The bulk of the regiment based in Dublin was therefore relocated to the racecourse at Leopardstown, on the southern outskirts of the city. With its stables and extensive grounds, it was ideal for their needs. In addition to this, race meetings were still being held at the course and so entertainment for the men was on their doorstep.[7] This didn't stop things going astray; for instance Lord Wicklow managed to 'mislay' his grey Aberdeen terrier on 27 March 1915, as posted in the 'Lost and Found' section of the *Irish Times*.

One slightly more serious incident occurred in the middle of January 1915, involving the Hon. Lieutenant and Quartermaster William Joseph Chilcott. He, together with Lieutenant Cyril Edmunds of the Royal Irish Regiment, was ordered to answer charges of being drunk on active service in the Theatre Royal on 23 January 1915, in front of a general court martial in the Lower Yard, Dublin Castle. They were both cleared.[8]

However, there were, as always, some detractors and in a letter to the *Irish Times* on 21 November 1914, 'Volunteer' complained about the cost of rail tickets to and from Leopardstown and the city.

In drawing attention to the fares charged to members of the South Irish Horse by the railway company … I do so with a view to a reduction in the present rate – viz 8d. return – as the fare is nearly two thirds of a private's pay, and seems excessive for a few hours recreation in the evenings. Numbers of men, with friends in town, visit the city every evening and all are unanimous that a reduction should be made. A soldier's privileges are few, and I have no doubt that, when attention has been drawn to what constitutes a grievance, a speedy reduction will be made.

A swift response came from A.G. Reid, from Dublin and South-Eastern Railway, Secretary and General Manager's Office, on 21 November 1914:

Referring to the letter ... I beg to say that ... this company agreed to convey officers and men of His Majesty's Forces (including Territorials, National Reservists and Legion of Frontiersmen) and of Ambulance Corps engaged with the Forces, when on short leave, at single fare for the double journey ... As it appears ... that this arrangement has not been notified to the officer commanding the South Irish Horse at Leopardstown, I am now sending him copies of the letters exchanged with the Major General in command of the Forces in Ireland....

Grievance addressed and situation resolved.

Away from the daily barracks life, an important part of supporting the troops abroad was the provision of 'comfort' parcels. Filled with socks, tobacco, sweets or scarves, these parcels were paid for from donations from the general public, through 'Comfort Fund' subscriptions, locally-organized bazaars and fetes. If they were lucky, the SIH Band would be available to play during the afternoon, or provide evening performances, concerts and accompaniments to soloists, all part of the drive for funds. The Red Cross, St John Ambulance and the regiment itself were all recipients of these drives. For instance, the then Major Burns-Lindow wrote, through his wife:

Major Burns-Lindow begs to thank the kind donors of comforts for the South Irish Horse which have already been received at the front, and for which they are very grateful. As many of these parcels have no name of the sender attached it is impossible to thank the donors separately.[9]

Further to that, a separate fund had been set up to purchase and furnish a motorized ambulance for the South Irish Horse, through the Red Cross. This was very successfully subscribed and, as a result, the ambulance was provided at the cost of £1,104 15s 3d (£86,362 at date of publication).[10] On 14 November 1914 the ambulance was used to help take 700 wounded men off the first hospital ship to land at Dublin, the SS *Oxfordshire*. Unfortunately, the ambulance was not destined for the regiment's use. Due to an 'excess' of ambulances on the Western Front, the SIH ambulance was not 'required'.

> When assistance was wanted towards the purchase of the ambulance, it was hoped to send it to the front with the squadron [A] of the South Irish Horse then under orders to proceed on active service. It transpired, however, that mounted men were not then required in Flanders, so the squadron was posted for service in the east coast of England [Doncaster]. It seemed, indeed, that there was no immediate use for the ambulance … from the War Office that they had plenty of ambulances at the front for the use of the Army. It appeared, however, that the French were not so well off … and Surgeon Major McCabe states … he arranged to send the South Irish Horse Ambulance to France to work with the French Army, for which it seems it has being doing splendid work. It has frequently been under shellfire, but so far escaped.

(The driver, Ferdinand Jules Vambeck, was commissioned in the South Irish Horse on 17 February 1917.[11])

The SIH Band was very active throughout the existence of the regiment, no more so than during the war years. The band played its part as a vital instrument for keeping up morale, spreading the word and supporting the numerous recruiting campaigns run throughout the war. From appearing in Dublin, Kingstown (Dun Laoghaire), in the park's bandstand, to playing at a Comforts Fund meeting in the town hall in Gorey on 2 January 1917, the band was kept busy. The Bandmaster, Mr Albert Fawcett RMSM (Royal Military School of Music), even managed to pen a new patriotic march entitled *The Emerald Isle* in 1915.

In June 1915 the resident troops billeted at Leopardstown were moved to the cavalry barracks in the centre of Carlow, having recently been vacated by 10 Signal Company Royal Engineers on 1 May. Their and some of the locals' disappointment was palpable. Rumours abounded that the squadron had interfered with the racing and that certain 'members' had used their influence to convince the War Office to relocate the men. Being a predominantly Dublin-recruited squadron, the men had friends and family in close proximity and had become used to visiting them on a frequent basis.[12]

However, this did not stop the officers from the squadron presenting Captain Quinn, the manager of the racecourse, with a gold cigarette case.[13] The move to Carlow was completed by the end of June. How long they were there is unknown. We know that they were there for the remainder of 1915 as Company Sergeant Major Edward Staunton was court-martialled for an unknown offence in Carlow on 27 October 1915. On 30 August 1915 Lieutenant Colonel the 5th Baron Decies was appointed Assistant Adjutant and Quartermaster General to the Adjutant General and Quartermaster-General's staff in Dublin Castle. That meant the command of the Regiment was passed to the then Major the Earl of Wicklow. He was appointed temporary lieutenant colonel to command the regiment. The Earl of Wicklow was to remain in charge of the regiment until he was posted to London to take up a position within the War Office on 14 June 1917. Major Burns-Lindow was then promoted to lieutenant colonel and commanded the regiment until its disbandment in 1922.

The life of the Depot Squadron at Carlow was rather innocuous. There was plenty of time to mingle with the locals, attend dances, fetes and variety performances.[14] Much was made in the local press about the attendance of a large detachment of the soldiers at a meeting concerning the reorganization of the United Irish League in the town hall at Carlow. At least twelve members of the regiment attended the annual march in the town to commemorate the Manchester Martyrs in December 1915.[15] More normal duties covered by the Depot were the attendance at and provision of an escort for the County Carlow Summer Assizes in July 1915.[16]

In June a small but notable brouhaha between the depot squadron, under the command of Lord Wicklow, and Carlow Urban District Council occurred over bathing rights in the River Barrow. It appeared that bathing by the men 'sans' bathing suits had been happening outside the council's prescribed hours for the soldiers, put in place in order to take into account the use and enjoyment of the river side by the people of Carlow. Naturally, naked soldiers frolicking in the river could quite possibly upset the good townspeople. A letter was written by the town clerk to the Earl of Wicklow stating the proscription and a reply was received that was felt by council members to be discourteous. The Earl of Wicklow had responded to the original letter stating that the council had no authority to set such rules on the Army and, as such, he would allow his men to bathe when and where he felt suitable! A great debate was held in the council chambers on this and it was decided that, in the words of the chairman, 'The Commanding Officer had sent the Council a challenge. The Major should be informed that he was not going to override the wishes of the people of Carlow, even with the Defence of the Realm Act in force.'[17] No more bathing 'in the nip' for the lads!

A tragedy occurred on the night of 11 December 1915 for Captain Anthony Loftus Bryan SIH, when his house burned down. Anthony Loftus was the son of Lieutenant Colonel Loftus Anthony Bryan JP, from Enniscorthy. Captain Bryan was at home on leave when a fire broke out. Having been awoken at 6:00am by smoke and the noise of fire from the basement, he vacated his upstairs apartments. It appears from the report of the incident that the hay and straw stored in the basement area must have caught fire and, as a result of this, the blaze ran throughout the building, eventually gutting the property. Limited access to firefighting equipment meant that there was little or no hope of survival for the building or its contents. Captain Bryan lived in Carrigmannon, approximately six miles north-east of Wexford, close to the River Barrow. He was a well-known and well-liked member of the community.[18]

At the beginning of January 1916 adverts were placed in national and local newspapers calling for more men to join the SIH, who were raising new squadrons at Cahir, County Tipperary. Just prior to this, the Depot Squadron enjoyed the Christmas festivities in Carlow town, reported in the local newspaper:

In Carlow the festival was celebrated in a very 'quiet' manner, and those buoyant feelings and general signs of outward rejoicings were conspicuous by their absence. In fact, the only section of the community who apparently 'bore their hearts light' was the South Irish Horse. On Christmas night a large contingent of these made a detour of the streets 'making jolly' and rending the air with the now famous *Tipperary* refrain. As per usual, they had a large following of the civil population of the young element, in which naturally enough the 'fair' sex were largely represented.[19]

Recruitment was not only targeted at the general public. The Royal Irish Constabulary (RIC), which had many army reservists within its ranks, was also a fertile ground for potential recruits. All in all, 752 RIC men served in the armed forces during the Great War. Of these, seventeen served with the South Irish Horse, mainly from the mounted police.[20] RIC Sergeant Martin Morgan joined the South Irish Horse on 28 April 1916, but it appears that he was too old to serve overseas and was subsequently discharged. On his return to the RIC, Sergeant Morgan was wounded on 3 September 1920 in Kilmacthomas, County Waterford, by the IRA. He succumbed to his wounds on the 27th, leaving behind a wife and two children. His attackers were (allegedly) shipped off to America to avoid prosecution.

The cavalry barracks, situated on the outskirts of Cahir, had been vacated by the Royal Artillery in August 1914 and had stood idle since then. Orders were received from the War Office that the South Irish Horse were to make the barracks their depot and so the regiment moved to Cahir that January. With an area of over twenty-three acres, purpose-made accommodation for horses and men, and all the necessary ancillary facilities for training, it was an ideal location for the reserve, or depot squadron. All headquarters staff were relocated there, including the regimental band.[21]

The regiment very quickly settled into local life at Cahir with sports days, boxing matches, fetes, war-related fundraisers and dinner dances all held throughout their stay. Football and cricket matches were also arranged between the townspeople and the regiment. Much use of the band was made at these occasions. The local businesses, naturally, did rather well out of the regiment, thankfully, as things would have been rather bleak following the departure of over 1,200 men of the Royal Artillery four months before.

Around this time, a rather sad, and fatal, accident occurred whilst training at Cahir. On 13 March 1916, No. 1702 Private John Joseph Reilly was thrown from his horse.

A very sad fatality occurred near the Royal Victoria Military Barracks, Cahir, on Monday morning, when Private J.J. Reilly, of the South Irish Horse, was thrown from his horse and received such injuries that death followed almost immediately. Deceased was one of the number out on horseback for exercise before 8 o'clock. Sergeant Conway was leading the troops while an officer brought up the rear. After passing a stream-roller on the Gallyclogher road, and when about half a mile was riding next [i.e. alongside] the deceased, noticed that deceased's horse seemed to get frightened—at what he knew not – and giving a side jump, threw the rider rather heavily to the ground. The riderless horse dashed on and was caught by Sergeant Conway. Several companions at once rushed to the deceased, who was bleeding freely, and still showed signs of life. The Royal Army Medical Staff were appraised of the occurrence, and Sergeant Ringwood, RAMC, soon came on the scene and applied artificial respiration, but unfortunately without avail. Dr Cusack JP, now Military Medical Officer, was telephoned for to the town, and arrived in a very short time, but only to pronounce life extinct. The remains were then reverently removed to the mortuary, and the matter was reported to the local police. Constable Keene visited the scene, and subsequently the facts were communicated to the district Coroner, Mr E. Cummins JP, Brookhill, Fethard. When the sad intelligence reached the town it created quite a sensation, for the SIH, since their advent to Cahir, have proved most popular with the townspeople, and this sad accident occasioned much regret. Inquiries made show that deceased was the son of Constable F. Reilly, RIC, who has been stationed for the past 12 years at Portarlington. Deceased was a splendid type of Irishman. He stood 6 feet 2 inches, and was of powerful physique. He was a teacher at the Military Barracks, having been a Monitor previous to his joining the Colours. He had been in the Army four months, and was most popular with his comrades, who deeply regret his loss. Deceased was only 20 years of age.[22]

A storm at the beginning of November 1916 in Cahir injured a member of the regiment when he was blown off his feet and landed on broken glass.

When there is a large military presence within a civilian area, there are bound to be disagreements between the two. Cahir was no different. A number of incidents, from theft to assault, were reported throughout the regiment's stay at the barracks. Cahir was not an isolated case, as C Squadron, whilst still at Moorepark in Cork, also attracted the unwanted attention of the civilian population. During a sweep by the military police on houses near and around the barracks, numerous items, clothing and military equipment was recovered. As a result a number of people were summoned to the Fermoy Sessions to answer for their 'indiscretions'. One such unfortunate gentleman was Mr John Daly, living at Kilworth, who was accused of possessing military blankets and biscuits discovered by Sergeant Taylor, Military Police. When in front of the bench on 26 September 1916, he defended himself by stating that the biscuits had been given to him by virtue of a contract with the South Irish Horse for the disposal of swill and disused biscuits. Sergeant Donegan, acting as mess sergeant for the regiment (I cannot find any reference to him as being a member of the SIH), confirmed that in fact Mr Daly did indeed have a contract to dispose of materials as stated and the case was dismissed.[23]

Every Irish regiment was affected either directly or indirectly by the events of Easter 1916, including the South Irish Horse. Although not directly present in numbers in Dublin at that time, some members were there, whether on leave or in transit at barracks. No doubt the service regiment at Cahir was put on the highest alert to provide assistance in the southern half of the country as required. I have little or no mention of the regiment in the archives with the exception of two instances.

On 24 April, whilst on leave at 51 Merrion Square, Captain Cyril G.P. Kirk was captured and held prisoner by the rebels and his field glasses taken. Luckily, he was released and returned to the front. He did not, however, forget to claim for the loss of the field glasses.[24]

Seamus Ua Caomhanaigh was a volunteer in the uprising, active in and around the General Post Office during the week of hostilities. Escaping via Moore Street towards the end of the week, he was eventually captured with the remainder of the volunteers when they were forced to surrender unconditionally. Having been captured, he was marched away on the Saturday with the other prisoners and corralled within the grounds at the front of the Rotunda Hospital.

We had not much rest that night as the space was too small to accommodate us and, in addition a crowd of *seoníns* (West Brits) called 'The South Irish Horse' kept flashing torches at us and poking rifles and clicking the locks every few minutes, until at last one of the sentries who could stick it no longer shouted 'Take no notice of these fellows, boy. If one of you had a gun the whole lot of them would run like the devil.' After that they came back no more.[25]

Meanwhile back at Cahir two men had been charged with assaulting two soldiers on 9 September 1916. Messrs James Holohan and John Reily were charged with assault on Corporal Matthew Clancey and Lance Corporal J.F. Pike respectively. A police officer, Constable Madden, was also involved in the fracas. (Again, unfortunately, Lance Corporal J.F. Pike does not show in any of my records. Newspapers at this time were notorious for misspelling names and, as such, Pike could be anyone.) As usual, drink had been taken by the defendants, one word led to another and a scuffle/fight erupted between the four men. After reporting this to the police, Holohan was remanded to the barracks, whereupon he attacked Constable Madden before being restrained. Holohan, being the main miscreant, was fined for his actions in court.[26]

Although the above is an example of a typical scuffle between soldiers and locals, this particular incident is of interest because of one of the participants, Corporal Matthew Clancey. As a reserve/training depot, Cahir would have had a training cadre. One member of the cadre, Ashleigh Cooper, was a training sergeant who remained at Cahir throughout most of the war. (He was awarded the British War Medal and Victory Medal at the end of the war, indicating that he was in France and Flanders with the regiment at some stage.) Cooper was described by Edward Mordaunt, who as a 17-year-old recruit came across him during his training, 'the extrovert Sergeant Cooper, who behaved as if recruits were put in his power to be targets for his wide repertoire of oaths and ribald humour'.[27] (It could well be construed as the typical description of a 'stay at home' training sergeant.) What has this got to do with Clancey? Clancey, as part of the training cadre, it appears, did not have any intention of being transferred from the safety of Cahir to the front line. For some, the front line would have been viewed as a bit of a nightmare, to be avoided at all costs. He, it appears, was having too much fun at home. This all came to a head when, on 19 January 1917, he was faced with court martial at Clonmel, the Regimental HQ of the Royal Irish Regiment. The Courts Martial record states he was charged with multiple thefts and sentenced to six months in jail. However, his medal roll indicates that he deserted on 27 January 1917 and I can only assume he escaped confinement. Desertion was not prevalent, but it did occur. Including Matthew Clancey, I have recorded eleven incidents of desertion. Although there appears to be at least twenty counts of desertion in the court's martial records, these cases were of men who were actually caught, charged and sentenced, unlike Clancey et al. The majority of the deserters survived the period when the regiment was mounted, but when dismounted and transferred to 7th (South Irish Horse) Battalion Royal Irish Regiment, desertions increased.[28]

SIH No.	R. Ir. No.	CofH No.	Rank	Surname	First Name	In theatre	Description
1719			Private	Clancey	Matthew		Deserted 26/1/17 As a Cpl was assaulted in Cahir 09/10/1916
1832	25091		Private	Coleman	Thomas		Deserted 3/1/18
		73587		Collins	Daniel	28/01/1918	Deserted 28/5/1918 enlisted RN 4/6/18 Demobbed 10/3/19
784			Bdm	Duncan	Donald William		Absent from mobilization 5/8/14 aged 40 was in C Sqn (Cork Division) and assumed he wouldn't be called up. Forgot about it until 1918 when attested C3 – looking for discharge papers 1936
2474	25243		Private	Dunn	Daniel George		Deserted 16/3/18
1619			Private	Enright	Patrick	07/06/1916	Deserted 6/6/1917
1691	25540		Private	Kinsella	Patrick		Deserted 11/11/1915 then fraudulently enlisted as McDonald, P.
1960			Sgt	Manning	Louis		Deserted whilst en route to join King's African Rifles
1621	25568		Private	McNulty	Joseph		Deserted 4/5/18
925	25615		Private	Monks	Michael	25/11/1915	Deserted 14/5/18

It appears that some of the desertions occurred whilst the soldier was at home on leave. Patrick Enright, for instance, deserted because he felt he hadn't received sufficient medical attention for his rheumatism. Due to this, he decided that he was no longer fit to serve. On the face of it, one could be excused for agreeing with his reasoning and be very well disposed to his plight. However, Patrick had previous form, having been with the Leinsters during the Boer War, enlisting on 23 November 1899. Whilst stationed in Pretoria, he deserted on 10 September 1903 and returned to Ireland where he was arrested on 13 April 1904. He subsequently rejoined the Leinsters on the 27 August 1904 and was finally discharged on the 3 April 1905. When re-enlisting at Cahir in 1915, he neglected to mention his previous record, assuming (quite rightly) that this may well have been held against him. This indiscretion only came to light when he unsuccessfully applied for his discharge papers and medals in 1936.[29]

Four of the above men deserted during or after the great German offensive of 1918. With tensions running high at home because of the proposals to introduce conscription in Ireland and the fallout from the 1916 rebellion, it's hardly surprising that some of the men felt disenfranchised and unwanted at the front. Naturally, the above men, when deserting, were not returned to service and so forfeited their right to receive a medal.[30]

Add to this being retrained as infantry and the loss of most of the regiment on the first day of the offensive, it appears that these men had had enough. It certainly didn't help that their performance on the first and subsequent days of the German offensive was under scrutiny by the General Staff and the English troops, who, quite wrongly, believed that they couldn't be trusted to fight. Haig's diary of 22 March casts doubt on 16th (Irish) Division's will to fight and calls into question the apparent lack of resistance put up by some units at the outset of the attack.[31]

All things considered, the desertion rate was very low, which is a good reflection on the leadership of the officers and NCOs and the quality of men still within the regiment. Having been mainly spared the brutal battles of the previous three years, there was still a good nucleus of 'cavalry' men.

One incident does stand out, though, and that is the desertion by Sergeant Louis Manning. Manning had been transferred to the King's African Rifles (KAR) who were fighting in and around German East Africa. The regiment was made up of mainly African troops, supported and commanded by European NCOs and officers. He was either thought good enough to be transferred away from the Western Front at a time when all the experienced NCOs were required, or he was a liability and not suited to the front. We know that he was transferred prior to the formation of the 7th (South Irish Horse) Battalion Royal Irish Regiment and through his actions we can safely say that he wasn't too enamoured with the prospect of serving with the KAR, as he disappeared (deserted) en route to East Africa.[32]

With the war continuing apace in France and Flanders, the training of recruits and replacements also continued. The command of the regiment was taken over by Major Burns-Lindow when the Earl of Wicklow was posted to the War Office in London in May 1917. Sporting events, fundraisers and fetes continued throughout 1917 and 1918, as did petty theft, larceny, desertion and assault. For instance, Trooper James Withers was charged with stealing a bicycle at the beginning of June 1917; two men, Michael Bolger and John O'Rourke were arrested for desertion in April 1917; a year later Joseph McKenna of Queen's County was arrested for desertion of over twelve months; and, on 28 September 1918, Trooper Dan Traynor was court-martialled for breaking into a public house and stealing whiskey. There are over seventy instances of a court martial being held to prosecute a member of the South Irish Horse from the period 1915–1919. Of these fifty-nine courts martial were held at home; the remainder were 'In the Field'. The majority of the home service courts martial were based in Cahir, together with Tipperary and Clonmel. At least four were held in and around Tickhill, Yorkshire, during A Squadron's stay there.[33]

Offence	No.	Where Courts Martial held
Desertion (and arrest)	20	All on home service.
Absence without official leave (AWOL)	17	16 on home service/1 in the field but found not guilty.
Absence and breaking out of barracks	3	In the field.
Assault/drunkenness	2	On home service.
Theft	5	On home service.
Disobedience	9	6 on home service and 3 in the field, 1 of whom was not guilty.
Insubordination	9	5 on home service, one of whom was not guilty and 4 in the field.
'Conduct to prejudice of good order and military discipline'	5	2 on home service; one not guilty and 3 in the field; two not guilty
Quitting or sleeping at post	1	On home service
Striking a senior officer	1	In the field
Fraudulent enlistment	4	On home service
Drunkenness	2	On home service and In the field; both found not guilty

The above does not include the 'mutiny' that occurred in March 1918 (See Chapter IX)

When the re-organization of all the mounted troops in the field occurred in July 1917 to form an infantry battalion, the training cadre at Cahir continued to train cavalry recruits. Those men not required for the infantry role at the front were sent back to Cahir for re-assignment or, in some cases, dismissal. Re-assignment could mean transfer to another mounted regiment, to the Labour Corps, or to a commission. Dismissal was generally for those who were time expired or no longer physically fit for service.

On Thursday 10 October 1918 the steam packet RMS *Leinster* was on her way between Kingstown (now Dun Laoghaire) and Holyhead carrying 771 passengers, 180 of whom were civilians, including women and children; the remainder were mainly military personnel going to and returning from leave. At around 10:00am she was torpedoed by the German submarine *UB-123* and sank about sixteen miles off the coast of Ireland. The sinking of the ship claimed 529 souls, of whom 115 casualties were civilian. Amongst the dead were three members of the regiment. Lance Corporal Augustus Doyle, A Squadron, Shoeing Smith Henry Quinsey, B Squadron and Staff Sergeant Frederick Megroff (Army Ordnance Corps attached 7th (South Irish Horse) Battalion Royal Irish Regiment).[34] This tragic event was made even more so, coming so close to the end of the war. The German submarine was subsequently to strike a mine on 18 October and sink with all hands.[35]

The 7th (South Irish Horse) Battalion Royal Irish Regiment – 49 Infantry Brigade – 16th (Irish) Division, Tunnel Trench, Ronssoy, Amiens – 21 Infantry Brigade – 30th Division – Locre, Wervicq, Courtrai – Disbandment

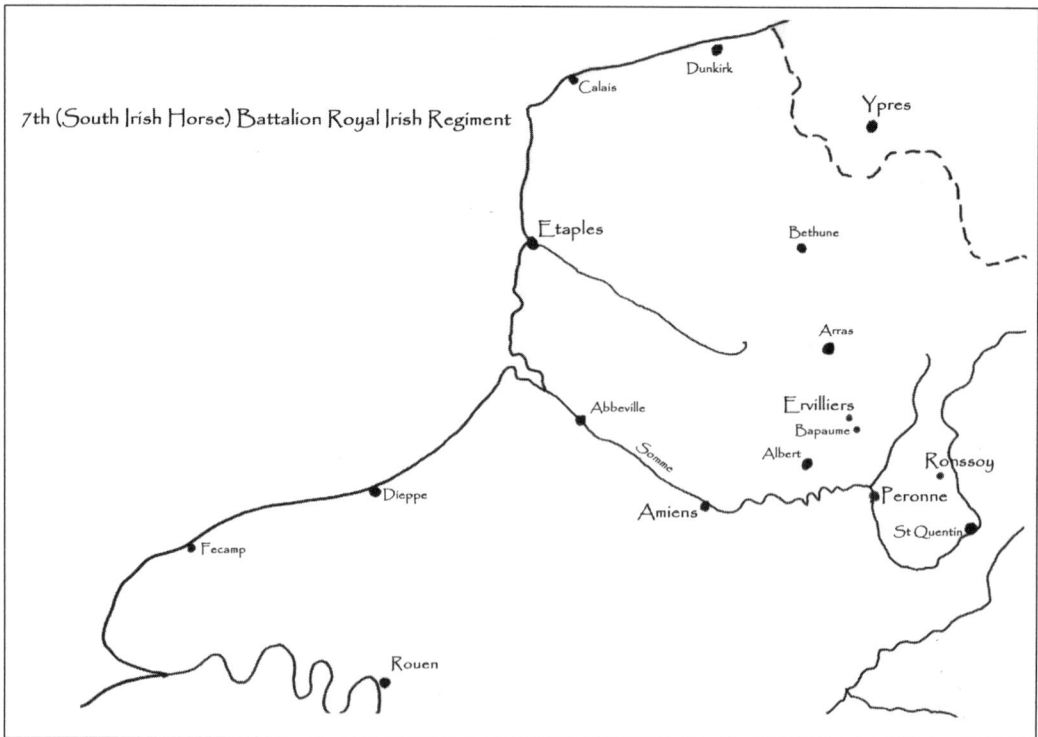

7th (South Irish Horse) Battalion Royal Irish Regiment

So, that was that; the horses had gone, saddlery and tack dubbined, packed and sent off to the base, men deemed necessary for mounted duties transferred elsewhere and the idle hands and 'useless mouths' (support troops, ASC etc.) returned to base. However, in Cahir, 3rd South Irish Horse was still recruiting and training men for mounted duties with the regiment. One consolation, if it could be viewed as a consolation for losing their horses, was that they still retained their higher rate of cavalry pay.

A regimental history of the 7th (South Irish Horse) Battalion Royal Irish Regiment has been published as part of the complete history of the Royal Irish Regiment, from their formation to disbandment in 1922. The history is somewhat brief and deals mainly with the events of 21 March 1918 and the latter stages of the war in October/November 1918.

Analyzing the non-commissioned officers and men using medal rolls, medal index cards and available service records shows that, from August 1914 to September 1917, out of the 1,351 men I have recorded, the following were:

Commissioned	84
Time Expired	42
Discharged unfit	38
Discharged underage	4
Transferred to other regiments/corps	114
Died at home or hospital	10
Died on service	1
Died of wounds received	10
Killed in action	21
Deserted	4
Sub-total	328
Transferred to 7 (SIH) R.Ir. Regt	641
Transferred to Corps of Hussars (inc SIH) and new number issued	376
Total ORs	1,345

Even these figures may be somewhat conservative, as there are no available muster books to confirm the total strength of pre- and post-re-organization that I have found. It would be safe to assume the remainder of the new battalion's strength would have been made up of men and officers transferred in from other regiments, both Irish and English. That said, the battalion still remained predominantly South Irish Horse and Irish.

From 1 September until 14 October 1917 the battalion was based in Maresquel, training to be infantry. Platoon drill, musketry, bayonet drill, bombing and Lewis-gun training were carried out again and again. When the battalion transferred to Ervillers, the training intensified with practising open ground attacks, interspersed with wiring and trench-digging duties (a skill they were already well trained for) and improvements to their camp. If they felt that they were fit when they were initially dismounted by the end of October they must have been 'fighting fit'. With the autumnal weather turning wintry and preparations for a move to the front line as infantry underway, they could only feel trepidation, especially as many of the men had experienced, or been present at, every major battle in France and Flanders since the retreat from Mons.[1]

A snapshot of how the battalion was organized at this stage (October), comprising four Companies A, B, C and S, as well as the Battalion Headquarters (BHQ) is outlined below:

A Company Commander	Captain Thomas E. Morton with Second Lieutenants J.A. Watts, Stokes and A.B.P. Hadden
B Company Commander	Captain Noel Furlong, Captain George Colvill, Lieutenant C.T. Stewart and Second Lieutenant W. Dwyer
C Company Commander	Captain John M Wardell, Captain Laurence Trant, Second Lieutenants N. Murphy and Wilks
S Company Commander	Captain J Roche-Kelly, Second Lieutenants W.S. Barrett, G.A. Harris and H. Brocklebank.
HQ Commanding Officer	Lieutenant Colonel C.M. Truman DSO, 2 i/c Major H.E. Norton, Adjutant Captain F.H. Brooke, Signals Officer, Intelligence Officer and Medical Officer [?Surgeon Major F.F. McCabe]
Lewis Gun Officer	Second Lieutenant Thornley
Bombing Officer	Second Lieutenant A.S. Wolfe-Smyth
Works Officer	Second Lieutenant Watts
Transport Lines	Second Lieutenants Penhale, Brown, Ferguson and Dignan
On leave	Lieutenants Fogarty, Dease and Smith.

Each company comprised approximately 200 men, divided into four platoons of fifty men each. The battalion headquarters would include non-front-line troops, such as signallers, runners, cooks, stretcher-bearers, a small section of medics under the Medical Officer, Surgeon Major McCabe, drivers and other ancillary specialist roles. To give an idea of the strength of the battalion, on the morning of 21 March 1918 there was a total of 1,012 officers and men.[2]

Surgeon Major Frederick Faber McCabe was an unsung hero of the regiment. Born in 1869, he was the son of Sir Francis McCabe, the first Irish Roman Catholic to be knighted for services to humanity (medicine). He qualified from Trinity in 1894 as a medical doctor.[3] He was no stranger to the privations of war, as he had served as a civilian surgeon in the Second Boer War, where he was captured. A keen horseman and amateur trainer, he joined the SIH at its inception and remained throughout. He was known for training the first ever Irish Derby winner, 'Orby' in 1907, being buttonholed afterwards by an old lady who reportedly said, 'Thank God and you Sir, a Catholic horse has won the Derby in my lifetime.'[4] His response to the win was to send a telegram to the regiment prescribing a glass of champagne for the troops. He was also the author of a number of books and articles relating to the health and upkeep of horses and men alike. Ever conscious of his duty to the men under his care, he was instrumental in fundraising and equipping the SIH ambulance (that the French Army used) and organizing fundraisers for the Red Cross. He arrived at the front on 1 June 1915 and was to serve with the regiment through all its incarnations until the end of the war. He was Mentioned in Despatches in September 1917. After the war he maintained his links with the Old Comrades Association. With the formation of the Irish Free State, McCabe continued to work as a military surgeon, offering his services as assistant medical surgeon for the Free State Army during the civil war. He was even appointed honorary Director of Medical Services for the Irish Brigade fighting in Spain in 1937.

As part of 16th (Irish) Division under County Tipperary born Major General Sir William B. Hickie, the battalion was transferred to 49 (Ulster) Brigade on 14 October 1917. For former members of C Squadron, returning to 16th (Irish) Division must have been like coming home. Shortly after joining, they entered the trenches for the first time, relieving 2nd Battalion Royal Dublin Fusiliers (2 RDF) in the support trenches on the north-western outskirts of Croisilles, a move to the front lines opposite Fontaine les Croisilles. On the 27th, the Battalion moved from the support trenches to the front line, relieving 7th/8th Battalion Royal Irish Fusiliers. It was here on the 29th that they suffered their first casualties, when a Lewis-gun emplacement received a direct hit from a German shell. The two casualties were 22-year-old Private 1242 Charles Barsby and 23-year-old Private 2049 John (Jack) Kelly. John Kelly had recently joined the battalion, arriving in theatre in September of that year. In all probability he was the 'Kelly' mentioned by Archibald Goodchild in his letter to the Marchioness of Waterford. On 31 October, the Battalion was relieved from the front line by the 10th Battalion Royal Dublin Fusiliers, thus ending their first full rotation in the trenches as an infantry battalion with two men killed and three wounded.

The beginning of November saw the battalion retiring to Belfast Camp (Ervillers) for the week. Training resumed with the emphasis on combat drills, close-order fighting, wiring, bombing and digging in. Lieutenant Colonel Truman left the battalion on 11 November to transfer to the Tank Corps. His replacement was Lieutenant Colonel H.E. Norton. The 12th saw the battalion training with 2nd Battalion Royal Irish Regiment and 7th/8th Battalion Royal Inniskilling Fusiliers in preparation for the offensive on Tunnel Trench timed for later that month. With the battalion returning to the front lines from the 14th until the 25th, patrolling, wiring parties and trench repairs continued.

As part of the preparation and subsequent attack on Tunnel Trench carried out by 7th/8th Battalion Royal Inniskilling Fusiliers and 2nd Battalion Royal Irish Regiment on the 20th, B and S Companies were ordered to construct a communication trench between Lump Lane and Tunnel Trench. In doing so, they unearthed a gas cylinder, damaging it in the process. Lieutenant Brocklebank and twenty-two other ranks were gassed as a result and had to be evacuated.[5] However, the trench was successfully completed in quick time. Enemy shelling in support of their counter-attacks along the front line wounded a further four men. The support given to the Allied attack by the battalion was very effective and even netted seven German prisoners from the 470th Regiment. Unfortunately, on 25 November, just as the battalion was being relieved, they suffered another casualty, that of 25420 Private Thomas Kearney, aged twenty-two. A native of County Tyrone, but living in Glasgow, he had only recently enlisted.

The men had a brief respite for five days back at Belfast Camp including much needed baths before returning to the front line to relieve 2nd Royal Dublin Fusiliers on the 30th. It was during this relief that the battalion suffered its greatest number of fatalities to date. As the men moved up the trench known as Mole Lane, behind Tunnel Trench, they were spotted and the Germans opened fire, shelling B Company.[6] The shelling killed one officer and seven men; 22-year-old Captain George Chaigneau Colvill, the second son of the Governor of the Bank of Ireland, Sergeant William Newman aged 29, Corporal Herbert Mitchell aged 23, Lance Corporal Christopher Shier aged 29, Privates Denis McCarthy, aged 26, and William Wilson. Christopher Shier's headstone carries the inscription 'Killed while helping a wounded comrade under heavy shellfire', taken from his obituary:

> He was universally popular with the men of the regiment, and had he lived must have received higher distinction. He was a father to his section, and they loved him as such. They are heartbroken about him, and wish me to convey their very deep sympathy to you. He was killed instantaneously by a piece of shell. But I know you will feel proud of him – as his company are – when I tell you it was while carrying down a wounded comrade under heavy shellfire, which act of devotion he volunteered to do. We brought him down from the trenches the same night, and buried him the following morning in a quiet spot behind the line.[7]

The war diaries indicate that five men were killed and a further two were reported as missing. I can only assume that one of the men listed here was one of the missing; the other is still unknown. However, 1691 Christopher Kiely is commemorated on the Thiepval Memorial and was reported missing, presumed dead, on 4 December. As the battalion was not in action on 4 December, it could be rightly assumed that Christopher was the seventh man killed on 30 November.[8] The following day was no better with Sidney Roe and John McNamee being seriously wounded in the line, only to die at the casualty clearing station. Sidney died on 1 December, John on the 2nd. Of Sidney Roe, Captain Furlong wrote:

I mourn his loss, for he was a gallant soldier and a good fighter and did not know the meaning of fear; he was bright and cheerful and a general favourite with both officers and men.[9]

Leaving Croisilles and Ervillers behind, the battalion marched out on 2 December and made its way over the next three days to the Peronne region of the front and, ultimately, to Villers-Faucon. Sixteenth (Irish) Division was to relieve 55th (West Lancashire) Division around the village of Ronssoy on a 4,500-yard front (approximately 2.55 miles/4 kilometres). The division (and battalion) were to stay there until 21 March 1918.[10] Initially billeted at Tincourt-Boucly, the battalion relocated to billets at Villers-Faucon, closer to the front line, for the remainder of their stay. Arriving at Tincourt on the 5th, the battalion manned the reserve outposts around St Emilie the following morning for a day, before relieving 1st Royal Dublin Fusiliers in the front line. Over the next few days the routine was established for manning the front-line trenches, reserve lines and rest.

The layout of this part of the front, as part of the Fifth Army under General Hubert Gough, was based on the premise of defence in depth with support from established artillery posts ranged on prefixed points. The front line was to be a series of fortified outposts and listening posts, joined with established trenches. At this location, the lines of defence were annotated as Blue Line (Outpost line), Red Line (Main Line – l'Empire), Yellow Line (Support – Ronssoy/Ephéy Road), Brown Line (Reserve – north-east St Emile) and Green Line (Tincourt). These were to be lightly held during daylight hours, with main strongpoints between the Red and Blue Lines to be manned in strength when under attack.[11] Reserve lines and fortified posts were located approximately 1,500 yards apart to the rear. This defence in depth, if manned in strength, would have presented a formidable obstacle for the enemy to penetrate. However, due to the general lack of manpower and incomplete protection on the ground, the situation at the end of 1917 and the beginning of 1918 would have left this part of the front very susceptible to attack. Added to that, winter weather was making the repair and upgrading of trench systems nigh on impossible. Snow, ice and intermittent thawing of the ground turned the trenches to sludge.[12]

It was into this environment that the battalion was placed. During his stay in the front lines, John Honner, together with his mates, would be standing duty four hours on and four hours off. He was bitterly cold all the time and suffered frostbite that was to stay with him for the rest of his life. He recalled one instance when he and two others lay down for a sleep in the frosty conditions. The trench rats (he mentioned them being as big as small dogs) kept him alive by sleeping either side of him for mutual warmth. His two colleagues died of exposure. (Unfortunately, I cannot find the names of his two colleagues.)[13]

Targeted shelling was experienced throughout December and an increase of activity by enemy aircraft, including bombing of the trenches and rear areas. Testing of the defences and artillery reaction to bombardments would have confirmed the apparent strength of this part of the line. The continual harassment of the front lines, and rear areas meant that the defending troops would find it difficult to settle. Whilst in the trenches, patrols, trench repairs and wiring parties continued unabated. On the night of 10 December, a small skirmish between the enemy and the battalion around the left-hand section of the battalion's area at Priel Farm occurred. Starting with an enemy bombardment, a group of German soldiers was noticed working around this area and after about half an hour was seen to be returning to the German lines. It was then that the observing outpost opened fire with their Lewis guns and bombs, wounding many of the twenty-five enemy troops and killing at least two of them. The battalion suffered two wounded.

The morning after the skirmish, the GOC 16th (Irish) Division, Major General Hickie, presented the Military Medal to No. 1498 Corporal C. Bolton and Parchment Certificates to four further men. Two of the soldiers receiving their Parchment were Corporal Charles Ryan and Private Gerald Carson. Ryan had been with the SIH for over six years, whereas Carson joined up at the outbreak of war in 1914. Both had been in the field for over two years. Both were from Dublin, Carson from North Earl Street (opposite the GPO) and Ryan from Emor Street, Portobello. (Charles Ryan and Gerald Carson were to be captured later in March and spent the remainder of the war as PoWs in Germany). Lance Sergeant G.J.T. Campbell, from Rathmines, who enlisted in the South Irish Horse in 1915, received two Parchment Certificates for Gallantry. The first was for action in 1917 (Tunnel Trench action) and the second for action on 10 January 1918 (patrolling no man's land).

During the relief of the battalion by 7th/8th Royal Inniskilling Fusiliers on the night of the 12 December 1917, C Company, along with members of the administration staff received a direct hit from a single shell as they were caught out in the open by their billets in St Emile. Sixty casualties were recorded, of whom forty were from C Company. Of the forty casualties, twenty-two were killed outright and a further six died of wounds the next day. Added to that, Captain Cuthbert Vernon and four ORs were also wounded during the relief and subsequent relocation of the battalion to new billets in the quarry to the north-west of the village by the railway station. (Captain Vernon was later to be attached to the Irish Guards and awarded the Military Cross for his actions on 26 September 1918). John Honner was one of those having to render first aid to the wounded that night. (A list of those killed is contained in Appendix III.)[14] Company Sergeant Major Thomas Fletcher, writing home on 17 December 1917, in one of his last letters to his sister, Harriet, broke the sad news of the death of two of their friends caught in the shelling; Corporal Tom (J.T.) Smith and Private Edward Farrell. In his letter he expressed the loss felt by the rest of the Company, and the consolation that 'their end was painless and they are buried in a nice little cemetery behind the line'. Fletcher's brother, Edward, was also wounded in the same attack, receiving wounds to his arm and leg, sufficiently bad enough to be considered a 'Blighty' wound (a wound bad enough for the casualty to be sent to Britain for treatment). Thomas thought this was a bit of luck as his brother could now spend Christmas 'in Blighty'.[15]

With the battalion in temporary billets (tents) at the railway station, time was taken to send the men off to Villers-Faucon in two sections for much needed baths before returning to their billets for fatigues, cleaning kit and the inevitable working parties up the lines to the front. Just prior to vacating these billets and returning to Villers-Faucon for a rest, the area was heavily shelled, wounding one man. Lance Corporal Michael Quirke, 30, died from wounds received the next day, exactly two years to the day since he had set foot in France with the rest of C Squadron. There were at least two other men who died of wounds in and around this date. It could be reasonably presumed that they died from wounds received as a result of the shelling on 12 December, as the battalion is not recorded as having any other fatalities about this time.

After resting for seven days, the battalion returned to the front, relieving 6th Connaught Rangers of 47 Brigade at l'Empire (Red Line) on 23 December, where they remained over Christmas before being relieved by

7th/8th Royal Irish Fusiliers, to retire to billets at Ronssoy village on the 29th. Working parties of forty-five men with an officer commanding for defensive works were supplied from each company throughout their stay in the support lines at Ronssoy. Unfortunately, on 1 January, the Germans spotted the working parties in the village and promptly shelled them. Anticipating further activity within the village, the Germans continued their bombardment throughout New Year's Day. On the 4th, a welcome relief by the 8th/9th Royal Dublin Fusiliers meant that the battalion could return to safer billets and rest in Tincourt. Five days of rest, training, baths, sports and, of course, the inevitable working parties ensued, with a return to the front and the Blue Line around Priel Farm. Apart from the usual trench routine and working parties, patrols into no man's land were stepped up with little result. No enemy was heard or seen. The patrols were quite substantial with up to twenty men in each, often going out at least three times in one night. That, together with a considerable thaw and heavy rainfall, made the trenches unbearable and would not have made for a pleasant new year.

A short respite in the brigade reserve at St Emile (Brown Line) for five days and then back to the front lines around Priel Farm followed. All the time the weather was inclement, trenches were in very poor condition due to rain, and the thaw, coupled with poor visibility from the mist and fog, meant that the conditions were extremely harsh. Several patrols were sent out, but again with little success. Intermittent shelling by the enemy was endured throughout their stay. However, early in the morning on 25 January, Heythorp Post was heavily shelled. Expecting an attack, a counter-barrage was called. A listening post manned by a small patrol of one NCO and six men in the ruins of Little Priel Farm to the north of Heythorp Post spotted and fired on an enemy patrol around the same time. When the listening post patrol returned, the patrol leader was missing. It is not clear whether he was caught in a friendly fire engagement underway at the time, or whether he was captured by the enemy patrol they fired on. One man was reported missing assumed dead on 31 January, Private James Coleman who is commemorated on the Thiepval Memorial. Was he the missing NCO? There is no documentary evidence that he was an acting NCO, but no other man was reported missing at this time. The brigade assumed the missing NCO was captured; however as PoW records are scarce, it is very difficult to confirm, let alone place a name against the man.[16]

Maintenance of the trenches and improvement of defences, strongpoints and wiring along the front throughout January and February was the primary focus for the whole division. It was well known that the defences were not as strong as they could be, so it was essential that they be improved with some urgency. Continual shelling of the forward, support and reserve areas continued throughout this period, sometimes sufficiently severe as to elicit SOS signals for counter-battery fire.

At the end of January and in early February 1918, an Army-wide re-organization was undertaken. As part of this, each infantry brigade was reduced from four battalions to three. This meant that some existing battalions within 16th (Irish) Division were disbanded and their men redistributed throughout the brigades where needed. One of these disbanded battalions was the 6th (Service) Battalion Royal Irish Regiment (Major William Redmond's former battalion). Six officers and 371 men were transferred to the 7th (South Irish Horse) Battalion Royal Irish Regiment on 9 February, bringing the unit up to strength.

Using the rough figures previously tabled, and Lieutenant Colonel Burns-Lindow's figure, I believe that, at the time of the German offensive, the battalion comprised thirty-two officers, based on the breakdown of each company previously highlighted, and 980 men as set out below:

641	Original complement transferred from 1st and 2nd South Irish Horse
57	Less those Killed, MIA, died at home up to 20 March 1918
371	Transfer of men from disbanded 6th (Service) Battalion Royal Irish Regiment on 9 February 1918
25	Estimated number of replacements
980	Estimated total ORs on 20 March 1918

(The above figure does not take into account any men wounded, on leave or on courses at that time and, as such, can only be an educated guess.)

On 18 February one incident stands out during an inter-company relief between S and A Companies at the front. The transport carrying rations up to the front for distribution was spotted by an enemy aircraft that dropped a bomb on the ration party. The bomb killed Corporal Victor Stoker and wounded Lance Corporal Hickey, Privates McGarvey and Hartery. Victor was hit by shrapnel to his back. His commanding officer stated, 'Your son was one of the nicest and most popular fellows in the regiment and his loss

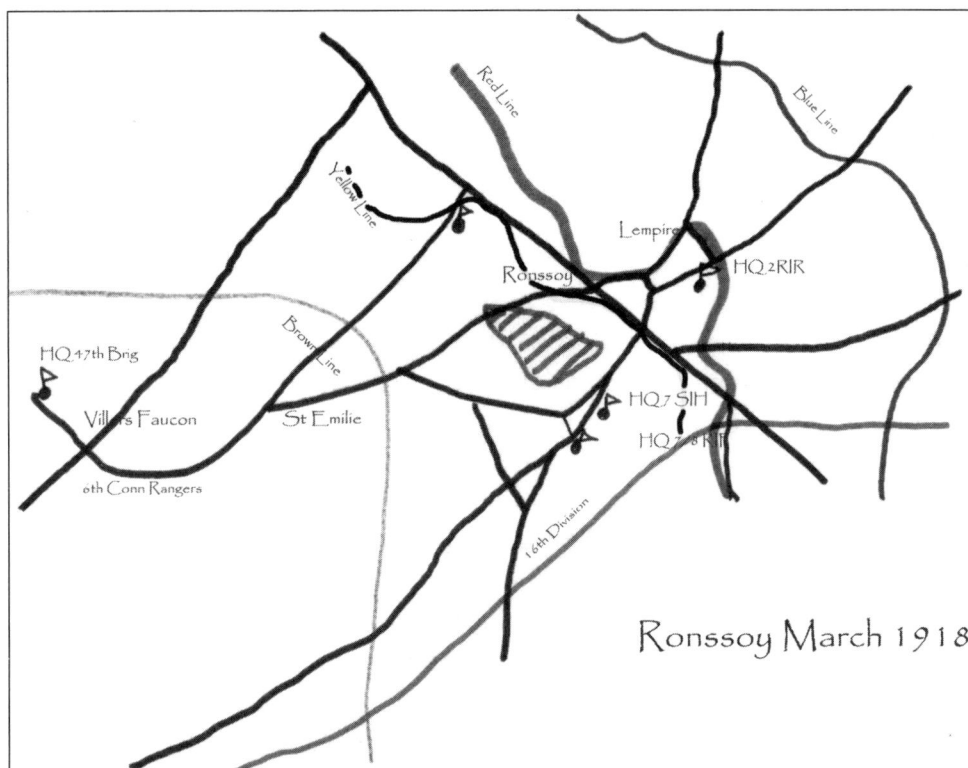

Ronssoy March 1918 (Based on 49 Brigade War Diaries).

is deeply felt by all.'[17] Three days later, heavy shelling of the front lines wounded a further five men of B Company, including Lieutenants Wolfe-Smyth, J. Smythe, Privates Byrne, Fitzgibbon and Rowden.

Now to the events of March 1918. The war diaries for this time, including any record of the battalion's strength, were destroyed by Captain Start, the Adjutant, on the afternoon of 21 March. Lieutenant Colonel E. Roche-Kelly, the CO of the battalion from 12 April, had to rely on information contained in the brigade and divisional diaries and any first-hand accounts from the surviving officers and men only. Later a written report was submitted, on 18 March 1919, by Major F. Call DSO, the battalion's CO from 7 March 1918 (who took over from Lieutenant Colonel H.E Norton on 3 March). Major Call had been captured with the majority of the battalion, on the first day of the offensive.[18]

Having spent much of its time on the left section of the divisional front around Epéhy, the battalion was relocated to the right section of the front around l'Empire and Basse Boulogne on 5 March, where they remained until the offensive, a matter of sixteen days. Facing them was the heavily fortified German 'Hindenburg Line', built on an undulating landscape with two shallow valleys running at right angles to the front line, ground ideally selected for defence by the Germans. Within this period, they moved up to the line and were in reserve, so only had approximately eight days at the most to acclimatize themselves to this section of the front. Yes, working parties had been up and around the lines, preparing and repairing trenches and wire, but no prolonged exposure to these lines had been experienced. At the same time, the other two brigades, 47 and 48, were in a similar situation, having taken over areas unfamiliar to them.

Moving up to this line on the night of 18/19 March, the battalion relieved 2nd Royal Irish Regiment. Aggressive patrolling was initiated during the night of 20/21 March. A seven-man patrol, sent out at approximately 0300 on the 21st, was led by Lieutenant Richard Gardiner Brewster (Intelligence Officer). Richard, originally a private with the South Irish Horse, was the son of the manager of the Independent Newspapers and a native of Dublin. He had been in France since August 1914. He was commissioned into the South Irish Horse on 16 February 1917. Leading the intelligence-gathering patrol back to their lines, they were caught in the initial bombardment. Only one man managed to get back.

That German bombardment commenced at 0430, directed on the outposts, the Red line, the HQ posts and lines of communication. Using what is understood to be a mixture of HE and gas shells, the bombardment coincided with heavy morning fog, reducing visibility to virtually nil. The defenders were forced to wear their cumbersome and visually very restrictive gas masks. It was reported that even the wire in front of the lines was obscured. Almost immediately, telegraph lines were cut and any visual form of communication, such as flags, lights or flares were made redundant by the lack of visibility. The only form of communication left to those in charge was through the use of runners (men assigned to carry messages by foot).

Typical 'dispositions' of the battalion in the front line are briefly outlined as follows. During the day, the front line was lightly held, with each company split with two platoons in the front-line posts (Blue Line) and two platoons in 'fixed posts', locations behind the front line, halfway between the Blue and Red Lines. The platoons in each company were rotated at dusk, reserve platoons to the front, front platoons to the reserve. In this instance, the two front-line platoons were located along the Blue Line, with the 'reserve' platoons in the 'fixed posts'. Standing orders stated that at 0400am each day, companies were to move into 'battle positions' in case of a dawn attack by the enemy. The two platoons manning the Blue Line retired to the 'fixed posts', the reserve platoons holding the Red Line and Yellow Line (fixed defences).[19] It was during these movements that the enemy's bombardment commenced. The men falling back from the Blue Line achieved their positions, but the men moving to the Red Line were caught out. A Company's two platoons lost thirteen men (one officer and twelve men) and C Company appears to have lost both platoons (approximately ninety men) with only a few men and one (wounded) officer reaching their allotted positions. At least one platoon of S Company failed to even reach their allotted station and retired to their

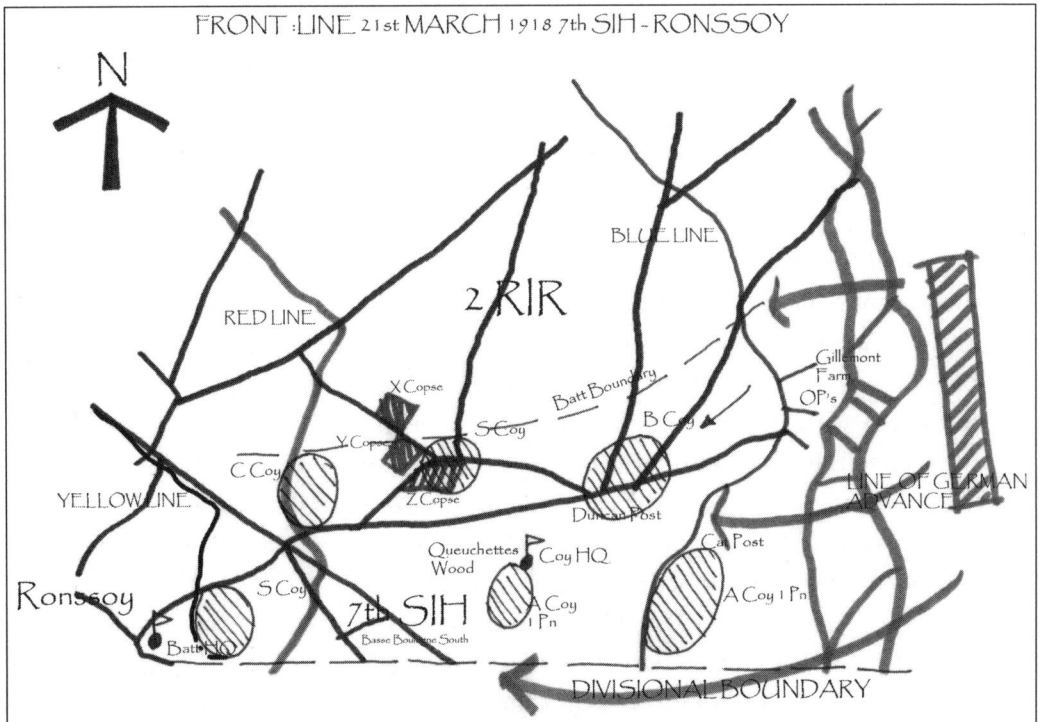

Attack at Ronssoy (Based on 49 Brigade War Diaries).

starting point where a platoon of 2nd Royal Irish Regiment (the battalion holding the Left section of the line) was located. There, at Z Copse, they remained fighting until 1500 that day, when they surrendered.

With the front platoons effectively isolated from support, they were soon surrounded when the German infantry attacked at 0930. However, they didn't give up the fight and continued to man their posts until they either ran out of ammunition, or men. With a divisional boundary between 16th (Irish) Division and 66th Division on the extreme right of the battalion, there appeared to be only a lightly-held section of the Blue Line and 'fixed posts', with the responsible battalion relying on the reserves to move up and hold the Red Line.[20] As such, the enemy managed to take advantage of this and push through to the Red Line, effectively rolling up the battalion's right flank. By 1100 the enemy had breached the Red Line and all available men at battalion HQ were rushed to defend the posts around l'Empire and Ronssoy. With a few men retiring from the front line, Major Call continued to fight on both flanks until around 1600, when he was forced to surrender.

One of these men, employed as a cook, was No. 1836/25851 Private Richard Tucker. Richard, or 'Dick', a dentistry apprentice, who had enlisted on 11 November 1915 in Dublin with the South Irish Horse at the age of 20. Dublin born, he became a cook and was transferred to the 7th (South Irish Horse) Royal Irish Regiment with the rest of the men in France at the end of July 1917. Having survived the initial attack by the Germans on that day, he was to become a prisoner of war for the duration, incarcerated in Limberg PoW camp with many of his colleagues.[21] Another casualty from the support troops was Lieutenant A.G. Dignan. Albert Guy Dignan, a native of Roscommon, born into a prominent Roman Catholic family, joined the regiment on 3 October 1915 and was gazetted as a probationary second lieutenant. Promotion continued with Albert becoming a full lieutenant on 2 July 1917. He was attached to the 7th (South Irish Horse) Royal Irish Regiment and became the transport officer. It was whilst carrying out his duties as the transport officer in Ronssoy that he was killed. As his body was never found, it can be assumed he died as a result of the artillery bombardment.

Second Lieutenant A.B.P. Hadden was to be very unlucky that first day. Addison B.P. Hadden, a native of Wexford, aged 22 in March 1918, had joined the South Irish Horse as an officer cadet, and was commissioned in the regiment on 21 December 1916. On the morning of the 21st, he was manning the command post at Cat Post. The enemy opened up on Cat Post with heavy trench mortars from around 0630. Very soon all communication with battalion HQ was lost and the men manning the post, together with Duncan Post to the north, suffered heavily. Around 0915 the barrage lifted, but with visibility still poor and no wired communications, Lieutenant Hadden sent his signallers to battalion HQ in Ronssoy village. In doing so, he walked into eight or ten Germans and was captured. He managed to escape and made his way towards Duncan Post to raise the alarm. However, he found the telegraph wires cut there and decided to try and retire to the red line, but ran into more Germans, was captured a second time and again escaped. He then made his way to Sart farm, to the east of Duncan Post, supposed to be held by 2nd Royal Irish Regiment. Unfortunately, the Germans had overrun the position and he was captured for a third and final time. On this occasion it was for good and he was sent to the rear as a PoW. Addison was released from captivity on 14 December 1918. For his actions on that day he was awarded the Military Cross.[22]

There were many acts of heroism on 21 March, some unrecognized. However, two men deserve a mention. Private 1562/25055 Arthur Horsford Browne was one such man. Arthur, a Cork man and a member of C Squadron, arrived in France on 18 December 1915. He transferred to the 7th (South Irish Horse) Royal Irish Regiment in August with many of his comrades. As a member of A Company, he was located at the company's command post in Queuchettes Wood, on the extreme right flank of the battalion's area of operations. This flank was the boundary between 16th and 66th Divisions. When the German attack commenced at 0930, the attackers encircled and isolated the forward posts of Duncan, Cat and Hew, taking advantage of the divisional boundary where lines of responsibility would be somewhat blurred. At least one platoon of A Company was lost in the initial attack, before the Germans concentrated their attack on the command post half an hour later. Company commander Captain J.M. Wardell, although wounded twice, co-ordinated the defence of his lines even though both machine guns were put out of action by the enemy. It was during this that 24-year-old Sergeant John (Martin) Rudge, a native of Walsall, and Arthur counter-attacked by bombing the enemy's machine-gun post and knocking it out. Rudge was fatally wounded and would die that day. A former 6th Royal Irish Regiment man, Rudge's body was never formally recovered and he is commemorated on the Pozières Memorial. When the position was eventually over-run, both the wounded Captain Wardell and Arthur were captured. Wardell was released on 6 December that year, Arthur on 22 November. For their actions on the day, Captain Wardell and Sergeant Rudge were Mentioned in Despatches and Arthur received the Military Medal.[23]

The other man was Matthew Henning. At the height of the attack Lieutenant Colonel Call at his battalion HQ in Ronssoy decided to strengthen the defences on the Red Line by using his HQ staff, about fifteen men or so, and abandoned his position to move forward. The men were spread along the Coleen Post/Basse Boulogne North Line (Red Line) Around 1215, Lieutenant Colonel Call's position was in danger of being surrounded, so he sent out two runners to brigade HQ to advise them of the position and request reinforcements. One of these runners was 27-year-old Private 1871/25367 Matthew Henning, a native of County Down. He successfully delivered the message to brigade HQ and had to avoid capture by the advancing Germans, passing through their front lines, to get back. For his devotion to his duty, he was awarded the Military Medal. I have been unable to ascertain whether he was captured with the rest of the battalion, but he did survive the war.[24]

Two further men who deserve to be recognized are Lance Corporal James J. McMaster DCM from Maghera, County Londonderry, and formerly of 6th Royal Irish Regiment, and Regimental Sergeant Major George H. Floater DCM. Both men showed great courage under fire. George, a Mons veteran, was formerly of the King's Royal Rifle Corps. McMaster led a counter-attack and drove the enemy back on the sunken road west of Ronssoy. Although initially successful, they were driven back in turn. McMaster was killed and is buried in Templeux-le Guerard Cemetery. George Floater, although shot through the jaw, continued to chivvy and encourage the men throughout the battle.

By the end of the day the losses of the battalion became clear when they were ordered to regroup just outside Tincourt, mustering only 132 men, including officers. The attack on 21 March was largely responsible for the destruction of the original 7th (South Irish Horse) Royal Irish Regiment; the majority of casualties were from the South Irish Horse. Lieutenant Colonel Call stated that 'the men of the South Irish Horse and 2nd Battalion continued to fight as long as it was possible to do so and maintained to the last and best traditions of the Regiment'.[25]

A re-organization of the three brigades making up the division was hurriedly carried out on the 22nd. As each battalion of the brigade could barely muster a full company, they amalgamated into the 49th Brigade Battalion, which comprised two companies of 2nd Royal Irish Regiment and 7th (South Irish Horse) Royal Irish Regiment under the command of Major M.C.C. Harrison 2nd Royal Irish. Over the next few days, the Brigade Battalion carried out a fighting retreat, to end on the 31st east of Hamel. Sufficient numbers of stragglers/reinforcements were gathered by the 24th to again re-organize the brigade into three battalions of 150 men each: 2nd Royal Irish Regiment, 7th/8th Royal Inniskilling Fusiliers and the 7th (South Irish Horse) Royal Irish Regiment. From this date, the brigade remained as three separate battalions throughout the March retreat.[26]

An interesting anecdote concerning the first few days of the retreat was recorded by a private in the Black Watch, Eric Linklater. During the retreat he fell in with a couple of soldiers from the 7th (South Irish Horse) Royal Irish Regiment, a 'band sergeant' and a young trooper. What is interesting about this is the conversation Eric Linklater heard between the two. The sergeant appeared to be a 'nationalist' who saw the war as a training exercise for the inevitable conflict between Ireland and Britain. As a training exercise, he felt it was his duty to impart his military knowledge to his prodigy, the young trooper.[27] The description of this meeting leads me to assume that the two soldiers may not have been in the front-line trenches at the time of the attack. I make this assumption as the sergeant is described as a band sergeant. Members of the regimental band were engaged as stretcher bearers, and would have been kept in reserve at Battalion Headquarters with the other non-front-line troops. As this was not overrun until later in the day, it would have been possible for both these men to have escaped. One suspects that the sergeant would have made every effort to avoid being captured. My feeling is that he (they) were not part of the original mounted contingent, but part of the 6th Battalion Royal Irish Regiment who were drafted in in February, following their disbandment. That is not to say that there weren't any nationalists within the ranks of the South Irish Horse, far from it, but the fact that the sergeant is a 'band' sergeant and the South Irish Horse prior to being dismounted didn't have a band in theatre, points to this assumption.

The report of the action from 21 to 31 March contained in the 16th Division war diaries makes sobering reading. On casualties alone, they reported that 47, 48 and 49 Brigades lost a total of 191 officers and 4,840 ORs either killed wounded or missing for the period 21–24 March. Of these, the battalion lost seventeen officers and 650 ORs. A further report on the permanently missing from 21 March to 3 April recorded a total of 277 officers and 6,672 ORs of which the battalion lost sixteen officers and 675 ORs.[28]

The fighting strength of the division on 31 March/1 April was seventy-eight officers and 1,977 ORs of which the battalion comprised two officers and forty-nine men. There were still casualties even after the end of March. Men died of wounds received, at both Allied hospitals and in enemy hands. One such man was 32-year-old 1838/25619 Private Michael Moran. Michael was considered to be Ireland's finest golfer before the war. He died in captivity at le Cateau, from wounds received on 10 April 1918. He was one of four men to die of wounds in le Cateau German Military Hospital, the others being: 21-year-old 1293/25757 Corporal Henry Eustace Rutherford MM MiD (died 24 March), formerly A Squadron; 23-year-old 1103/25590 Private Thomas Carleton Mainwaring (died 6 April), formerly S Squadron; 21-year-old 2099/25178 Lance Corporal Thomas Coveney (died 28 April), formerly C Squadron.[29]

A strange incident occurred on 29 March at Aubigny. While stragglers, reinforcements and replacements were being gathered to attempt to rebuild the division, 130 ORs refused to carry wire up to the line and subsequently were paraded on the 31st and marched off in charge of the Assistant Provost Marshal (APM).[30] This mutiny by elements of 49 Brigade was mainly by men of the Royal Irish Regiment and 7th/8th Royal Inniskilling Fusiliers. Timothy Bowman, in his book *Irish Regiments in the Great War: Discipline and Morale*, suggests that the mutiny was a military rather than a political statement, due to the reduction of the two battalions to a cadre. He points out that the sentences given out at the subsequent courts martial were more lenient than would have been expected and were, in all cases, suspended. He also suggests that the mutiny was similar to that suffered by the Australian Imperial Force (AIF) in September 1918. In that case, four battalions of the AIF refused to fall out on parade because the military authorities planned to break up the battalions in order to provide reinforcements to other AIF units.[31]

Using the figures from the Field General Courts Martial records, I estimate that of the 130 soldiers who mutinied at least thirty-one of 7th

(South Irish Horse) Royal Irish Regiment were arrested for mutiny, two of whom were found not guilty. Three of these men would have been men from the 'original' regiment, rather than transferred men and reinforcements from outside the 'regiment'.[32]

The first few days of April saw a complete re-organization of the divisional resources, men and matériel. During this time, the battalion's strength of officers and men fluctuated from just thirteen ORs on 1 April to six officers and 130 ORs on the 4th. They moved from Aubigny on the 3rd, Saleux, via Tours-en-Vimeux, Woincourt, arriving at Wavrans on the 11th. On the 13th, divisional orders were issued that the remaining battalions be re-organized into a composite battalion comprising:

Major R. Kerr MC, Royal Iniskilling Fusiliers
HQ of Royal Inniskilling Fusiliers
Second in command Captain H.M. O'Reilly, 2nd Royal Irish Regiment
Adjutant Second Lieutenant J.J. Nulty, 7th/8th Royal Inniskilling Fusiliers
Quartermaster Lieutenant H. Egan, South Irish Horse
Transport Officer Lieutenant Wilks, South Irish Horse
Medical Officer Lieutenant Kinsey Royal Army Medical Corps (attached 2nd Royal Irish Regiment)
A Company – 2nd Royal Irish Regiment
B Company – South Irish Horse
C Company – 7th/8th Royal Inniskilling Fusiliers
D Company – South Irish Horse/Royal Irish Fusiliers
All companies had an approximate strength of 130 men each
Transport from South Irish Horse.

This was all completed by 2130 that day. A further march by the composite battalion to Delettes was ordered on 14 April and completed by the battalion by lunchtime of the 15th where they remained. During this time, the 7th (South Irish Horse) Battalion Royal Irish Regiment were digging along the GHQ lines at Steenbecque south-west of Hazebrouck. On 18 April a complete overhaul of 16th (Irish) Division was carried out. In order to maintain a useable fighting strength, it was decided to retain 2nd Royal Irish Regiment, 2nd Leinster Regiment, 1st Royal Munster Fusiliers and 1st Royal Dublin Fusiliers at full strength by stripping the remaining battalions and transferring those four units' men to bring the others up to complement. The remaining battalions, including 7th (South Irish Horse) Battalion Royal Irish Regiment were to be reduced to a 'training' cadre of eight officers and fifty men. Of the 262 men in B and D Companies, 106 men were transferred to 2nd Royal Irish Regiment. It would be reasonable to assume that the majority of these men were from the original 6th Royal Irish Regiment, disbanded in February. Of the remaining 156 men, 112 were transferred to the cavalry base at Rouen under the command of Captain Blackett. These were the surviving cavalry trained men of the South Irish Horse. At Rouen, they were again re-organized in order to provide reinforcements for other cavalry units, or to return to Cahir. As noted previously, some of these men were sent to Palestine and Egypt to join the Queen's Own Dorset Yeomanry.

The timing of the relocation of these three parties is a little hazy, as the 7th (South Irish Horse) Battalion Royal Irish Regiment war diary indicates that all the men left for their respective destinations on 18 April, whilst the 49 Brigade diary records that the Rouen-based party left on the 25th, having provided working parties up until then. On 12 April Major James Roche-Kelly MC took over command of the battalion. James Roche-Kelly had been with the original S Squadron when they arrived in France on 17 August 1914 as a lieutenant. He was Mentioned in Despatches in February 1915, had transferred to 2nd Royal Munster Fusiliers in 1915 and then to the Royal Irish Regiment later that year as Captain and Adjutant. He was awarded the Military Cross in January 1917 and again Mentioned in Despatches in May of that year.

The 7th (South Irish Horse) Battalion Royal Irish Regiment 21 Infantry Brigade – 30th Division – Locre, Wervicq, Courtrai –Disbandment

In essence, that was that. The 7th (South Irish Horse) Royal Irish Regiment was no longer the battalion it had been in August 1917. Gone were the men of the South Irish Horse with a few exceptions, the vast majority either killed in action, wounded, missing or prisoners of war. Those men remaining had been transferred either to other cavalry units or back to Cahir. For the men behind the wire in the German prisoner of war camps, life was extremely harsh, contending with poor food and atrocious living conditions.

Punishments and beatings were rife, with some prisoners being used as forced labour in ammunition dumps behind the German lines, often under fire. A South Irish Horse prisoner who was forced to work in the German veterinary stables said, 'In some senses we used to wish we were working on ammunition dumps, because there was some chance of being killed and put out of our misery there.'[33] With that, and the constant fear of disease, some of those prisoners captured during the German offensive succumbed. Richard Tucker, behind the wire in Limburg writing his one letter allowed a week to his mother said:

> Well Mother, I often wonder how you feel about my been (sic) a prisoner well its far from sunshine but never the less I often thank God that I was taken prisoner that day and not killed or wounded as so many of the lads of my regiment.[34]

More importantly, for Richard, were the parcels from home, containing food, clothing and cigarettes. There was still a small nucleus of former South Irish Horse men still in the battalion (fifty or so) of whom half were to lose their lives fighting later in the year.

For those fifty men that remained, together with their eight officers, an uncertain future awaited. Having formed the training cadre, they paraded and sent off their twenty-six man strong transport section to Elnes on 20 April.[35] A short period of 'intensive training' for the men was undertaken (to teach them how to train other troops) between 20 and 29 April before travelling to Theroaunne, to the east of Mametz. On 1 May 1917 they moved to Pecquer in order to supervise a draft of 700 reinforcements comprising men from the Royal Munster Fusiliers and Royal Dublin Fusiliers digging defensive lines, under the direction of the Royal Engineers. This lasted for two weeks until the draft of reinforcements was handed over to the training staff of 8th Battalion King's Royal Rifle Corps. Over the next week the training cadre marched from Pecquer to Frencq, just north of the main combined Expeditionary Force base of Étaples, arriving on 21 May 1918. On arrival, the cadre commenced training the American troops from 12th Machine Gun Battalion and 4th Engineer Regiment US Army in rifle skills, bombing, the machine gun and gas drills. The training continued throughout the month of June with various American battalions rotating through the training schedule. Over that time eight battalions were trained from the two American divisions, 4th Infantry Division and 30th Infantry Division.

On 22 June 1918 the cadre received notification that the strength of 7th (South Irish Horse) Battalion Royal Irish Regiment now stood at zero. This seems a little strange as there were still eight officers and fifty-one men in the training cadre – in effect, the battalion. The war diary for the battalion states that 'all Cavalry Personnel having been transferred to the Corps of Hussars and posted to the South Irish Horse and all infantry personnel having been transferred to the 7th (South Irish Horse) Battalion Royal Irish Regiment'. This appears to be a paper exercise in order to recommission the battalion and 'balance the books', as the following day, the cadre moved to Widdebrouck (Widdebroucq) with orders to form a battalion and took over the Irish reinforcements they had left digging defensive lines at the beginning of May. The reinforcements now comprised 500 men from the Royal Dublin Fusiliers, 250 men from the Royal Munster Fusiliers and eighty-five from the Royal Irish Regiment. The reinforcements numbered 835 men, and when the fifty men of the training cadre are taken into account, the battalion would have been almost up to strength. By the end of the month, the battalion had thirty-one officers and 830 men on strength, including one officer from the Royal Naval Division and a medical officer from the American Army. Due to the mix of reinforcements the battalion was organized into four companies around their parent regiment:

A Company   Royal Irish Regiment and Royal Dublin Fusiliers
B Company   Royal Dublin Fusiliers
C Company   Royal Dublin Fusiliers
D Company   Royal Munster Fusiliers

The 7th (South Irish Horse) Royal Irish Regiment was now, although still Irish in its roots, a 'proper' Infantry of the Line battalion.[36] On 24 July 1918, Lieutenant Colonel James Roche-Kelly MC left for a month's leave. Temporary command was handed over to Major F. Naden DSO MC from 1/6th Cheshire Regiment.

Now complete, the beginning of July saw the battalion join 21 Brigade, 30th Division, X Corps, at Oxelaere, south-east of Cassel to commence intensive training to bring the battalion up to fighting proficiency. This training continued until August, the following month, when the division moved to the Locre area to relieve 35th Division. As part of 21 Brigade, the battalion became the support battalion relieving 104 Infantry Brigade on 8 August and remained in support until ordered to relieve 2/23rd Battalion London Regiment in the front line. They stayed in the front line for five days. On the night of 19/20 August the enemy tried to attack one of the manned outposts, but were fought off. During the skirmish two men were wounded. The war diary does not indicate who was wounded, but I believe at least one of the men subsequently died as a result of the attack. Second Lieutenant Robert Courtois Lloyd, aged 43, originally from Dublin, travelled from Brazil in April 1917 in order to volunteer. He was commissioned into the Royal Irish Regiment and was transferred from the 4th (Reserve) Battalion Royal Irish Regiment to join the 7th (South Irish Horse) Battalion Royal Irish Regiment, arriving in France on 26 June 1918. At 43, he would have been one of the oldest subalterns in the battalion.[37] He was taken to the casualty clearing station where he died of his wounds.

The battalion left the front line on the night of 22/23 August and moved to the brigade reserve. On 24 August, whilst in reserve, they were heavily shelled and suffered seven casualties, four fatal. Privates William Flynn, James O'Shea, Edward Walsh and T. Dewhurst were all from A Company and are buried side by side in Godewaersvelde British Cemetery.

With only four days in brigade reserve, the battalion again moved up to support positions, relieving 1/6th Cheshire Regiment who moved forward to the front lines on the night of 26/27 August. On 30 August news came in that the enemy had retreated along this sector of the front line and 1/6th Cheshires were ordered to send out patrols and then to advance the following morning. Providing close support 1,500 yards behind 1/6th Cheshire Regiment, the battalion relieved them at dusk on 31 August and dug in approximately 500 yards farther in front. They remained in position throughout the night. At dawn they were ordered to advance on Wulverghem and, whilst initially they met with little opposition, by 0900 the enemy had managed to slow down the advance with flanking heavy machine-gun fire from the nearby Neuve-Église ridge directed on the right flank of the battalion. Although the battalion's Stokes Mortars managed to knock out the German positions closest to the right flank, when a further attempt to advance was made at 1030, B Company and C Company took the brunt of the enemy fire and suffered many casualties. By 1130, the advance had halted just over a mile from its start point and could not progress any further until the Neuve-Église ridge had been cleared.[38] Whilst waiting for the ridge to be cleared, Major Naden DSO MC was hit in the shoulder and was evacuated. Temporary command of the battalion was handed over to Captain and Adjutant H. White MC, until Major J.S. Brothers, battalion second in command, could reach the front and take over. During the night of 1/2 September, Neuve-Église Ridge was finally taken by the adjacent division, so that the following morning a combined push of two companies of 7th (South Irish Horse) Battalion Royal Irish Regiment and 2/23rd London Regiment eventually took the village of Wulverghem. The battalion was relieved that night and sent to the rear to re-equip and re-organize. The action of the last few days had cost the battalion two officers and twenty-eight ORs killed. The war diary records two officers and fifteen ORs killed, with three officers and fifty-five ORs wounded and a further five ORs missing. The difference in the two figures for those killed can be explained by men who subsequently died of their wounds but weren't accounted for in the original diary entry. (At least one man, Private Edward Spires, 24 and from Dublin is mentioned on the Tyne Cot memorial, indicating that he has no known grave.) With just under two weeks in reserve, the battalion was again moved up to the line (now west of the village of Wulverghem) on 15 September where they had so recently lost so many men. They remained there until the night of 22/23 September when they were relieved by 7th/8th Battalion Royal Inniskilling Fusiliers and sent to Divisional reserve.

On the night of 18/19 September the battalion was ordered to carry out two patrols to establish the identity of their opposition. Two patrols were formed, one comprising No. 9 Platoon under the command of Second Lieutenant W.J. Trueman and the other a smaller patrol of twelve ORs from D Company under the command of Second Lieutenant W.H. McNeight. McNeight's was the first patrol to leave at 0130 and, although reaching the enemy, the attempt to breach the enemy's defences was unsuccessful. The second patrol left their lines at 0300 and were luckier. The war diary reports that they entered the enemy's trenches, captured two prisoners and a machine gun and killed a number of the enemy.[39] Although no 'friendly' casualties were recorded as a result of the raid, Sergeant James Lane MM is listed on the Tyne Cot Memorial as killed in action, no known grave, on 19

September 1918. James Lane, 32, volunteered with the Army Cyclist Corps under the pseudonym of Clarke. Originally from Slane, County Meath, he then transferred to the 6th (Service) Battalion Royal Irish Regiment where, I believe, he was awarded his Military Medal before being transferred to the 7th (South Irish Horse) Battalion Royal Irish Regiment. Of those who survived the raids, Second Lieutenant W.J. Trueman was awarded the Military Cross and 26503 Sergeant J. Higgs and 4434 Private L. Doyle were awarded the Military Medal.[40]

With the battalion in reserve, they used their time to train and improve tactics, as it now appeared the fighting on the front line was becoming more fluid. This was especially evident as, whilst in reserve, the rest of the brigade had moved forward again, requiring the battalion to move its reserve billeting forward on 30 September in response. As soon as they had bivouacked, orders were received for them to move to the Wervicq area of the front, approximately seven miles to the east of their current location. Arriving in the Houtherm area on 1 October, the battalion took over the front line in front of Wervicq and immediately started aggressively patrolling no man's land. They were in the front line for seven days before being relieved. The war diary does not record any casualties occurring during this stay in the trenches, but there are three fatalities from the battalion (Privates J. Howard, Vincent McCabe and W.H. Bunbury) buried in cemeteries close to their frontline positions during 1 to 6 October 1918.

The battalion returned to the front line on 12 October 1918 in preparation for the planned offensive along the Belgian front, the Battle of Courtrai. Thirtieth Division was on the extreme right of the line of attack, with 21 Brigade the pivot. The battalion was right at the 'end', facing the town of Wervicq. The battalion was spread over an 1,800-yard front, with B Company attacking on the left and D Company on the right. A company was on the left support and C Company on the right support, behind B and D Companies. Zero hour was set at 0535. Approximately an hour and a half earlier, one platoon of C Company, No. 12 Platoon, commanded by Second Lieutenant T. Lucas, had managed to work their way forward and occupy an enemy trench approximately 500 yards in front of the right flank. When the attack commenced, this platoon was able to counter any German fire directed on the advancing troops and, in doing so, caused a great many German casualties. The initial barrage prior to the attack contained some gas shelling, so it was important that the advancing troops did not advance too quickly, lest they were affected by the gas themselves. (The Germans, incidentally, had been shelling the front line with gas the previous day.) Despite initial resistance from the German machine-gun posts along their front, B Company managed to advance to their objective by 0630. Such was the speed of their advance that the creeping barrage had not yet lifted over their objective and they had to retreat roughly 500 yards and dig in until it had cleared. Machine-gun posts in Crucifix Farm held up the left-hand section of D Company for a considerable time but were cleared as the remaining objectives were reached along the battalion's front at 1000. Patrols were pushed out towards Wervicq and the River Lys, but these met with stiffer opposition and had to be withdrawn. Directed artillery fire for the rest of the day and overnight on those positions meant that more patrols were able to push forward at dawn on 15 October and by 1000 had reached the northern bank of the River Lys. The battalion, along with the brigade, was relieved that night and spent it in very poor dug-outs, before being ordered to move forward again, as the enemy continued to retreat and the division needed to keep in touch with the advancing troops. It was a rather unsettling time as whatever rest the troops managed was negated by the continual forward movement of the front. After six days of advance, support and rest again, the battalion was ordered to continue the advance in the area of Helchin, on the River Escault.

The battalion's attack had been extremely successful with all objectives taken with a reported loss of two officers wounded and thirteen ORs killed. A further forty-three ORs were wounded and four men missing. An additional nineteen men were gassed (quite possibly as a result of B Company's speedy advance).[41] An examination of the Commonwealth War Graves Commission records shows that twenty men were reported killed during 14 and 15 October, three of whom are commemorated on the Tyne Cot memorial as killed in action, no known grave. The battalion managed to capture 194 German soldiers and a number of machine guns, trench mortars and anti-tank rifles.[42]

The battalion found itself along the Helchin-Bossuyt road facing the west bank of the Escaut river on the night of 21 October in preparation for a river crossing the following morning. The battalion was ordered to attempt a river crossing using rafts and then advance towards their objectives over the river.

A Company was to commence the attack with D Company following behind with the rafts. The remainder of the battalion was to cross the river using a pontoon in the village of Helchin later. A short bombardment of high explosive (HE) and smoke shells commenced at 0900 and A Company began their advance. After reaching the main Helchin–Bossuyt road, the company came under heavy machine-gun fire from the wood in front of Bossuyt and the village itself. They were then subjected to heavy artillery fire and as a result had to retire to their original starting positions, leaving behind one platoon, under the command of Second Lieutenant Robert Switzer, that had lost touch with the rest of the company. He and his platoon were left isolated for the rest of the day, but during that time Switzer gathered as much intelligence as he could, before retiring under cover of the night. For his gallantry, he was awarded the Military Cross.[43] Sergeant H. Smythe, Lance Corporal E. Ince, Privates G. Slaeter, J. Scott and J. McCormack were all awarded the Military Medal.

This was to be the last action of the war for the battalion. They were relieved on 25 October to rest and refit. The strength in the line on 26 October was nineteen officers and 272 ORs including battalion headquarters.[44] The beginning of November saw the continuation of refitting and training for the men, including special training for crossing rivers with rafts. At 1100 on 11 November 1918, hostilities officially ceased across the whole of the Western Front. The war diary recorded that the troops showed very little excitement on hearing the news.

Over the next few months the battalion moved from Belgium, eventually reaching Boulogne on 11 January 1919. During this period the men were subjected to general training, routine and ceremonial inspections and physical activity, when all they wanted to do was go home. That said, 123 men re-enlisted for two, three and even four more years, and fifteen men volunteered for a further year as part of the army of occupation.[45] The battalion remained at Boulogne, billeted at Escault Camp, a convalescent camp, whilst acting as the disciplinary battalion for the Boulogne area. The strength of the battalion at the end of January was thirty-five officers and 593 ORs. The routine remained the same throughout February and most of March. The battalion was presented with the King's Colour on St Patrick's Day (but no King's Colour for the South Irish Horse Regiment). The end of March saw the battalion travelling to Étaples to carry out escort duties and guard duties at various prisoner of war camps around Étaples. Guard duties were also performed at various hospitals and ordnance dumps in the area. The routine for the remaining men of the battalion was the same throughout the summer until 10 September 1919, when orders were received that the battalion was to be reduced to a cadre. By then all men eligible for demobilization had been sent home and the remaining men who had re-enlisted were transferred to other units. At the end of the month the strength of the battalion stood at twenty-seven officers and ninety ORs. At the beginning of October the demobilization of the battalion commenced, with all stores and equipment packed ready for transfer to the Royal Irish Regiment's depot at Clonmel, County Tipperary. These, together with the Colour Party, travelled to Clonmel on 24 October 1919. The 7th (South Irish Horse) Battalion Royal Irish Regiment was disbanded.[46]

Mention should be made of those men who died in captivity from wounds received when captured, ill treatment, suicide and disease (I have recorded twenty-one). One of these men, 25-year-old 988/25886 Private William Wilby, was to die of heart failure as a result of wounds received whilst a prisoner of war in hospital, following his capture during the battle of Courtrai on 14 October 1918. He now lies next to Lieutenant M.J. Dease VC in St Symphorien Military Cemetery, Mons (an Irishman and the first VC of the First World War).[47] Michael Moran, 32, was one of Ireland's finest golfers and had joined the South Irish Horse in 1915. He was captured during the retreat of the 21 March 1918 and died of wounds received whilst being treated at the German hospital in le Cateau. He is joined by Lance Corporal Thomas Coveney, Privates Thomas Carlton Mainwaring, Henry Eustace Rutherford MM and Herbert Jelly in le Cateau Military Cemetery.[48]

A number of men were to die following the Armistice, either from their wounds, the influenza epidemic sweeping the continent during 1918–19 or from disease brought on as a result of their time at the front (TB, bronchitis, etc.). One such man was 1376/25855 Private Frederick Turner. Frederick, aged 22, originally from Dublin, had joined the Limerick-based B Squadron and arrived in France on 23 November 1915. Transferring to 7th (South Irish Horse) Battalion Royal Irish Regiment in August 1917, he was one of many men captured during the German offensive of 21 March 1918. Taken prisoner, he survived the privations of the PoW camp at Limburg, was repatriated, but only got as far as London, where he fell ill. Moved to hospital, he remained there until his death on 9 December 1918. It can be presumed that he succumbed to influenza, unable to fight the infection, following his incarceration at the hands of the Germans. He is buried in Brookwood Military Cemetery.[49]

Chapter 10

South Irish Horse – April 1918 to 12 June 1922

From April 1918 onwards the state of the regiment becomes a little more difficult to establish. The lines become blurred between the South Irish Horse, the cavalry regiment and the 7th (South Irish Horse) Battalion Royal Irish Regiment, the Infantry of the Line battalion in France. Surely at this stage in the war, there wouldn't appear to be any need for the cavalry depot in Cahir. Yet it was still operating, training and recruiting cavalrymen for the South Irish Horse. We can see through newspaper reports, courts martial reports and the partial recruiting records that are available that, in fact, the South Irish Horse was still a substantial force at home. For example, the last record relating to a court martial of a member of the South Irish Horse is from 9 May 1919.[1] It was reported that when a section of the South Irish Horse marched off to the railway station on 10 October 1918, large crowds from Cahir came to see them off.[2] According to the medal rolls, there were still some members of the regiment serving with it as late as 12 December 1919. For example, Sergeant Ashley Cooper, the training sergeant at Cahir, was demobbed on 2 June 1919.

After April 1918, mounted or dismounted, the South Irish Horse (as a regiment or squadron) was never to fight on the Western Front again. Although still producing and training recruits, the garrison at Cahir in the latter stages of 1918 was facing a difficult and uncertain future. With the 'declaration' of an Irish Republic in December 1918, following the success of Sinn Féin in the general election of that year, there was increased civil and armed unrest throughout the country. 1919 is widely considered as the start of the Irish War of Independence with the murders by the Irish Republican Army (IRA) of two RIC constables escorting explosives at Soloheadbeg, County Tipperary. Cahir was still maintained by the South Irish Horse up to at least August 1919. The Royal Field Artillery (RFA) returned to the barracks after the war and were present there with a company of the Lincolnshire Regiment until they evacuated the barracks on 30 January 1922.[3]

The lightly-armed RIC also had the British Army to assist them in maintaining law and order. The 'flying columns' of the IRA at the height of the War of Independence were very successful in the southern part of the country (Waterford, Cork, Tipperary, Kerry etc.) and it would safe to assume that the garrison was called on to assist the RIC. The ability of mounted troops to move swiftly through the countryside, especially when the riders knew the land intimately, and provide armed support for the RIC would have been essential. In fact, the apparent success of the garrison was a continual thorn in the side of the IRA. Lancers, the South Irish Horse and the Cyclist Corps covered the by-roads around Tipperary used by the 'flying columns' in an attempt to disrupt them.

> Liam Lynch travelled to Davins of Rathsallagh, near Cashel, (our Brigade Headquarters) and complained with what seemed to me to be a good deal of pent up feeling and politely suppressed indignation that the South Irish Horse (a British Cavalry Unit stationed at Cahir Military Barracks) was continually raiding southwards into his Brigade area. He informed me in measured terms that it was the duty of the O/C of the area in which Cahir was situated, to put an instant stop to the irksome, disconcerting raids – by sealing them off from the South. I told him that these same SIH had been doing the same thing north, east and west into our territories from 1918 until a few months previously when they gave up coming our way because they had got nothing but headaches from us.[4]

Not only were the activities of the IRA affecting the retained troops, but also the recently demobilized members of the regiment. Lieutenant (formerly Sergeant) William Roe, having returned home to manage the family farm in Rathmore, Queen's County (Offaly), was subjected to intimidation with his cattle being continuously driven off his land. Things came to a head when seven men were charged with cattle raiding and sentenced to three months' imprisonment. Another, more serious, incident occurred involving former Sergeant Michael J. Shanahan. Shanahan was a well-established Roman Catholic farmer living with his family in Coolfin House, Coolfin, County Waterford. He was a veteran of the Boer War, having served with the 74th Company Imperial Yeomanry and after returning from South Africa, served in the newly formed South of Ireland Imperial Yeomanry for four years. He rejoined the South Irish Horse on 25 January 1915 and was posted as a sergeant to France on 18 May 1917. He was transferred to the Labour Corps in November 1917, having been assessed as not fit enough to be an infantryman (with 7th (South Irish Horse) Battalion Royal Irish Regiment). He was demobbed in February 1920 and returned to his house in Coolfin. On 15 May 1920 the family was visited by IRA members looking for weapons. In his witness statement for the Bureau of Military History, the leader of the raid, IRA Vice-Commandant William Keane recalled:

All the time we were constantly on the lookout for arms of which we had very few and, as a result of information received from a friendly servant, I heard that there was a service rifle and ammunition in the house of a man named Shanahan, at Coolfin, a district about 12 miles north-west of Waterford city. I decided to raid the place. This Shanahan was just after leaving the British Army where he held a commission in the South Irish Horse Regiment [*That obviously is not true. Interestingly the local newspaper also reported that he was a 'Captain in the SIH'.*] and he had the reputation of being a tough man.... Each of us was armed with a loaded revolver. Approaching the house, we saw Shanahan standing at a gate in front of the building, so we left our bikes with Darmody. Duignan and I went on foot into a field near the house to look at some calves there. Shanahan was watching us. After examining the calves, we walked up to him and I asked him if he had any of the calves for sale (this was a blind to put him off the scent). As he made to reply, I whipped out my revolver and gave him 'hands up', adding 'and be quick about it or I'll let you have it'. He immediately raised his hands and I instructed Duignan to tie him up with a rope I had brought with me. I then left him with Duignan and went into the house through the open door. There were three ladies inside whom I locked in a dining room. [*Presumably Frances, his wife, and his two daughters, Frances P. and Mary.*] I went upstairs to search for the rifle and, on looking into a wardrobe, I found concealed up two legs of the trousers two Lee Enfield rifles in perfect condition. I also found two bandoliers loaded with ammunition and a pair of field-glasses. I took away all the stuff, went outside and warned Shanahan not to leave his position for 20 minutes or I'd shoot him dead from the road.[5]

Not all returning soldiers were keen on retaining the status quo and joined the IRA. Even as early as 1915, recruitment for Irishmen who opposed British rule incarcerated in the German prisoner of war camps was taking place. At least one man from the South Irish Horse, named Joseph Kavanagh, a farrier, was recruited into what was known as the 'Irish Brigade' (an idea devised by the Irish nationalist Roger Casement).[6] James McSorley was also a victim of the War of Independence. A native of Ulster, having enlisted in the South Irish Horse on 2 November 1915, he was transferred to the 7th (South Irish Horse) Battalion Royal Irish Regiment and discharged from the Army as a lance corporal on 12 April 1919 as a result of wounds received. He was eligible for the Silver War Badge, having been honourably discharged. It was not until 1921 that James resurfaced. Living at Dunteague (Dunteige), County Antrim, he was fatally involved in a somewhat mysterious run-in with the police. Officially, he was involved in a shoot-out with the police, leading to his death on the night of 8 July. A police patrol was fired on and returned fire, killing James with a single shot to the chest. His brother maintained that he was off to meet a girl, but the police stated he was part of a gang who opened fire on the patrol. The military tribunal held into the circumstances of his death in Omagh later that month accepted the findings of the police report. The majority of returning soldiers were susceptible to abuse and attacks from the IRA and as such kept themselves to themselves.[7]

Another man who returned and joined the IRA was John Joseph Groark. Born in 1899, in Hartlepool, he was the son of John Joseph Groark, a native of County Mayo. The family moved back to Mayo in or around 1905. He joined the South Irish Horse in 1916 and trained at Cahir Barracks. After being demobilized in 1919, John returned to County Mayo and at some stage joined the IRA. As a trained soldier, he would have been useful, especially as other members of his family appear to have been members of the IRA too. Most of his time was spent fighting with the East Mayo Brigade as part of one of the 'flying columns', rising to the rank of captain within the brigade. However, John did not agree with the terms of the treaty ending the War of Independence and fought on the anti-treaty side in the ensuing civil war. In the end John migrated to America in 1924, where he started his family.

In order to provide a 'safe' meeting place and to facilitate members and former members of the South Irish Horse, an old comrades club was established in January 1920. It is not clear whether the original members club was incorporated with the new old comrades club, or whether it was separate from the original, located in Mount Street. The new location was at 20 Merrion Square, Dublin. It appears to have been well used, but however, not for all the right reasons. It was noted by the IRA that the club was used by 'spies' and 'informants'. One of the more notable visitors was former Captain Parcell Rees Bowen MC DFC and Bar. An undercover agent, he was targeted and killed after spending time (presumably socialising) in the South Irish Horse Club on the night of 26 October 1920.[8]

Unfortunately, due to the increasingly fraught situation in and around Dublin as the War of Independence reached its height, including the curfew, the club was forced to close on 4 May 1921 and the contents auctioned off on the 11th.[9] The formation of the club in 1920 by the 'CO of the South Irish Horse, Beggars Bush Barracks' would point to the fact that the South Irish Horse as a regiment was still in existence until at least May 1921 when the club was closed. To what extent the regiment was operating is more difficult to establish. With the majority of the 'original' members having left and/or served their time, and members who signed on for the 'duration' having been demobilized, one can only assume that any remaining men would be permanent staff and senior officers – in effect a small cadre, based, presumably, at Beggars Bush Barracks.

Chapter 11

Into Obscurity?

As part of the negotiations for the creation of the Irish Free State in late 1921 and early 1922, the existence of the southern Irish regiments came under intense scrutiny. (The continuation of *all* the Irish regiments was considered by the Geddes Committee as part of their work, reporting on means of reducing supply services expenditure.[1] As it was, the committee recommended reductions in the Army's strength.) Political minds were firmly focused on enabling the new state, not on standing armies, foreign or otherwise. As a result, it was decided to disband all the southern Irish regiments, including the South Irish Horse. This was announced in February 1922 and was to be completed by the end of July 1922. On 11 March 1922 the War Office ordered the disbandment of all southern Irish regiments,[2] the Royal Irish Regiment, Connaught Rangers, Prince of Wales's Leinster Regiment (Royal Canadians), Royal Munster Fusiliers, Royal Dublin Fusiliers and the South Irish Horse. The Royal Irish Regiment, for example, was still on active service (1st Battalion in Upper Silesia and 2nd in India) when the orders for their disbandment arrived.[3] For the South Irish Horse, with possibly only a cadre of permanent staff in Beggars Bush Barracks, the winding up of the affairs of the regiment would have been a lot less onerous, but still just as poignant as that of the Royal Irish Regiment.

On Monday 12 June 1922, in an emotional ceremony, the Colours of the five disbanded infantry regiments were handed over to King George V at Windsor Castle.[4] The South Irish Horse, having no Colours, presented the King with an engraving given to them by the people of le Havre in commemoration of their landing at the port in August 1914. (Whilst the infantry regimental Colours reside in Windsor Castle, having survived the fire in 1992, the South Irish Horse's engraving does not appear to be with them.) The King's address, made available to all serving members of the regiment appears below:

TO THE OFFICERS, WARRANT OFFICERS, NON COMMISSIONED OFFICERS AND MEN OF THE SOUTH IRISH HORSE

It is with feelings of no ordinary sorrow that I address you for the last time; for I know that I am taking leave not merely of a fine regiment, but of great memories and great traditions which hitherto have been kept alive and embodied in you.

You came forward at a time of danger to the Empire, and stood by it honourably and faithfully then in the most deadly peril of all.

Your life, alas! has been far too short, but few regiments in so brief a span could have crowded it with more honourable achievements.

I am very proud to receive from you the Engraving presented to the Regiment by the City of Havre in commemoration of its landing there in August, 1914. You may rest assured that I shall always preserve this as a perpetual record of your noble exploits in the field.

Meanwhile, be very sure that, with or without external monument, the fame of your great work can never die.

I thank you for your good service to this Country and the Empire, and with a full heart I bid you – Farewell.

George RI – 12th June 1922[5]

Armistice Day parades in Dublin from 1919 were always well attended with the South Irish Horse Old Comrades' Association representing the regiment. The mid-1920s also brought back the traditional regimental St Patrick's Day dinner and dance, together with a further regimental dinner prior to the Armistice Day parades. These two occasions carried on well into the mid-1930s and were always very well attended. The annual dance on 9 November 1928 was described as 'one of Ireland's most popular functions' and 'the scene in the ballroom was brilliant, and beautiful frocks and fancy dresses, combined with the many Orders and decorations worn by most of the gentlemen, made a spectacle which is not often seen in Dublin'.[6]

These dances were not only for the old comrades to meet up, but were also used as fundraisers for various memorials to their fallen comrades. A memorial window to the regiment in the Garrison Church at Ypres was funded by the Old Comrades' Association Fund and completed on 15

May 1928. Major Gilmore O'Grady and Lieutenant Colonel Isaac William Burns-Lindow were chosen to the represent the regiment at the unveiling of the memorial at Ypres on Sunday 24 March 1929.[7] The St Patrick's Day dance of that year was held to fund a hospital bed in Dublin's Royal City Hospital, Baggot Street, Dublin, in memory of the officers and men of the South Irish Horse, who fell during the Great War. The memorial bed was unveiled on Monday 17 March at 4:00pm, with Lieutenant Colonel Burns-Lindow presiding over the ceremony:

> The South Irish Horse has already one or two memorials; there is one in Ypres Garrison Church, another in the Cathedral, Westminster [Chapel of St Patrick and the Saints of Ireland], and, I hope, very shortly there will be a memorial brass plate in St Patrick's Cathedral [Dublin]....
>
> It is not time for boasting, but I happen to have just heard from my old friend Dr McCabe that there is an idea in Dublin that the regiment was never abroad. I can tell you that the South Irish Horse went abroad at the beginning of the war. They were at Mons and at the time of the Armistice there was a small and very battered band of the South Irish Horse still in France and Flanders. We had the honour of heading the roll of casualties for the mounted army. Of the 2,500 who went abroad 385 never returned and 2,000 were wounded.[8]

The following year's St Patrick's Day with around 2,000 people attending, raised further funds for the hospital bed. The autumn reunion dance before Armistice Day at the Phoenix Park was held on Friday 7 November 1930, attended by about 800 people. The Association was reckoned to be one of the largest for former regimental comrades in and around Dublin at the time. In 1931 the St Patrick's dance accommodated almost 1,000 guests. Meanwhile in the 'Roll of Honour – In Memoriam (1914–1918)' columns of the *Irish Times*, the same names were to be found year after year: Brewster, Dignan, Hall, McGovern, Stone et al.

Up until the 1940s the dances and subsequent Armistice Day services continued. In 1943 the commemoration of the twenty-fifth anniversary of the signing of the Armistice was held at the Garden of Remembrance in Islandbridge rather than the Phoenix Park. Having been completed in 1938, it was not until 1940 that the first commemoration was held in the Garden. (It was never formally opened by the Irish Government.)[9]

In 1936 the then King Edward VIII (Prince of Wales during the war) was trying to locate his wartime groom, No. 740 Trooper Robert Bell. Robert was one of the 'Old Contemptibles', arriving in France on 17 August 1914. In an interview he gave to the *Irish Times* on 18 March 1936, he said, 'Well that beats all. Now I know why I have been dreaming about the King these three nights. I dreamt last night I was shaking hands with him once again, as I did many times during the War.' He was then employed as a groom and driver in Londonderry, having married and settled in the city after the war. During the conflict, he was posted as the Prince's orderly and then as his groom for the remainder of the war. Needless to say, they managed to contact each other.

The last parade for the disbanded Irish Regiments was held in Whitehall on Sunday 4 June 1972.

Throughout the 1920s and 1930s, news of former members of the regiment cropped up in the newspapers, often reporting on their demise. No. 1273 Herbert C. Evans died when riding in the Hunt Cup during the 'Black and Tans' Hunt's point-to-point races, Limerick, on 30 March 1926. He was only 31 years old. Herbert, the only son of Thomas and Adelaide Evans of Ranelagh, Dublin, joined the regiment in 1914 during their annual camp at the Curragh. Being deemed 'under-age' for service overseas when he first joined, he transferred to S Squadron in France on 10 August 1915 and was wounded during his service there. He was one of the men retained as a cavalryman when the regiment was re-organized in September 1917 and returned to Cahir. Having been promoted to staff sergeant by the time he was demobilized, he went on to complete his training as a veterinary surgeon and practised in Limerick where he started his family.

The wife of Major McCalmont, adjutant of the South Irish Horse from 1912 to 1914, had £20,000 of jewellery stolen from their home, Mount Juliet, following a day at the races in Carlow on 15 April 1926. Martin Kelly, ex-South Irish Horse and ex-Dublin Metropolitan Police, was found guilty of forging a letter in to order receive £30 under false pretences and was sentenced to twelve months' imprisonment with hard labour on 28 May 1927.

Life was still hard for those who remained, whether from the land-owning classes, or working classes. Attacks on homes and livestock were endured. John Honner's daughter recalled that, during the Second World War,

> Once at a threshing on a local farm some derogatory remark was made about the Allies and Dad, who never feared speaking out, had a large clump of soil thrown at him – unfortunately it was a bad shot and the poor unfortunate man standing beside him received a nasty blow on the face and a dreadful nose bleed.

John, having served throughout the war, came home to a rundown farm with very little stock, the majority having been stolen, and in debt to the bank.

In late June 1946, Lieutenant Colonel Isaac William Burns-Lindow DSO died. The main driving force behind the regiment, both during the war years and afterwards, he was remembered in the following obituary:

> Ex-Service men in this country have learned with regret of the death, which took place at Ingwell, Moor Row, Cumberland, last week, of Lieutenant Colonel I.W. Burns-Lindow DSO, who commanded the South Irish Horse in the First World War. Lieutenant Colonel Burns-Lindow was well known in Dublin and the South of Ireland. He was MFH of the South Union Hounds, Cork, from 1908 to 1917: later leaving to live in England. He was the eldest son of J.L. Burns-Lindow, and he was educated at Christ Church Oxford, afterwards entering the Army. He reached the rank of captain in the 8th Hussars in 1898, and served throughout the South African War, in the course of which he was severely wounded. He gained the Queen's Medal [Queen's South Africa Medal] with six clasps. In 1903 he was promoted major; with that rank the next year he went to the South Irish Horse [then the South of Ireland Imperial Yeomanry], of which he became Lieutenant Colonel Commanding. [Succeeding the Earl of Wicklow] When the First World War broke out he went at once on active service. He won the DSO in 1915, and was mentioned four times in despatches. In 1922 he relinquished his commission. For many years past he came to Dublin each year to attend the annual reunion of the South Irish Horse, the members of which will mourn his loss. He took a great interest also in the work of the British Legion. He is survived by his widow.[10]

Burns-Lindow's death was followed closely on 11 October 1946 by that of Ralph Francis Howard, the Earl of Wicklow. Howard had been a member of the regiment from its early days and throughout the war. He had seen action in the Boer War with the 2nd Life Guards. During the war he served as the acting CO in the absence of Lord Decies from 1915,[11] firstly at Leopardstown, Carlow, and finally at Cahir, until April 1917. After a short time in London, he transferred to the War Office in July 1917. He lost his first wife, Lady Gladys Hamilton, on 12 March 1917. He was promoted to lieutenant colonel in 1920. Following the war, he was elected to the first Seanad and served in the Seanad for six years between 1922 and 1928. He married again in 1942, shortly before his death.

On 26 November 1950 the Regimental Standard was handed over to St Patrick's Cathedral in Dublin to hang above the regiment's Memorial Plaque. Unfortunately, in the 1970s or 1980s, someone took offence at the Union flag in the top corner of the standard and cut it out, destroying the standard in the process. Where it is now, I have no idea. A replica of the original standard was presented by the North Irish Horse and now hangs in its place. The memorial itself suffered from the attentions of vandals. A bronze shamrock had been fitted to each corner of the memorial. These have been unscrewed and taken, presumably because they were shamrock. It is a sad state of affairs when a public memorial commemorating the supreme sacrifice of Irishmen is desecrated in such a fashion, even when in the sanctuary of a church.

As the 'old soldiers' passed away, so did the regiment. The memory of the regiment had been kept alive by the Old Comrades' Association up until the 1970s, until they amalgamated with the Royal Irish Regiment Old Comrades' Association to become the XVIIIth The Royal Irish Regiment and South Irish Horse Old Comrades' Association, until that too discontinued in the mid-1980s. It has now been succeeded by a modern association, The 18th Regiment of Foot Royal Irish Regiment Association.

As mentioned before, no formal history of the regiment was ever published and with the situation in Ireland in the immediate aftermath of the war, I can well understand why not. During the War of Independence, it is believed that at least 200 ex-servicemen were killed by the IRA just for being ex-servicemen. Whether they were Roman Catholic, from nationalist families, or wanted to help in the War of Independence, all ex-servicemen were considered legitimate targets and suffered accordingly. All the returning soldiers wanted was to return to their pre-war jobs and families and get on with their lives. For some men, the only option to escape these turbulent times was to emigrate. Many ex-soldiers packed their bags, and families, and set off to all corners of the Empire, as it still was, to start new lives. Australia and Canada both self-governing Dominions although not part of the Empire, were favourites as well as mainland Britain. No. 1164 Private Thomas Styles was one of those men. Trained as a blacksmith in Dublin, he joined the South Irish Horse and served in France and Flanders, arriving in theatre on 28 November 1915 with B Squadron. After the re-organization in September 1917, he was transferred to the Northumberland Hussars until his demobilization on 12 March 1919. He moved to Belfast and started a family. In 1926 he decided to move his entire family and settled in Victoria, Australia, where he remained until his death at the age of 88 in 1984.

A final assessment of the role of the regiment throughout its twenty years could be, on the face of it, inconsequential. They never fought as a mounted cavalry regiment, were sent to France and Flanders piecemeal and, in the end, when re-organized as an infantry regiment, were effectively wiped out in approximately three hours, six months later. However, this would be totally wrong, for a number of reasons.

Together with its sister regiment, the North Irish Horse, they were the first yeomanry regiments to be raised in Ireland since 1834, a feat in itself when the word 'Yeoman' was held in such distain and hatred by the Irish people. Being able to overcome the intransigence of the War Office with regard to the colour of the uniform was instrumental in achieving the success of the regiment. The Marchioness of Waterford's ceaseless campaigning for the green jacket and sand-coloured breeches, instead of the more conventional khaki worn by the majority of the Army, gave the impression that the regiment was more 'Irish' than British and, therefore, more acceptable. In fact, the uniform was so 'acceptable' that recruits joined, not to train as yeomen, but because the walking-out dress was so smart. Not only was the regiment a yeomanry regiment, but it was filled with men of all religions serving as officers and troopers. For example, Major Stern was Jewish, Surgeon Major McCabe Roman Catholic.

Secondly, the regiment, again along with the North Irish Horse, were the first non-regular force to arrive in France at the beginning of the war. Lord French, when describing the conduct of the Territorial Force towards the end of 1914, indicated that the Oxfordshire Hussars and the London Scottish were the first Territorial units in theatre. However, in a footnote appended to this statement, he noted, 'The North and South Irish Horse went to France much earlier than these troops but were employed as special escort to GHQ.'[12] He also went on to indicate that, without the Territorial units arriving from October 1914, it would have been increasingly difficult to hold the line. Both the North and South Irish Horse had spent time in the trenches prior to this, not just as 'escorts to GHQ'. Furthermore, the squadron took over all despatch work for I Corps from 31 October until they were taken out of the line in December. Much was made by the North Irish Horse that they had more squadrons in theatre than the South Irish Horse, and felt this was an example of the south of Ireland 'not pulling its weight'. Philip Tardiff quotes Major Cole, OC A Squadron North Irish Horse: 'Another N. Irish Squadron has just come out with the Highland Division. This makes three out here whereas the South have only one. Of all the shitinest etc. etc.'[13] As Tardiff rightly indicates, the South Irish Horse had three squadrons in England ready to transfer to theatre, A, B and C Squadrons. Additionally, Burns-Lindow stated in his address during the dedication of the hospital bed that the regiment had more than enough men ready and willing to form another overseas squadron at the beginning, but were not allowed to.

Thirdly, the regiment, in one form or another, had been present at every major battle from 1914 to 1917 and, as the 7th (South Irish Horse) Battalion Royal Irish Regiment, up until November 1918. They had been ready and waiting when the tanks were first used on the Somme and had attacked following the successful use of the tank during the clearing of Gird trench on 26 September 1916. As previously mentioned, Lieutenant Bence-Jones' troop were part of a small but very successful use of cavalry to exploit the confusion at short notice, when they were called to reconnoitre over open ground and hold the village of Gueudecourt. These successes were very few and far between.

Fourthly, when the regiment was dismounted, they only had a month and a half to re-train as infantry, before being transferred to 16th (Irish) Division as the 7th (South Irish Horse) Battalion Royal Irish Regiment. They suffered fifty-eight casualties, up until 21 March 1918 – the shelling of the battalion when relieving 2nd Battalion Royal Dublin Fusiliers and when hit by a 'casual' shell(s) outside their billets in St Emile. In neither instance were they in combat. They were accused of not fighting by Haig in his now infamous diary entry of 22 March 1918. Without having the correct information, Haig deduced, incorrectly, that 16th Division and, in particular, the Royal Irish Regiment, ran away in the face of the enemy.[14]

The accounts of the battalion during that fateful day from Major Call and others rightly show that this was not the case. The weather, mist and the thinly-manned defence positions all contributed to the German breakthrough. A rather large finger could be pointed to General Gough, the commander of Fifth Army for not appreciating the principle of defending in depth, by providing sufficient manpower in order to make it work. In fact, the battalion held on to their positions against overwhelming odds, often surrounded with no chance of relief, until they ran out of ammunition or were overrun by the enemy. One Military Cross and two Military Medals were awarded for that day's work, bearing in mind that the battalion lost 880 men killed, wounded, and missing (PoW) in one day. The remainder of men surviving the March offensive and forming the cadre of eight officers and fifty ORs were no less proficient. When the battalion was re-formed in May 1918, this core of South Irish Horse men played their part just as effectively as the 'proper infantry' replacements (500 Royal Dublin Fusiliers, 250 Royal Munster Fusiliers, eighty-five Royal Irish Regiment) with John James Craigie (Temporary Regimental Sergeant Major) earning a Bronze Medal for Military Valour (Italy)[15] and a Distinguished Conduct Medal during the attack at Wervicq on 14 October 1918:

He went about, regardless of personal danger, cheering and encouraging the men, and by his example gave them confidence. It was also through his resourcefulness that rations and ammunition were got up to an isolated platoon during the action. He has always displayed great gallantry and devotion to duty in action.[16]

A further five men from the original 'South Irish Horse' whilst serving in the 7th (South Irish Horse) Battalion Royal Irish Regiment were to receive the Military Medal: 25002 Private George Adams (later to transfer to 15th Hussars),[17] 25133 Corporal John Claxton,[18] 25136 Private Victor Cleary,[19] 25989 Sergeant J. McCarthy,[20] and 25789 Lance Sergeant Henry Smyth.[21]

Whatever their reasons, from the men who first joined the yeomanry in 1902 to the final recruits in 1918, the story of the regiment remained untold. All in all, although the regiment was not as exposed to the privations of the front line as often as 'line infantry' regiments and many regular cavalry regiments, when called on, they answered with courage, determination and selflessness. In the words of Lieutenant Colonel Isaac Burns–Lindow DSO, 'Of the 2,500 who went abroad 385 never returned and 2,000 were wounded.' I have tried to provide a snapshot of what happened throughout their twenty years of existence (and beyond), a story that I am sure will continue to grow if given the exposure. Given the now changed political landscape in Ireland as a whole, I hope this allows their descendants to take pride in their achievements and encourage them to delve deeper into their family history.

Appendix I

The Strength of the South of Ireland Imperial Yeomanry, circa 1905

Honorary Colonel		Field Marshal HRH Arthur Duke of Connaught and Strathearn KG KT KP GCB GCMG GCIE GCVO, Col Grenadier Guards and ASC and Col-in-Chief 6 Dgns, HLI, RDF and RB, Personal ADC to the King
Lieutenant Colonel		Lt Col Henry de la Poer Beresford, 6th Marquis of Waterford KP
Major (Second in command)		Major Richard St Leger Moore
4 Majors (OC Squadrons)	Limerick Squadron Cork Squadron Kildare Dublin	Major Francis Hubert Wise Major Henry Charles Villiers Stuart Sir Kildare Borrowes Isaac Burns-Lindow
Captains		James O'Grady Delmege
		Hon Edward B.L.H. Stopford
		Aylmer Coghill Somerville
Lieutenants:		Lionel Charles Warren
		Desmond John L. Fitzgerald, Knight of Glin
Second Lieutenants		Lionel Lloyd Hewson MVO
		Randall Kingsmere Moore
		Noel Charles Bell Furlong
		Edgar Lecky Phelps
		Hon. Vere Brabazon Ponsonby
		W.H. Ball
Adjutant		Captain F M Jennings 8th (King's Royal Irish) Hussars
Quartermaster		James William Bayliss (Hon. Lieutenant)
Medical Officer		Surgeon-Lieutenant Frederick Faber MacCabe MB

	A Squadron Beggars Bush Barracks Dublin	B Squadron Artillery Barracks Limerick	C Squadron Glen House Ballyvolane Cork or Glanmire or Victoria Bks	D Squadron Beggars Bush Barracks Dublin
Squadron Sergeant Major	1	1	1	1
Squadron Quartermaster Sergeant	1	1	1	1
Sergeant	5	4	4	5
Lance Sergeant	2	2	2	1
Sergeant Farrier	1	1	1	1
Trumpeter Sergeant			1	
Saddler Sergeant		1		
Corporal	4	6	4	5
Lance Corporal	7	11	7	7
Shoeing Smith Corporal		1		
Shoeing Smith		1	2	
Trumpeter	2	1	2	3
Saddler	1			
Trooper	80	63	80	81

Regimental Sergeant Major J. White; Regimental Quartermaster Sergeant M. Hall; Farrier Quartermaster Sergeant J.G. Evans.
Permanent Staff: 1 Regimental Sergeant Major and 4 Squadron Sergeant Majors; the Band were also included on the muster roll.[1]

Appendix II

The Diaries of Trooper George Dixon covering January, February and March 1915

Date	The Diaries of 870 Tpr George Dixon A Troop, S Squadron, SIH Transcribed from the Newsletters of the XVIIIth The Royal Irish Regiment and South Irish Horse OCA May 1977, November/December 1977, March 1978, May 1978, August 1979, November 1979, March 1980, May 1980, March 1981, May 1981, August 1981, March 1982, May 1982 and May 1983.
Friday 22 January 1915	Change in routine, first parade Physical Exercises which did not go down well with some after the celebrations winning the Boxing Tournament the night before. Usual work, fatigues and exercise horses during remainder of day.
Saturday 23 January 1915	No PT today. Clean up equipment etc. Exercise horses in the afternoon under [William Joseph Pogue McCoombe, commissioned 2/Lt 19 July 1915 14th Bn Notts and Derby, KIA Battle of Arras 23 April 1917] McCombe who was sporting a new pair of breeches and let everyone know about it.
Sunday 24 January 1915	I am on Provost Marshal duty and keeping my ears open for scraps of information at HQ. Heard that men were now going to get leave in UK. Heard also that [IV] Corps was for Egypt. But doubt very much if either item is true. The bread appears to be getting very short, two days ago we were put on half rations, yesterday quarter rations- same today. They seem to be attempting to starve us out.
Monday 25 January 1915	Main business the exercising of horses in the Morning and afternoon under McCombe again, who was not so objectionable this time. It is reported that my old horse is to be got rid of at the last moment, he is lame. No news any leave or the move of [IV] Corps to Egypt. Front Line trenches were lost this morning but regained at 2 pm. Heavy casualties on both sides. In evening washed [Joe M.J.] Foley's and [Charles or Albert] Williams' kit, they paid me for my efforts with fried chips for supper. Heavy German ship sunk, but the story of our smaller boat being sunk is untrue. [A reference to the previous day's Battle of the Dogger Bank, between squadrons of the RN's Grand Fleet and the German *Hochseeflotte*, during which the German armoured cruiser *Blücher* was sunk and the British cruiser *Lion* damaged.]
Tuesday 26 January 1915	More early Physical Exercises. After breakfast mounted exercises with spurs. Got fifteen francs as pay today and received long overdue Christmas parcel from home; Sweet cake, pudding, cigarettes and sweets, with letters from Mother and Sam. Also Christmas cards. Artillery firing very heavy all day. In evening attend Boxing, [William] Harvey and [Stephen?] Sullivan win on KOs. Evening very calm, but plenty of rifle and machine-gun fire. Horse very panicky this morning but not lame. Gave him good cleaning that he will OK in the morning. Joe and Jimmy quite tight.

Wednesday 27 January 1915	Troop drill all morning, then exercising spare later. In the evening presents from the officers were given out, chocolate, matches, socks, soap, tooth powder etc. All were welcome as these items are short. Joe and Jimmy go sick. Jimmy gets two pills from the doctor, one to swallow to gargle throat with. He swallows the one that should be used to gargle and complains of pains in the stomach.
Thursday 28 January 1915	Normal exercises and cleaning of kit. It was good to get moving as the weather is intensely cold. Field exercise afternoon, which made us very hungry, so went down to town with [Private S.] Leonard and Joe for a feed of beefsteak and chips in a cafe and returned home broke.
Friday 29 January 1915	[William] Jago, [J.] Fulham, [Patrick] Coyne, the two [Joseph and James] Kings and myself on bearer parties for Burial Escort during morning. Coffins almost cut my shoulder with their sharp corners, quite uncomfortable. Weather still very cold. Exercise horse and clean saddles with dubbin during afternoon. No rest tonight, detailed for guard duties. Issued with a new soft cap. ['Gor Blimey' Cap]
Saturday 30 January 1915	Another burial party escort, three chaps of the Rifle Brigade [Cpl A. Boyce, Cpl Arthur James Gilding and Rfn H. Hogg, Merville Communal Cemetery]. Heard that the Germans lost 40,000 men last few days and that our losses were heavy too. Hence no doubt the spate of funerals. Afternoon exercise horses, roads very slippery with ice. Intended to go to photographers this evening but whole Troop stuck with cleaning out stables. Extra guard of three men per Troop to patrol some road all night. Glad I was on guard last night now, so missed this. Still very cold. Got a nice parcel from home; good cake, which was soon gone, and other useful items. Too many friends perhaps.
Sunday 31 January 1915	Early spit and polish for Church parade, which went off quite well. On return from Church exercised horses until dinner time. Sleet fell all day, very mucky and cold. In evening took washing to where we used to sleep, found Williams there, had some fried spuds and coffee before returning to billets.
Monday 1 February 1915	On Provost Marshal Duty, had to go into town in afternoon, so had photograph taken while there, ordered 12, will collect on Thursday. Nothing new in the way of news to be gained from stay in PM's office.
Tuesday 2 February 1915	Early morning exercise of horses, again in afternoon, very lame. Received from [Private John] Pick, he says Todd and Wilson are to go to Grenadiers soon. Boxing Competition in the evening, which proved to be quite good.
Wednesday 3 February 1915	Weather very wet, cold and generally rotten, but we take our horses for exercise as usual. My horse not good. Todd and Wilson departed for Grenadiers. Heard they were put through their paces by a Sergeant Major who swore in great style. Take the old horse to the Vet who prescribes medicines and exercises, but really the horse only fit for base duties. In the evening, on road patrol and piquet. I take 9pm to 12 midnight for Patrol and 5am to 7am for piquet, which gave me a few hours' sleep at least. Cpl Buckley mentioned that he was thinking of applying for Irish Guards, but reports of Todd's and Wilson's reception have caused me to seriously think about it. [Alexander Buckley did indeed transfer, but to the King's Royal Rifle Corps on 24 September 1915, commissioned as a second lieutenant. Later he transferred to the Royal Air Force as a flying officer and survived the war.]

Thursday 4 February 1915	Again early morning exercise of horses. Sergeant [J.] Peat, while jumping through gap in hedge, got badly torn about the eyes by thorns. Took him to hospital. While there heard that Cavalry were for the trenches on 13 February and that Kitchener's Army is on the way here, hope they dodge the German submarines. Went to collect washing from cottage and had some more fried potatoes and coffee. On guard all night.
Friday 5 February 1915	Weather an improvement today, not so cold and quite dry. Exercise horses early morning and afternoon, clean up equipment and rifle. Ejector spring of rifle broken, must report this. Aeroplanes active overhead and heavy artillery duel going on in the distance. Wonder whether we shall ever get into a real scrap? Went into town and saw proof of photographs. On return got [Private M.] Walsh to clip [Private John] Pollard's horse. Bed early.
Saturday 6 February 1915	Up to clean out stables. Horse exercises morning and afternoon. Long walk from billets to stables makes one feel tired having to go there so often. Got paid 10 Francs today, got a feed of potatoes. Heavy artillery firing all day. Still thinking of Irish Guards. At bedtime Thrustler (Brewster)[Theo], [W.] Mitchell and Walsh start telling yarns about ghosts, lots of them very creepy, which makes Joe Hubbard [Transferred Army Ordnance Corps 3 August 1916] rather frightened.
Sunday 7 February 1915	Much spit and polish about for Church Parade this morning. They all must have done it properly as no complaints at the inspection. Heavy artillery duel going on all day. Took old horse out for exercise this afternoon, murky day, makes one feel fed up. Wish Spring would get a move on and help to cheer us up. Got some newspapers from home and see that there is a great windup over submarines. In evening strolled into town with [T.] McDonald and had a feed.
Monday 8 February 1915	Detailed for Bearer Party, but found out that we were not needed on arrival. That was pleasing as it is a mournful job. On return to unit took horses out for usual exercise. My old horse became all swollen. I am afraid he is almost done. The artillery are not so active today. [D.] McMillan [transferred RE Sig Section 23 July 1917] and [T.] McClean go to town and get drunk and are arrested and put in the Clink.
Tuesday 9 February 1915	On Provost Marshal duty today with Cpl Buckley. Warned to keep a tight watch as two prisoners broke out yesterday and got away. Put handcuffs on them and later found that we had lost the key. Poor devils had to wear them until late at night, until another key could be obtained. This made us miss the Boxing Tournament, where B[rereton] got KOed in the 5th Round against ? Rawlins, a much heavier man than himself. Hear old horse is improving. Farrier Sergeant said he had been neglected. I am afraid I had to call him a liar [Farrier Sergeant C. Sheehan.]
Wednesday 10 February 1915	Early morning and usual exercising of the horses. My old horse is left to graze in the field. I think he is done for but the vet thinks he's not. In afternoon put on relief from 1pm to 3pm at Provost Marshal's. Wrote to Tess and Farrell. German aeroplane comes over, we all open fire on it but fail to get it. Fine warm day, after tea went to cottage near old billet to collect washing. Hear the Germans have retired seven kilometres from the Béthune area and that 80,000 Kitchener's Army troops have landed at Ostend.

Thursday 11 February 1915	Lots of refugees passing today. Sounds of heavy rifle and machine-gun fire not too far away. More rumours that the SIH are to relieve the Scots Greys in the trenches later on. This will be a welcome diversion. Thus we get several parades of sword exercises, don't think swords will be much use up there. This evening went into town and collected photos. Not satisfactory, but will have do, then had feed and returned.
Friday 12 February 1915	Woke very early to a sound like thunder. It was artillery fire, continuous for two hours, never heard like this before, so continuous and reverberating. Exercised horses about 7.30 breakfast, then cleaned stables. Detailed for Night patrol, which uneventful and quite boring. Later played draughts with Hubbard, finished all even. Then had some supper and to bed.
Saturday 13 February 1915	Bad night awful cold, never slept a wink. Rifle inspection by [Second lieutenant C.T.] Stewart at 9:30am, all in good order. Exercises in afternoon, very wet, very rotten horse and am sore can hardly sit down. Some 10,000 of Kitchener's Army passed here for la Bassée. Many rumours going round, one that we are moving on 3 March and the Guards Brigade is to go home after they have taken la Bassée. Our other Squadrons are coming over and we all shall eventually end up in the trenches. [A Squadron, the next, did not arrive until 11 September 1915, although there were numerous replacements for men time expired, transferred, casualties etc.]
Sunday 14 February 1915	Still raining very hard, but it does not stop exercises, all got drenched, then Church Parade, and the rest of the day to ourselves. Heard we are to be all detailed to supply the Guards tomorrow, so asked Brereton for the Orderly Room job again. Surprisingly he agreed. Took washing to old billet, coffee and sandwiches there which was welcome. Get back to billet at 9.30pm. Sullivan informs me all guards cancelled for us tomorrow.
Monday 15 February 1915	Still raining hard, exercises as usual, then saddlery inspection. Three night guards to be detailed, so see Brereton and get appointed acting Corporal to check stables each night.
Tuesday 16 February 1915	On Provost Marshal duties with Cpl [G.E.] Evans, get detailed for Burial Escort party. In evening went to Boxing Tournament which was quite good. Brewster and Co. started yelling 'DIXON' at the top of their voices, Walsh started this game, but I am saying nothing at present, waiting my time.
Wednesday 17 February 1915	All very quiet today. Exercises morning and afternoon, then groom horses and bed them down. Boys very much quieter, not a murmur from them.
Thursday 18 February 1915	Up early, raining very heavily, don't feel too well, must be a cold coming on. Exercise horses despite rain, come back drenched, will probably make cold worse, cleaned out stables, groomed horse, and got a new pair of boots. Rumour has it that there is a big battle going on in the North Sea. Bed early.
Friday 19 February 1915	Awake feeling somewhat better, much to my surprise. However, Mitchell gone sick instead, so I am detailed to take his place at Provost Marshal duty. Still lashing down with rain. Lots of motor cars pass through, probably from England. Detailed for guard in the evening, not my lucky day.

Saturday 20 February 1915	Marvels will never cease, the rain has, just for a change, and it is quite dry if wet underfoot. My rifle needs some attention by an armourer, but find Scots Greys Armourer has gone to trenches, so Marsh had nothing to do, and took it to him to fix up. Hear chap we handcuffed and lost key on the 9th has been shot. The cook excelled himself today and a fine dinner of steak, potatoes and greens so no need to venture out tonight to find something worth eating. Marsh returns with rifle fixed and tells us that two ships have been sunk in Mersey by submarines. [Two ships were reported sunk in the Irish Sea close to the mouth of the Mersey, the *Cambank* and the *Downshire*, both attacked by *U-30*.] To crown this I am detailed for guard again, with Cpl Buckley as Guard Commander. No peace for the wicked.
Sunday 21 February 1915	Early Church Parade, then exercises. Took Cpl Evans' horse, could not get him jumping over a fence. Harvey then had a go, again refused, so Harvey gave horse awful hiding and got him over at last. Horse in an awful state and Evans had quite a lot to say about it which was not complimentary. 2/Lt Jago had a big row with [Private Anthony Francis] McCann over his bacon which had been given to us. McCann is an ignorant ass. [McCann commissioned into 11th Royal Dublin Fusiliers on 28 August 1917.] Boots not broken in yet so put them on and went to cottage at our old billet to collect laundry. Man at this cottage mobilises tomorrow, so no more of that. [J.] Pollard has been made L/Cpl while at HQ and goes home on leave tomorrow. Hear all leave stopped after 1 March, so Pollard is doubly lucky. Hear also we are to attack on the 28 February.
Monday 22 February 1915	Reveille 5am. Early breakfast, spit and polish for Camp Commandant's full inspection. Much rushing about to no point at all, for in the end he fails to put in an appearance. Detailed for Town patrol and found that [Private F.] Flower and Wilson had arranged for first relief. I was detailed with [Private T.] Fletcher and [Private Jeramiah – arrived 20 January 1915] Kelleher. We made them all toss for reliefs and got 3rd relief for ourselves. Pretty hectic night as the troops were paid today. Picked up Sullivan and McClean who were both quite tight and gave them a night's lodging in the Guard Room.
Tuesday 23 February 1915	Breakfast late this morning, cooks must have had a night out too. Sullivan and McClean for Troop Orders, they get ordered a Court Martial by Captain Smythe and placed under close arrest. Usual exercising of horses then cleaning out stable. In the evening went to the Boxing Tournament, very good. Later hear all leave stopped for good.
Wednesday 24 February 1915	Sullivan and McClean Court Martialled at 10 am by Camp Commandant. A month's detention – goodbye to them for a few days. Cpl Evans takes out A Troop on exercises, very wet, return drenched and a lot of work cleaning up horses, mud everywhere on saddlery and horses. Had a good row with Walsh, he objected to me calling the names out in the room; eventually I gave in and when Walsh got on with the job, he had a reception from the others who did not like him trying to boss the room. The result was he had a fight with Hubbard and then Williams and Foley joined in. I went out and decided to collect my washing from the cottage, and while there had a good feed. Later rumours are saying we are for Armentières to be used as Despatch Riders.

Thursday 25 February 1915	Exercising horses from 8 am till 11 am. Boots got into a shocking state, need a new pair. Went to stores to change my old pair, none available that will fit me, so had to borrow a pair from Jago until they get some replacements. Detailed for firing party at 2pm. Five poor souls buried one after the other. Took place three miles from base and snow fell immediately afterwards. Mud and slush everywhere, in a fine state when we got back. Scots Greys return from trenches for a break, showed one of them where the Shebeen was. Received cigarettes and tobacco from *War Illustrated*.
Friday 26 February 1915	Usual exercise with horses. Scots Greys moved back from trenches and billeted near. Very cold today, have to keep moving to keep warm, so rode over to Scots Greys to try and find an armourer [to] fix the safety catch on my rifle, but was unlucky. On way back looked for some souvenirs in ruined cottages, but could not find anything interesting. Very cold and fed up, decided not to go into town, so went to [bed] early and borrowed two of Hubbard's blankets, who was on guard, to keep warm. Soon very comfortable and fell asleep.
Saturday 27 February 1915	Up early, still very cold. Exercise horses at 7 am, gave my horse a good rub down after cleaned out stable. Breakfast at 8.30am. Dismounted parade at 9.30. Several got told off for dirty boots and buttons etc. Lucky gave my own a good clean when I got up. Fatigues rest of morning. Dinner of stew, very warming. Mounted parade at 2.30 went a long way and did not get [back] until 5.30. Had a letter from Mother saying that Kathleen was very ill and hoped she would be all right. In Canteen that night the rumour was that war would last another three years, not a very cheering prospect. [How right they were].
Sunday 28 February 1915	Reveille 7 am, quite nice, clean up for Church Parade, which went rather well, everybody spick and span, no charges. In afternoon went to the cottage to collect washing, took some of the cake I got from Aunt Lillie and Mother a few days ago. Good company, so stayed all night. The rumour there that we were leaving Wednesday.
Monday 1 March 1915	On Provost Marshal duty with Cpl Bradley all day. Much warmer today felt much better. Nice easy guard, no unpleasant duties.
Tuesday 2 March 1915	Exercises at 8:30, but was detailed to move stables, as 1st Army was coming in to take them over. This took up the whole day, what with fodder and harness and cleaning up after. New stables much nearer billet, which will save much time. Would sooner have gone on exercises, as I was very tired after all the lugging of stuff about. Went to Boxing at 6:30pm, the first event was a wrestling display by Cpl Evans, got rather fed up with it so left early and went Bed.
Wednesday 3 March 1915	Move was only a rumour, nothing happened. Exercise horses till 12.30, rest of day on fatigues. Lots of Canadians passing through today. [1st Canadian Division]

Thursday 4 March 1915	Field Day started 9 am, great fun, and a lot criticism from higher ups. Learned something useful. Halted at noon to feed horses and to eat sandwiches, good warm tea, returned 3 pm. Detail stated that all soldiers to be in billets at 8 pm, which was taken with some disagreeable remarks.
Friday 5 March 1915	More funerals, detailed for firing party at 8.30am Joseph [Jacobs] made a mess of the present Arms from the Order and detailed for special Arms Drill, very annoying. As soon as this was over the exercising of horses, followed by fatigues day. On guard at night, a happy day, I don't think.
Saturday 6 March 1915	Raining heavily, and far too bad to exercise horses this morning, so spend time on cleaning kit, get issue of Regimental Cloaks so have to sew Regimental buttons on same. Rain ceases about noon. After dinner exercise horses and spend much time rubbing them down and clearing harness after. Rumoured that we are to join B and C Troops and become Divisional Cavalry [13 April 1915 2nd Division Mounted Troops]. Hope this is correct, it will make a nice change. Brewster reports that he finds some of his things missing; we suspect H_____ but no evidence.
Sunday 7 March 1915	All spit and polish again, but everyone comes through without any reports. After Church Parade exercise horses, very wet, hard job cleaning up again. Rumoured la Bassée to be taken tonight, then town had fallen, both false. Sergeant Switzer [Robert MC and MSM] over from C Troop all well there. [Private Arthur] Ashman and McDonald fight, good scrap. [Arthur Ashman after his Time Expired 4th May 1916 was then commissioned into the Queen's (Royal West Surrey) Regiment]. McDonald had the best of it. Fool around with Evans, Brewster and Jago, tie Evans up good fun. Brewster still losing things.
Monday 8 March 1915	Very cold this morning but get warmed up on exercising horses. Plenty to do after in cleaning up. A parcel and a letter from Mother. Kathleen much better now, which is good news. Someone lifted my pot of jam and the candy from the parcel. I shall go for H_____ when he comes in.
Tuesday 9 March 1915	Detailed for Provost Marshal duty with Cpl Buckley. La Bassée at last taken and 2,000 prisoners reported taken. Troop detailed for Road Patrol from 6am to 6pm. Went to boxing in the evening, some good fights, only one dud one.
Wednesday 10 March 1915	Still detailed for Provost Marshal duties. There is great activity in the town, not too easy to control flow of traffic. Miles of ammunition trucks, limbers, new guns passing through, lots of Canadians and Naval personnel in armoured cars. Have been told that an attack is about to start and we will not be relieved until Lille is taken. [The Battle of Neuve Chapelle started on 10 March 1915]. News of good work in the Dardanelles and that all German submarine crews when taken will be treated as awaiting trial for murder. I agree with this, a good idea. McCombe sent home with skin disease, after all his baths and boasting that he would be immune from such troubles. Kept on duty until 10.30 pm, as hundreds of German prisoners are being taken and passed down. Some very young indeed, while others appear to be very old looking. Sergeant McMillan said he would have a try to get us relieved of this job, but no luck all. Williams is going to have another try tomorrow.

Thursday 11
March 1915

Williams also failed, and have done all I could to rid of it, so now I must resign myself to the inevitable and accept it. We could be on this for another few weeks or more at least. Seems to me that those who do not wish to take part in any action are in it long before those that want to get into the thick of things. I wish I had joined the Royal Dublin Fusiliers now that would have got me into it. More German prisoners roll in today, it seems things are moving. My knee is giving some trouble lately and appears to be rather weak. If it does not pass soon I will report sick and get it seen to, also if we are in this job much longer. It is dreadful when there is a real job of work to be done. At 4pm went to billet and took old horse out for a trot, on return met Captain Smyth, gave him receipt for boots and asked to be relieved. He said he would see what he could do about it.

Friday 12 March
1915

Captain Smyth worked the miracle. I am relieved by Cpl Evans. Reveille was at 5am and we were turned out at 7am to escort 600 German prisoners to base, later on went with a Royal Marine to an Estaminet about 5 miles away from the front line. Crowds of wounded being brought in, saw the 3rd Cavalry Brigade and several armoured fighting trains going up. At 6:30pm escorted another 500 German prisoners to Merville, getting back to billet at 9pm. Never saw chaps so mucky and filthy as chaps from trenches, both our own and the Germans. Wilson hit in head by shrapnel and Todd reported dead, hit in stomach. Had a bad headache and sore throat, so went to bed early.

George Dixon got his wish and was commissioned into the East Yorkshire Regiment on 23 July 1917 and was awarded the Military Cross on 31 May 1918 (*London Gazette* 31 May 1918 *Supplement 30716* Page 6465).

Honours and Rewards

South Irish Horse
7th (South Irish Horse) Battalion Royal Irish Regiment

The following awards and rewards were given to the officers and men of the South Irish Horse Regiment and those members of the South Irish Horse who transferred to the 7th (South Irish Horse) Royal Irish Regiment. (I have also included men who were serving with the Regiment in France and Flanders but were then either transferred or commissioned to other regiments.)

DISTINGUISHED SERVICE ORDER

Lieutenant Colonel Isaac William Burns-Lindow

BAR to the MILITARY CROSS

Lieutenant A.O.C. Patman

MILITARY CROSS

Lieutenant Colonel J Roche-Kelly
Major A.H. Watt
Captain A.V. Fitzherbert
Lieutenant Addison Barnes Penott Hadden
Lieutenant A.O.C. Patman
Lieutenant F.J. Vambeck
Second Lieutenant J.A. Watts
Second Lieutenant R.F. Switzer

MILITARY CROSS (serving with other regiments)

1111	Trumpeter	P.C. Bell	Commissioned Royal Field Artillery 24 March 1917
592	Private	F.W. Dalton	Commissioned Royal Garrison Artillery 13 September 1916
870	Private	G. Dixon	Commissioned 3rd Bn East Yorks 23 July 1917
689	Private	P. Dunne	Commissioned Royal Engineers 23 February 1917
587	Sergeant	W.H. Good	Commissioned Connaught Rangers 28 March 1917
711	Corporal	M. McDonough	Commissioned 5th Bn Royal Irish Regiment 4 October 1915
579	Private	J.R. Plowman	Commissioned Leinster Regiment 28 August 1915
1664	Private	F.G. Ross	Commissioned 5th Royal Dublin Fusiliers 30 October 1917

DISTINGUISHED CONDUCT MEDAL

Lieutenant R. Ludgate (Formerly Private 757)
Commissioned Royal Munster Fusiliers
2173 (25182) Temporary Regimental Sergeant Major J.J. Craigie

BAR to the MILITARY MEDAL

93	Sergeant	J Ryan

MILTARY MEDAL

1980	(25002)	(73680)	Private	G. Adams	Transferred 15th Hussars
1498	(25039)		Sergeant	J.C. Bolton	KIA
1562	(25055)		Corporal	A.H. Browne	
1199	(25136)		Private	V. Cleary	Transferred Royal Fusiliers
1287		(73119)	Private	W.F. Gore	Commissioned Royal Irish Regiment KIA
1871	(25367)		Private	M. Henning	
239			Sergeant	R. Jago	Commissioned South Irish Horse
1109		(73090)	Sergeant	W.S. Smith	Commissioned South Wales Borderers
1049		(73082)	Corporal	R.E. West	Commissioned Reserve Cavalry Regiment
903		(73053)	Private	M. White	Awarded attached Dorset Yeomanry
93			Sergeant	J. Ryan	Attached Mounted Military Police
1293	(25757)		Corporal	H. Rutherford	Died of Wounds
1558		(73881)	Private	P.J. Loftus	Northumberland Hussars
1591	(25789)		Sergeant	H. Smyth	
1198		(73819)	Sergeant	S. Magill	S Squadron
1998	(25133)		Corporal	J. Claxton	

MERITORIOUS SERVICE MEDAL

439	Sergeant	G.O.H. Beveridge	Formerly (S) Sqn	Awarded MSM with MMP
1028	Lance Corporal	A.S. Craig	Formerly B Sqn	Awarded MSM with MMP
862	Acting Company Quartermaster Sergeant	J.J. Pollard	(S) Sqn	
544	Temporary Regimental Sergeant-Major	J.E. Yarnell	South Irish Horse and 7th (South Irish Horse) Battalion Royal Irish Regiment	
	Second Lieutenant	R.F. Switzer	South Irish Horse	
747	Corporal	A. McBeath	South Irish Horse and 7th (South Irish Horse) Battalion Royal Irish Regiment	

MENTIONED IN DESPATCHES

Lt Col I.W. Burns-Lindow (x4)	73961 Acting Corporal J.W. O'Driscoll	1016 Sergeant J. Keegan
Major Hamilton Stubber	1293 Corporal H. Rutherford	1552 Lance Corporal J. O'Driscoll
Major A.H. Watt	Captain J.M. Wardell	943 Private E. Burke
Lt B.B. Bellow	1400 Private T. Wilks	811 Acting Quartermaster Sergeant R.C.W. Airey
783 Cpl L.P.J. Allen	299 Sgt T.B. Mitchell	Captain P.N. Smith
798 Private J. Ardill	1342 Sgt W. Rawlins	Lieutenant J. Roche-Kelly
852 Private P. McCarthy	1525 Cpl C.Lowry	783 Private J. Johnston
476 Lance Sergeant C.L. Taylor	417 Sgt J. Spittal	

Appendix IV

Roll Of Honour

South Irish Horse Regiment and Members Who Transferred to Other Regiments (Listed)

SIH No.	R.Ir. No.	Corps of Hussars. No	Rank	Name	First Name(s)	Died	Age	Sqn	Comments	
970			Pte	ALLEN	Matthew	26/09/1916	21	B	Only casualty of action at Gueudecourt, no known grave.	
			Lt	ALLGOOD	George	15/04/1917			Joined SIH then commissioned in Royal Dublin Fusiliers. Killed in action, no known grave	
798	25007		Pte	ARDILL	John	23/08/1918	25	S	Died in captivity PoW	MiD
2452	25023		Pte	BARRETT	Thomas	21/03/1918	20		Missing, presumed dead Ronssoy	
1242			Pte	BARSBY	Charles	29/10/1917	22		Killed in action Tunnel Trench Croisilles Sector	
1608	25026		Pte	BATEMAN	Samuel	12/12/1917			Killed in shelling of billets St Émilie	
1992	25027		Pte	BATEMAN	Charles	21/03/1918			Missing, presumed dead Ronssoy	
1742			Pte	BENTLEY	James Edward	14/05/1917	22	1 SIH	Killed in action at battle post, Somme front	
3088			Pte	BICKER		22/03/1918			Transferred to Royal Dublin Fusiliers. Killed in action Ronssoy	
1498	25039		Sgt	BOLTON	John C	21/03/1918	26		Killed in action Ronssoy	MM
2110	25083		Pte	BRAZIL	Michael	09/06/1918			Died in captivity PoW	
1626	25047	73697	Pte	BRENNAN	Patrick	09/10/1918	29		Transferred 10th (Prince of Wales's Own Royal) Hussars Killed in action	
655			2/Lt	BREWSTER	Richard Gardiner	21/03/1918	25	S	Commissioned 16/2/17 South Irish Horse. Killed in action Ronssoy	
1942			Pte	BROWNE	John	29/03/1917	27	(B) 1SIH	Enlisted Limerick. Died of pneumonia.	
634			Pte	BROWNLOW	Robert	04/12/1914	24	S	Died on Service Hazebrouck	
2087	25057		Pte	BRYAN	Arthur Patrick	21/03/1918	26		Missing, presumed dead Ronssoy	
1299	25059		Pte	BUCKLEY	William	06/08/1918	29	C	Missing, presumed dead Ronssoy	
2121	25063		Pte	BURKE	Michael	12/12/1917			Killed in shelling of billets St Émilie	

SIH No.	R. Ir. No.	Corps of Hussars. No	Rank	Name	First Name(s)	Died	Age	Sqn	Comments
983			Pte	BYRNE	Thomas	12/10/1916	20	B	Missing presumed dead whilst attached to Corps Intelligence, no known grave, Somme Front
1213	25070		Pte	BYRNE	Michael	21/03/1918		B	Killed in action Ronssoy
1587	25097		Pte	CAHALIN	Francis	21/03/1918			Missing presumed dead Ronssoy
3151	25101		Pte	CAMERON	David	17/12/1917	26		Died of wounds received from shelling of billets St Émilie
2673	25109		Pte	CARR	Albert E.	19/01/1918			Died of wounds, Kilkenny
1877	25116		Pte	CASEY	Joseph	13/12/1917	21		Died of wounds received from shelling of billets St Émilie
1518	25140		Pte	CLYNCH	Joseph	12/12/1917		C	Died of wounds received from shelling of billets St Émilie
1495	25145		Pte	COATES	William Alexander	27/03/1918	25		Missing presumed dead during retreat from Ronssoy
935	25096		Pte	COFFEY	Thomas	12/12/1917	20	A	Died of wounds received from shelling of billets St Émilie
73207		73207	Sgt	COGHLAN	Thomas	24/10/1918	26		Commissioned 25 June 1918 Royal Irish Fusiliers. Died of wounds.
1829	25152		Pte	COLEMAN	Patrick	12/12/1917	25	B	Killed in shelling of billets St Émilie
2399	25153		Pte	COLEMAN	James	31/01/1918			Missing presumed dead Ronssoy
1534	25154		Pte	COLLEARY	John	12/12/1917	22		Killed in shelling of billets St Émilie
2455	25157		Pte	COLTON	Frederick William	22/02/1918	21		Killed in action Ronssoy.
			Capt.	COLVILL	George Chaigneau	30/11/1917	23	B	Killed in action Tunnel Trench Croisilles Sector
1983	25159		Pte	CONDON	John	12/12/1917			Killed in shelling of billets St Émilie
1617	25161		Pte	CONLON	Andrew	12/12/1917			Killed in shelling of billets St Émilie

SIH No.	R. Ir. No.	Corps of Hussars. No	Rank	Name	First Name(s)	Died	Age	Sqn	Comments
1179			Pte	COONEY	Edmond	04/06/1917	27	C	Arrived 18 December 1915 and commissioned 11 Royal Dublin Fusiliers 21 April 1916. Killed in action Messines
1540				CORRIGAN	George Henry Sykes	21/03/1917	21	C	Died of wounds/pneumonia in hospital Manchester
1532			Pte	CORRIGAN	Alfred	19/06/1917	22	C	Killed in action at Cavalry Trench, Liévin (Loos sector)
2133	25175		Pte	COSGROVE	John Joseph	20/12/1917	21		Died of wounds from shelling of billets at St Émilie
2099	25178		L/Cpl	COVENEY	Thomas	28/04/1918			Died of wounds whilst in captivity PoW
695			S/ Smith	COYLE	Alfred	27/08/1917		B	Discharged 16/4/17 then died, buried Nicholastown
1409	25199		Pte	DALY	John	14/10/1918	22	C	Killed in action at Wervicq
2196	25205		Pte	DAWSON	John	27/03/1918	21		Killed in action during retreat from Ronssoy
1541	25209		Pte	DE BERG	Eric	21/03/1918	24		Killed in action Ronssoy, previously received gunshot wound on left forearm 12 June 1917
1383	25211		Pte	DE RUYTER	Phillip	13/12/1917		C	Died of wounds received from shelling of billets St Émilie
965	25207		Pte	DEA	Patrick	11/11/1918		S	Died of wounds whilst serving with 19th Hussars
2151	25214		Pte	DEVANNY	Barry	15/03/1918	24		Missing presumed dead Ronssoy
			Lt	DIGNAN	Albert Guy	21/03/1918	23	B	Killed in action Ronssoy
1710	25229		Pte	DOYLE	Joseph	21/03/1918			Missing presumed dead Ronssoy
73104		73104	L/Cpl	DOYLE	Augustus	10/10/1918		A	Drowned, RMS Leinster
1787	25239		Pte	DUGGAN	Martin	12/12/1917			Killed in shelling of billets St Émilie
1711	25242		Pte	DUNBAR	Oliver	21/03/1918	19		Missing presumed dead Ronssoy

SIH No.	R. Ir. No.	Corps of Hussars. No	Rank	Name	First Name(s)	Died	Age	Sqn	Comments	
855	25244		Cpl	DUNNE	John James	21/03/1918	21	S	Missing presumed dead Ronssoy	
			2/Lt	EAVES	Frederick William D.	21/03/1918			Killed in action Ronssoy	MM
1419	25248		Pte	EDGHILL	Edward	31/05/1919		S	Died. Previously wounded in February 1917	
2272	25259		Pte	FAIRTLOUGH	Edward	21/03/1918	29		Missing presumed dead Ronssoy	
901			Pte	FARRELL	Matthew	12/07/1916	24	A	Killed in action, no known grave, Thiepval Memorial	
1817	25266		Pte	FARRELL	Edward	12/12/1917	26		Killed in shelling of billets St Émilie	
1074	25262		WOII	FARRELL	Francis	21/03/1918	23		Missing presumed dead Ronssoy	
1084			Pte	FAUSSET	Robert Clifford	16/11/1916			Commissioned Royal Field Artillery. Died in UK	
1280	25269		Pte	FEELEY	Thomas	15/03/1918			Missing presumed dead Ronssoy	
1965		73785	Pte	FLEMING	Joseph	24/02/1919	32		Died at home Naas County Kildare	
561	25281		WOII	FLETCHER	Thomas	11/04/1918	23	S	Died of wounds received Ronssoy	
			Capt.	FOGARTY	William	21/03/1918	23	C	Killed in action Ronssoy	
1555	25320		Pte	FAYLE	Edward	31/08/1918		E	Missing presumed dead Ypres Salient	
1919			Pte	FREENEY	Patrick J.	08/10/1918			Commissioned 29/5/18	
2388	25311		Pte	GAFFNEY	Adam	21/03/1918			Missing presumed dead Ronssoy	
2102	25313		Pte	GANNON	James	21/03/1918			Missing presumed dead Ronssoy	
920	25309		L/Cpl	GIBSON	Robert	12/12/1917		C	Killed in shelling of billets St Émilie	
1287		73119	Pte	GORE	William F.	27/09/1918	25	B	Commissioned Royal Irish Regiment 26/3/18. Killed in action	MM
1852	25325		Pte	GORMAN	Arthur	21/03/1918	30		Missing presumed dead Ronssoy	

SIH No.	R. Ir. No.	Corps of Hussars. No	Rank	Name	First Name(s)	Died	Age	Sqn	Comments
942		73062	Pte	GRAY	George	11/10/1918		S	Died serving with Dorset Yeomanry, Palestine/ Egypt. Buried Haifa War Cemetery
1160	25329			GRAY	Robert Kingston	02/11/1918		A	Enlisted at the outbreak of war with the SIH. Transferred to Royal Flying Corps in 1917. Died of influenza. Buried in Deansgrange Cemetery
1297			Pte	GREEN	John Redfearn	21/03/1918	24		Missing presumed dead Ronssoy
1261			Pte	GREGAN	John	21/06/1917	24	1 SIH	Died from gunshot wound to the head at Cavalry Trench, Liévin (Loos sector)
1404	25334			HALL	Ellis	21/03/1918	21	C	Missing presumed dead Ronssoy
1309	25333		Pte	HALL	Ernest	28/10/1918		A	Died in captivity of Pneumonia PoW
1707	25344		L/Cpl	HARMON	Philip	01/04/1918	23		Died in Rouen hospital from wounds received at Ronssoy
1775	25920		Pte	HARRIS	Aylmer	21/03/1918	24		Missing presumed dead Ronssoy
833			Pte	HARVISON		09/02/1919		S	Commissioned 3rd Royal Munster Fusiliers 29/1/18
1909	25355			HAUGH	Francis	27/02/1920	22		Wounded 10/2/18, died at home, Ennis County Clare
1410	25356			HAYES	Michael	23/10/1918	25	B	Died of Pneumonia, whilst in captivity PoW
73173		73173	Cpl	HEENAN	Timothy	10/10/1918	25		Drowned RMS Leinster
1110	25362		Sgt	HEFFERNAN	Edward	01/06/1918	33	A	Died in Rouen hospital from wounds received at Ronssoy
1698	25370			HICKEY	John	28/10/1918			Died in captivity PoW
1862	25376			HOBBS	John	21/03/1918	22		Missing presumed dead Ronssoy
1473			Pte	HOGAN	Martin	27/10/1917			Killed in action, Tunnel Trench, Croisilles Sector

SIH No.	R. Ir. No.	Corps of Hussars. No	Rank	Name	First Name(s)	Died	Age	Sqn	Comments
510			Cpl	HURST		04/04/1917	25	S	Died of TB: originated in September 1914; aggravated by exposure on active service. Buried Drumcondra
1070	25385			HUTCHINSON	James Samuel	21/03/1918	24		Missing presumed dead Ronssoy
1759	25402		Pte	JACKSON	John D.	12/12/1917			Killed in shelling of billets St Émilie
2441	25403			JELLY	Herbert	14/09/1918	30		Died in captivity PoW
648			Sgt	JESTIN	Martin	07/06/1917	27	S	Killed in action. Commissioned 2/Lt in 7/8 R.Ir.F. 12/2/17
1246	25412		Pte	JOHNSTONE	William	23/03/1918		S	Missing presumed dead during retreat from Ronssoy
1401			Pte	JORDAN	John Charles	31/03/1917	23	1 SIH	Killed in action Loos sector
867	25501		L/Cpl	LUDGATE	Joseph	30/10/1918	25		Died of Pneumonia, Armentières
3148	25420		Pte	KEARNEY	Thomas	25/11/1917	22		Killed in action Tunnel Trench Croisilles Sector
2049			Pte	KELLY	John (Jack)	29/10/1917	23		Died of wounds Tunnel Trench Croisilles Sector
1378	25429		Pte	KELLY	Richard	12/12/1917		C	Killed in shelling of billets St Émilie
1319	25439		Pte	KENDALL	Cecil	13/12/1917	27	A	Died of wounds from shelling of billets St Émilie
1771	25445			KENNY	Edward	16/11/1918			Died serving with 3 (R) R.Ir.Rgt in UK
2089			Pte	KERRIGAN	Thomas Joseph	13/04/1917	20	C	Died of wounds. Hit by a shell at an OP or 'battle post'; only arrived a few weeks before –Somme sector
1249	25447		Sgt	KERRISON	Donald	16/07/1918		B	Died in captivity PoW
1696	25469			KIELY	Christopher	04/12/1917			Missing, presumed Dead, Ronssoy
2412	25451			KILKEARY	Roderick	15/03/1918			Missing presumed dead Ronssoy
1951			Pte	KING	William	19/06/1917	20	1 SIH	Killed in action at Cavalry Trench, Liévin (Loos sector)

SIH No.	R. Ir. No.	Corps of Hussars. No	Rank	Name	First Name(s)	Died	Age	Sqn	Comments
1670	25460		Pte	KINNEAR	James	13/12/1917	42		Died of wounds from shelling of billets St Émilie
1068			Pte	LARKIN	Frank	22/12/1915	22	A	Killed in action at Mushroom Trench, Armentières
			SSM	LARKIN	William James	25/12/1916	39	B	Commissioned Lincolnshire Regt 14 November 1916. Killed in action Loos Sector
1073			Pte	LE BAS	Leopold C.	22/12/1915	19	A	Killed in action at Mushroom Trench, Armentières
1668			Pte	LEAHY	Samuel	27/05/1917	22	1 SIH	Killed in action Loos Sector
2338	25492	73380	Pte	LLEWELLYN	William	28/03/1918	20	A Coy	Killed in action during retreat from Ronssoy
2759		73362	Pte	LOUGHLIN	Joseph	07/10/1918			Transferred Dorset Yeo Palestine/Egypt. Died, buried Damascus
971	25512			LOUGHRAN	Francis	23/03/1918		C	Died of Wounds whilst in captivity PoW
710			S/ Smith	LYONS	Albert	15/03/1915	19	S	Died in hospital, Rouen
1945	25578		Pte	MACKEY	Denis	21/03/1918	29		Missing presumed dead, Ronssoy
1256			L/Cpl	MACMULLEN	Victor James	02/10/1916	28	A	Died of Wounds – wounded by shellfire Somme sector
1210	25581		Sgt	MAGILL	William	21/03/1918	25	B	Killed in action, Ronssoy
1607	25587			MAHER	Thomas	22/10/1918			Died in captivity PoW
1237				MAHOOD	Robert	10/11/1917	26	S	Rheumatoid Arthritis. Died at home
1103	25590			MAINWARING	Thomas Carleton	06/04/1918	23	S	Died of wounds whilst in captivity PoW
1239			Pte	MARCHANT	Charles	04/06/1917	21	S	Commissioned Royal Dublin Fusiliers 21 November 1916 Killed in action Locre

SIH No.	R. Ir. No.	Corps of Hussars. No	Rank	Name	First Name(s)	Died	Age	Sqn	Comments	
1007	25518		Sgt	MCBRYDE	Henry	08/12/1918		B	Died whilst in captivity PoW	
1430	25519			MCCABE	William	14/12/1917		C	Died of wounds from shelling of billets St Émilie	
2039	25525		Pte	MCCARTHY	Denis	30/11/1917	26		Killed in action Tunnel Trench, Croisilles sector	
1415	25523		Pte	MCCARTHY	Fred	12/12/1917	20	C	Killed in shelling of billets St Émilie	
1930	25524		Pte	MCCARTHY	Timothy	12/12/1917		C	Killed in shelling of billets St Émilie	
539			Pte	MCCOMBE	William Joseph Pogue	23/04/1917		S	Killed in action. Commissioned 19/7/15 Notts & Derby	
2231	25541		Pte	MCDONALD	Joseph	12/12/1917	24	C	Killed in shelling of billets St Émilie	
1491	25544		Pte	MCDOWELL	Ernest	21/03/1918		C	Suffered shellshock in Dec 1917 St Emilie; then wounded in leg. Missing presumed dead, Ronssoy.	
1216	25548		Pte	MCGOVERN	Thomas	21/03/1918	27	A	Missing presumed dead, Ronssoy	
1391	25553		Cpl	MCGREGOR	Alfred	21/03/1918	30		Killed in action, Ronssoy	
1901	25565		Pte	MCNAMARA	Francis	27/09/1918	21		Died in captivity PoW	
2433	25566		Pte	MCNAMEE	John	02/12/1917			Died of wounds, Croisilles sector	
2140	25602		Pte	MEEHAN	Daniel	17/10/1918			Died in captivity PoW	
2247	25605		Pte	MILLETT	Frederick	26/03/1918			Killed in action retreat from Ronssoy	
1268			Pte	MITCHELL	Patrick Charles	16/02/1915	28	A	Died in hospital, Doncaster	
1597	25610		Cpl	MITCHELL	Herbert	30/11/1917	23		Killed in action Tunnel Trench, Croisilles sector	
1533	25613		Pte	MOLLISON	Charles E.	13/12/1917		C	Died of wounds from shelling of billets St Émilie	
1814	25617		Pte	MOORE	Michael	03/11/1918	24		Died in captivity PoW	

SIH No.	R. Ir. No.	Corps of Hussars. No	Rank	Name	First Name(s)	Died	Age	Sqn	Comments
1838	25619		Pte	MORAN	Michael	10/04/1918	32		Died of Wounds whilst in captivity at le Cateau Hospital
1177			Cpl	MORAN	Samuel Frederick	01/10/1918	29		Commissioned 26/6/17 Royal Irish Rifles. Killed in action
			Capt.	MORTON	Thomas Edward	26/03/1918			Died of wounds, no known grave, Ronssoy sector
1825			Pte	MURPHY	Patrick	22/06/1917		1 SIH	Killed in action at Cavalry Trench, Liévin (Loos sector)
2369	25637		Pte	MURRAY	George Irkington	12/12/1917	25		Killed in shelling of billets St Émilie
976			Pte	MURTAGH	Thomas	13/07/1916	18	B	Died of wounds, Somme sector
1896	25653		Sgt	NEWMAN	William	30/11/1917	29		Killed in action, Tunnel Trench, Croisilles sector
2235	25692		Pte	OAKLEY	Frederick William	21/03/1918	19		Missing presumed dead, Ronssoy
1821	25657		Pte	O'BRIEN	William	21/03/1918			Missing presumed dead, Ronssoy
2061			Pte	O'CONNELL	Francis	19/03/1917	20	B	Killed by a mine explosion Ransart whilst on police duty
2147	25665		Pte	O'DEA	Daniel	12/12/1917	22		Killed in shelling of billets St Émilie
2340			Pte	O'GRADY	Robert	09/12/1917			Died in Birmingham
2075	25678		Pte	O'MAHONY	Richard	21/03/1918	23		Missing presumed dead, Ronssoy
2478	25687		Pte	O'SHEA		12/12/1917	18		Killed in shelling of billets St Émilie
445			Pte	O'SULLIVAN	Joseph Alphonsus	22/06/1917	26	S	Killed in action at Cavalry trench
1876			L/Cpl	PASLEY	John Vincent	05/03/1919	22		Died of pneumonia in Cologne. (Military Mounted Police)
2124	25700		Pte	PHELAN	Patrick	21/03/1918			Missing presumed dead, Ronssoy

SIH No.	R. Ir. No.	Corps of Hussars. No	Rank	Name	First Name(s)	Died	Age	Sqn	Comments	
2101	25699		Pte	PHELAN	Thomas	23/10/1918	20		Died in captivity, PoW	
1579			Pte	PIERCE	Thomas	22/06/1917	25	1 SIH	Killed in action at Cavalry Trench	
579			Pte	PLOWMAN	James	29/04/1918	27	S	Killed in action. Commissioned 28/8/15 Leinster Regt	
1987	25708		Pte	PURCELL	John F	21/03/1918			Missing presumed dead, Ronssoy	
1239		73120	S/S	QUINSEY	Henry	10/10/1918	37	B	Drowned RMS *Leinster*	
1440	25719		L/Cpl	QUIRKE	Michael Francis	18/12/1917	30	C	Died of wounds received from shelling of billets St Émilie	
2267	25720		Pte	QUIRKE	Michael	21/03/1918			Missing presumed dead, Ronssoy	
861			Pte	RANKIN	Joseph	16/10/1914	22	S	Died on active service: first casualty of S Squadron	
727	25725		Sgt	RANKIN	William	02/04/1918	31	S	Died of wounds received at Ronssoy, hospital in Rouen	
1342			Sgt	RAWLINS	William	30/09/1917	27		Killed in action Tunnel Trench, Croisilles Sector	MiD
1702			Pte	REILLY	John Joseph	13/03/1916			Died after falling from horse in Cahir, County Tipperary	
1849			S/ Smith	REILLY	Michael	29/06/1916	34		Died at home, buried Tullow	
2409	25732		Pte	REILLY	Patrick	21/03/1918	25		Missing presumed dead, Ronssoy	
449	25753		Cpl	RIORDAN	William	21/03/1918	26	C	Missing presumed dead Ronssoy	
915	25742		Pte	ROE	Sidney George	01/12/1917	29	B	Died of wounds 113 Field Ambulance, Tunnel Trench action, Croisilles Sector	
1285	25744		Pte	ROSE	William	06/10/1918		C	Died in captivity PoW	
1293	25757		Cpl	RUTHERFORD	Henry Eustace	24/03/1918	21	A	Died of wounds, whilst in captivity PoW	MM
1443			Pte	RYAN	John	25/11/1917	23		Died at home. Buried Glasnevin	
660	25754		Pte	RYAN	Daniel	08/12/1917	26	S	Died of wounds, Ronssoy sector	

SIH No.	R. Ir. No.	Corps of Hussars. No	Rank	Name	First Name(s)	Died	Age	Sqn	Comments
1512		73159	Pte	RYAN	Patrick Cornelius	13/10/1918	21		Commissioned East Lancs Regt 30/4/18 Killed in action Arras sector
1144			Pte	SADLEIR	William	22/12/1915	22	A	Killed in action at Mushroom Trench, Armentières
1425	25761		L/Cpl	SANDERSON	Charles Henry	14/10/1918			Died of flu in PoW camp Sennelager
1485			Pte	SAUL	Michael	09/04/1916	18		Buried Deansgrange
73380		73380	Pte	SEARLES	Henry	01/01/1919	19		Died on service, with 6th Dragoon Guards
884			Pte	SHANAHAN	Daniel	11/01/1916	22	A	Killed in action at Mushroom Trench, Armentières
2355	25771		Pte	SHAUGHNESSY	Michael	21/03/1918	21		Killed in action, Ronssoy
1610	25772		Pte	SHEA	Patrick	12/12/1917		C	Killed in shelling of billets St Émilie
1921	25781		Pte	SHIER	Christopher	30/11/1917	29		Killed in action whilst helping a wounded comrade, Croisilles Sector
1574	25782		L/Cpl	SIMPSON	Alan	15/03/1918	22		Missing presumed dead, Ronssoy
1868	25785		Cpl	SMITH	John T.	12/12/1917	27		Killed in shelling of billets St Émilie
1564	25793		Pte	SPOONER	James	21/03/1918		S	Missing presumed dead, Ronssoy
1782	25796	74010	Cpl	STANNAGE	Thomas	09/10/1918	26		Died serving with 10th Hussars, Somme sector, no known grave
1679	25800		Cpl	STEADMAN	Thomas	22/03/1918	23	C Coy	Died of wounds received, Ronssoy
909	25806		Cpl	STOKER	Victor Carmichael	18/02/1918	22	C	Died of wounds from bomb fragment dropped by aircraft adjacent ration cart, Ronssoy sector
1476	25809		Sgt	STONE	Frederick	21/03/1918		B	Missing presumed dead, Ronssoy
1544			Pte	SULLIVAN	James	12/06/1917	19	S	Died of wounds, Béthune/Loos sector
1977	25816		Pte	SULLIVAN	Michael	03/03/1918	28		Missing presumed dead, Ronssoy
2239	25823		Pte	SWIFTE	Albert	12/12/1917	26	C	Killed in shelling of billets St Émilie

SIH No.	R. Ir. No.	Corps of Hussars. No	Rank	Name	First Name(s)	Died	Age	Sqn	Comments
1186	25838		Pte	THOMSON	Arthur Bell	12/12/1917	21	C	Killed in shelling of billets St Émilie
724			Cpl	TODD	Benjamin	10/03/1915			
1376	25855		Pte	TURNER	Frederick	09/12/1918	22	B	Died of Influenza in London after release as PoW
1275	25918		Pte	VENABLES	Alfred	21/03/1918		S	Missing presumed dead, Ronssoy
1888	25865		Pte	WALDRON	Patrick	21/03/1918			Died of wounds received Ronssoy
1538		81200	Pte	WARD	Douglas	22/08/1918			Killed in action serving with Northumberland Hussars, Somme sector
927			Pte	WHITFORD	George	18/09/1917	25	B	Killed in action Belgian coast sector
988	25886		Pte	WILBY	William	23/10/1918	25	S	Died of wounds received. Captured and died in hospital at Mons. Buried next to Lt Dease VC
950			Pte	WILKES	Harry Edward Rahkal	18/09/1916	21	A	Died of wounds received on the Somme on observation duty. Enlisted first week of the war
680		70461	Pte	WILLIAMS	Albert	24/09/1918	24	S	Killed in action serving with Northumberland Hussars, Somme sector
			2/Lt	WILLIAMSON	John George	02/09/1918			Killed in action, Wulverghem
2736			Pte	WILLIS	Joseph William	29/10/1918		B	Died in Newcastle
1497			Pte	WILLOUGHBY	Charles	20/06/1917	22	1 SIH	Killed in action at Cavalry Trench Liévin (Loos sector)
789				WILSON	Cecil Vere	31/07/1916	32	S	Was at the retreat from Mons. Transferred Grenadier Guards 5/2/15. No. 22485. Commissioned in Royal Berkshires; died of wounds
1968	25894		Pte	WILSON	William Edward	30/11/1917			Killed in action at Tunnel Trench, Croisilles Sector
933	25907		Pte	YARNELL	Victor	27/03/1918		A	Killed in action on retreat from Ronssoy, no known grave

Notes

Introduction
1. *The Irish Sword* Vol XIII No.50, Summer 1977 F. Glen Thompson; and Vol XXIII No.94, Winter 2003 Pat Dargan.

Chapter 1
1. Interestingly, the 7th (South Irish Horse) Bn Royal Irish Regiment were presented with their own Colours.
2. *The Irish Times*, 5 September 1908 p. 8.
3. www.angloboerwar.com – David Biggins.
4. *Hansard 1803–2005* HC Deb 20 June 1843 vol. 70 cc176–9.
5. Quarterly Army List 31 March 1914, p.6.
6. *The London Gazette*, 7 January 1902, p.151.
7. *London Gazette* 25 February 1902, p. 1204.
8. General Letter to prospective members of the regiment 1902, Private Papers 6th Marquis of Waterford, Curraghmore House.
9. Letter from Deputy Adjutant General, Dublin to Marquis of Waterford dated 14 March 1902, Private Papers 6th Marquis of Waterford, Curraghmore House.
10. Marchioness of Waterford's unpublished personal diaries 1902–1906 transcribed by Lady Katherine Dawnay.
11. Ibid.
12. Copy letter to King Edward VII from Lady Waterford dated 1902, Private Papers 6th Marquis of Waterford, Curraghmore House.
13. Copy Letter to St John Brodrick from Lady Waterford dated 28 August 1902, Private Papers 6th Marquis of Waterford, Curraghmore House.
14. F. Glenn Thompson has written an extensive article on the uniforms of the South Irish Imperial Yeomanry and South Irish Horse, published in *The Irish Sword* Vol XIII Summer 1977, No.50.
15. Marchioness of Waterford's unpublished personal diaries 1902–1906 transcribed by Lady Katherine Dawnay.
16. Copy letter to St John Brodrick from Lady Waterford dated 15 August 1902, Private Papers 6th Marquis of Waterford, Curraghmore House.
17. *Hansard HC* Deb 29 September 1909 vol 11 c1260. The Militia and Yeomanry Act, 1902, gave power generally to raise regiments of Yeomanry under Section 3 of the Militia Act, 1882, under which no regulations were required. Section 1, Sub-section (2) of the Militia and Yeomanry Act, 1902, relates to the regulations required for the reserve divisions of the Militia and Yeomanry (under Section 1, Sub-section (1) which may be found in Army Order 36 of 1903, and were laid before Parliament. Militia and Yeomanry Act (Irish Horse).
18. Marchioness of Waterford's unpublished personal diaries 1902–1906 transcribed by Lady Katherine Dawnay.

19. *The Irish Times* Wednesday 19 August 1903, p.7.

20. Ibid, Saturday 22 August 1903, p.22.

21. Ibid.

22. Letter to Colonel the Marquis of Waterford from Richard St Leger Moore dated 19 September 1903. Private Papers 6th Marquis of Waterford, Curraghmore House.

23. Patricia Jeffares. Unpublished notes from conversations with her father.

24. Various letters outlining the raising of a loan dated 1903 and estimates for uniforms Sandon and Co., Savile Row. Private Papers 6th Marquis of Waterford, Curraghmore House. Later, in 1907, the Dublin Industrial Development Association wrote a letter to the Marquis of Waterford complaining that the uniforms for the regiment were being made in England and not Ireland. Captain Burns-Lindow had, however, already offered Irish companies the opportunity to tender for the production of the uniforms in 1903. No Irish company showed any interest, so the regiment were forced to look elsewhere.

25. Letter from Bandmaster C.H. Allen replying to Dr McCabe on the procurement of the band dated 18 January 1904. Private Papers 6th Marquis of Waterford, Curraghmore House.

26. *The Irish Times*, 14 May 1904, p.13.

27. Ibid., 13 June 1904, p.9.

28. Ibid., 2 July, p.19.

29. South of Ireland Yeomanry Club Report of proceedings at the preliminary meeting of the South of Ireland Yeomanry Club. Private Papers 6th Marquis of Waterford, Curraghmore House.

30. *The Irish Times*, 6 January 1905, p.3.

31. Ibid., 25 March 1905.

32. Letter to Marquis of Waterford from A. White dated 29 April 1905. Private Papers 6th Marquis of Waterford, Curraghmore House.

33. 'Haldane's Reform of the Regular Army: Scope for Revision' Edward M. Spears *British Journal of International Studies*, Vol. 6, No.1 (April 1980), pp.69–81.

34. Notes from meetings between Lord Shaftsbury and Colonel E.S. May of the War Office dated 23 August 1907. Private Papers 6th Marquis of Waterford, Curraghmore House.

35. South of Ireland Imperial Yeomanry Conditions for joining the Special Reserve written by Colonel Lord Waterford undated. Private Papers 6th Marquis of Waterford, Curraghmore House.

36. *The Irish Times*, 11 July 1908 p.7.

37. Letter from Earl of Shaftsbury to Marquis of Waterford dated 17 July 1908. Private Papers 6th Marquis of Waterford, Curraghmore House.

38. *The Irish Times*, 21 November 1908, p.14.

39. Ibid., 9 September 1908, p. 7.

40. Ibid., 28 June 1909, p. 8.

41. Ibid., 19 May 1910, p.10.

42. Ibid., 27 June 1910, p.9.

43. Ibid., 19 August 1910, p.4.

44. Letter to Colonel the Marquis of Waterford dated 1 November 1910 in the Private Papers 6th Marquis of Waterford, Curraghmore House.

45. Letter to Officer Commanding South Irish Horse from Brigadier General 3 Cavalry Brigade 14 August 1911: Private Papers 6th Marquis of Waterford, Curraghmore House.

46. Letter to Marquis of Waterford from Captain Bankes dated 15 August 1911: Private Papers 6th Marquis of Waterford, Curraghmore House.

47. *The Irish Times* 9 December 1911, p. 1.

48. Ibid., 23 January 1912, p. 6.
49. Ibid., An Irishman's Diary, 14 January 1987.
50. Ibid., 18 May 1912, p.15.
51. Moorepark (House) was owned by the War Office having been purchased in 1903. The house itself was burned down by accident in 1908. http://landedestates.nuigalway.ie/LandedEstates/jsp/estate-show.jsp?id=2923.
52. The Curragh *The Curragh Incident* , Matt McNamara – www.curragh.info/home.htm.
53. *The Irish Times* 29 May 1914, p.8.
54. Ibid., 25 May 1914 p.7.

Chapter 2
1. 'With the South Irish Horse, Belgium 1914' by Major G.R. MacDonald, November 1974 *RIrRegt and SIH OCA Newsletter*.
2. *The Irish Times* 14 January 1987, An Irishman's Diary.
3. Letter to *The Irish Times* 26 April 1924.
4. The Diaries of Trooper George Dixon, A Troop S Squadron SIH, May 1977 *18th RIrRegt and SIH OCA newsletter*.
5. Typewritten copied diary entries of Trooper Louis Paul J. Allen, B Troop S Squadron SIH, National Library of Ireland, Wicklow Papers MS 38,626/8.
6. Unless indicated all movements of S Squadron are taken from their war diaries, series WO 95/2380 National Archives Kew.
7. The Diaries of Trooper George Dixon, A Troop S Squadron SIH, op. cit.
8. Typewritten copied diary entries of Trooper Louis Paul J. Allen, op. cit.
9. The Diaries of Trooper George Dixon, A Troop S Squadron SIH, op. cit.
10. Typewritten copied diary entries of Trooper Louis Paul J. Allen, op. cit,.
11. *Haig's Medical Officer – The Papers of Colonel Eugene 'Micky' Ryan CMG DSO RAMC* – Kindle Version ISBN 978 1 47382993 0 Pen and Sword – Location 655.
12. Typewritten copied diary entries of Trooper Louis Paul J. Allen, op. cit.
13. Ibid.
14. Ibid.
15. Ibid.
16. *The Irish Times* Wednesday 14 January 1987, An Irishman's Diary.
17. Typewritten copied diary entries of Trooper Louis Paul J. Allen, op. cit.
18. *The Irish Times* Wednesday 14 January 1987 An Irishman's Diary – Kevin Myers.
19. Parnell Kerr, *What the Irish Regiments Have Done*, Third Impression, T Fisher Unwin Ltd, April 1916, p.71.
20. The Diaries of Trooper George Dixon, , op. cit.
21. Ibid.
22. Gladys Costello Letter to 'Granny', *The Irish Times* Saturday 4 December 1915, p.12.
23. Typewritten copied diary entries of Trooper Louis Paul J. Allen, op. cit.
24. MacDonald, 'With the South Irish Horse, Belgium 1914', op. cit.
25. Typewritten copied diary entries of Trooper Louis Paul J. Allen, op. cit.
26. Spears, *Liaison 1914*, Cassell and Co., 3rd Ed, 2000, p,299.
27. Hurst, discharged from service as Time Expired on 24 April 1916, later died at home on 17 August 1917 of TB aggravated by his service in France. He is buried in St George's Burial Ground, Drumcondra.
28. Jago, commissioned into the South Irish Horse on 24 August 1917.
29. Typewritten copied diary entries of Trooper Louis Paul J. Allen, op. cit.
30. Ibid.

31. Ibid.

32. Ibid.

33. A troop typically comprised thirty-two men: therefore four troops would equal 128 men with 6 officers = 134 officers and men. The medal roll for S Squadron records 6 officers and 179 other ranks (ORs). Assuming each troop was up to strength, that would leave two officers and fifty ORs. An escort of approximately eight men and one officer would have also been required for General Haig. That left the Squadron at troop strength, albeit an enlarged troop until the prisoner escort returned.

34. Typewritten copied diary entries of Trooper Louis Paul J. Allen, op. cit.

35. National Archives Kew, WO95/1287, war diary 2nd Division.

36. Typewritten copied diary entries of Trooper Louis Paul J. Allen, op. cit.

37. French Light Infantry, recruited from Algeria, its members wearing Moorish dress.

38. National Archives Kew, WO95/1311 War Diary 2nd Cavalry Division.

39. Typewritten diary entries of Trooper Louis Paul J. Allen, 20 September 1914, op. cit.

40. National Archives Kew WO95/1287, op. cit. They were sharing the billet with the Highland Light Infantry (HLI) at the time. According to the war diary of 2nd Division the Worcestershire Regiment were in the billets when shelled, but it is acknowledged that two men of the HLI were hit.

41. Typewritten diary entries of Trooper Louis Paul J. Allen, 29 September 1914, op. cit.

42. Ibid.

43. These two infantry battalions, acting as GHQ troops, were much reduced following their heroic action at le Cateau.

44. Doyle, *The British Campaign in France and Flanders*, p.242 3rd Edition Hodder and Stoughton, 1916.

45. Typewritten diary entries of Trooper Louis Paul J. Allen, 22 October 1914, op. cit.

46. Commonwealth War Graves Commission Newsletter, October 2012.

47. *Evening Express*, 27 December 1917.

48. Ryan, op. cit., Kindle Locations 1456–1459).

49. *New York Times*, 15 September 1918.

50. Gould, *Locations of British Cavalry, Infantry and Machine Gun Units 1914–1924*, Heraldene Ltd 1977.

51. *Freeman's Journal* 24 November 1914, p.7.

52. Sheffield & Bourne, *Douglas Haig War Diaries and Letters 1914–1918*, p.77.

53. *Nenagh Guardian*, 12 December 1914.

54. Prendergast, *Cork Voices of WW1*.

55. Typewritten diary entries of Trooper Louis Paul J. Allen, 4 November, op. cit.

56. *London Gazette*, No. 29202, 22 June 1915, p.6134.

57. UK, Citations of the Distinguished Conduct Medal, 1914–1920 Regiment, Corps, or Unit: Yeomanry, p.9.

58. Typewritten diary entries of Trooper Louis Paul J. Allen, op. cit.

59. *Nenagh Guardian*, 12 December 1914.

60. National Archives Kew, MH106/282, No. 3 Casualty Clearing Station records.

61. *Nationalist and Leinster Times*, 28 November 1914, p.6.

62. The Diaries of Trooper George Dixon, May 1977 *18th RIrRegt and SIH OCA Newsletter*.

63. Ibid.

64. Ibid.

65. Ibid.

66. No. 828 Pte Thomas Jestin was one of three brothers. Martin (Sergeant), also serving in the Squadron at the time, was later to be commissioned in 7th/8th Royal Irish Fusiliers

but did not survive the war. He was killed in action on 7 June 1917. John Thomas, who emigrated to Canada before the war, served with 43rd Canadian Infantry and died in action north-west of Courcelette on the Somme on 8 October 1916.

67. Even though the fourteen men arrived in 1914, they were not entitled to the 1914, or 'Mons Star', as they had not been present in France or Flanders between the dates of 5 August and 22 November 1914, the qualifying date for this award under Army Order 350 of November 1917; the 1914–1915 Star was awarded to those men who were in a theatre of war up until the end of 1915.
68. *Nationalist and Leinster Times*, 12 February 1916.
69. National Archives Kew, WO95/1287, op. cit.
70. National Archives Kew, WO95/1324/2, war diary 2nd Division Mounted Troops, S Squadron S. Irish Horse, 1 May 1915–28 February 1916; all movements relating to the Squadron for May 1915 to February 1916 relate to this document unless indicated otherwise.
71. National Archives Kew, WO95/1287, op. cit. The enemy bombarded 2nd Division's rear lines very heavily between 12:45 and 1:45pm at Rue de l'Esprite.
72. *Nationalist and Leinster Times*, 12 February 1916, p.5.
73. Ibid.
74. Ibid.
75. Ibid.
76. National Archives Kew, WO95/1287, op. cit.
77. Tardif, *The North Irish Horse in the Great War*, p.92.
78. National Archives Kew, WO95/1287 and WO95/1097, op. cit.
79. Of the 186 men entitled to the 1914 Star (Mons Star), two men arrived in theatre later than the original August contingent, as replacements on 30 October 1914.

Chapter 3
1. National Archives Kew, WO/95/2141, war diaries A Squadron South Irish Horse, 1 September 1915–May 1916. Unless indicated, the dispositions and actions of the Squadron relate to this document.
2. *Yorkshire Telegraph and Star* Thursday 18 February 1915, p.5.
3. National Archives Kew, WO95/2128, war diary, 21st Division .
4. *The Irish Times*, 2 October 1915, p.4 .
5. *The Irish Times*, 9 October 1915, p.1.
6. National Archives Kew, WO95/2128, op. cit.
7. *The Irish Times*, 9 October 1915, 'South Irish Horse Under Fire'.
8. National Archives Kew, WO95/2128, op. cit.
9. National Archives Kew, WO95/2141, 21st Division Cyclist Company war diaries.
10. Haythornthwaite, *The World War One Source Book*, p.92.
11. National Archives Kew, WO95/2141, op. cit.
12. The National Archives of Ireland 1911 Census.
13. *The Irish Times*, 31 December 1915, p.9.
14. The National Archives of Ireland 1911 Census.
15. *Irish Independent*, 21 January 1916, p.6.
16. Ibid.
17. National Archives Kew, WO95/43112/2, war diary 21st Division Cyclists.
18. National Archives Kew, WO/95/2141/1, war diary A Squadron South Irish Horse September 1915–May 1916.

Chapter 4

1. Tardif, op. cit., p.77.
2. National Archives Kew, WO95/2380/1, war diary, B Squadron South Irish Horse 25 November 1915–31 May 1916.
3. Murland, *Departed Warriors,* p.135.
4. National Archives Kew, WO 213; Piece Number 6, pp.309–10 Judge Advocate General's Office: Field General Courts Martial and Military Courts, Registers.
5. *The Irish Times*, An Irishman's Diary, 15 September 1993.

Chapter 5

1. Johnstone, *Orange Green and Khaki – The Story of the Irish Regiments in the Great War 1914–1918*, p.97.
2. *Freeman's Journal*, 17 December 1915.
3. National Archives Kew, WO95/1962/1, war diary for C Squadron December 1915– May 1916.
4. National Archives Kew, WO95/2563, war diary June 1916, 39th Division.
5. National Archives Kew, WO95/2574/1, war diary for E Squadron 1 March–30 April 1916.
6. National Archives Kew, WO95/2563, op. cit.
7. *The Irish Times*, 29 July 1936 Irishman's Diary, p.4.

Chapter 6

1. National Archives Kew, WO95/930, war diary entries for I Corps Cavalry Regiment, unless otherwise indicated.
2. Patricia Jeffares, Unpublished notes from conversations with her father.
3. *Freeman's Journal*, 27 April 1917, p.3.
4. 'He was one of ten children. One of his sisters was my grandma. She told me that he was a young man, only eighteen. He was in the trenches, actually. The men around him told him to stay down but he wanted to get into the fray. He bolted up to shoot but, sadly he was shot and killed.' – Kathy Davis.
5. National Archives Kew, WO95/2664, war diary, 46th Division.
6. Recollections of Patsy Gregan relating to his Uncle John.
7. National Archives Kew, WO372, Medal Card Index and Rolls; National Archives of Ireland, 1911 Census.
8. National Archives Kew, WO363.M2/021160, Wilfred Avery Collins, Army Service Corps.
9. National Archives of Ireland 1911 Census; Commonwealth War Graves Commission.
10. National Archives Kew, WO95/2664, op. cit.
11. Europeana Collections 1914–198 Identifier 205315, 18096 Joseph Clynch http://www.europeana1914-1918.eu/en/contributions/18096.
12. Badsey, *Doctrine and Reform in the British Cavalry 1880–1918*, p.281.

Chapter 7

1. National Archives Kew, WO95/930/1, war diaries A and B Squadrons.
2. Ibid.
3. Baker/Milverton Associates *The Long Long Trail*.
4. National Archives of Ireland 1911 Census; Commonwealth War Graves Commission.
5. National Archives of Ireland 1911 Census; Commonwealth War Graves Commission.

6. Badsey, op. cit.
7. National Archives Kew, WO95/930/1, op. cit.
8. Stern, *Tanks 1914–1918 The Log Book of a Pioneer Lieutenant*, p.94.
9. Ibid., p.97.
10. National Archives Kew, war diary XV Corps Cavalry Regiment.
11. *Dover Express and East Kent News*, 14 September 1916, p.1.
12. National Archives Kew, WO95/2131/1, war diary, 21st Division, 1 August 1916–31 March 1917.
13. Ibid., WO95/1178, war diary, 19th Lancers (Fane's Horse).
14. Ibid., WO95/1213, war diary, HQ 1 Guards Brigade.
15. Ibid., 21st Division, op. cit.
16. National Archives of Ireland, 1911 Census; *The Irish Times*, 4 November 1916, p.1.
17. *Irish Independent*, 10 October 1916.
18. National Archives Kew, WO95/930, war diary, A Squadron Corps Cavalry.
19. Ibid.
20. Ibid., WO372, Medal Card index and Rolls.
21. National Archives of Ireland, 1911 Census; National Archives Kew, WO95/930, war diary A Squadron Corps Cavalry; Commonwealth War Graves Commission.
22. Honner, Unpublished recollections.
23. Moore, *Images of War – Animals in the Great War – Rare Photographs from Wartime Archives*, p.149.
24. National Archives Kew, WO95/623/1, war diary, I Corps Troops: HQ SIH and A, B, F & S Squadrons.
25. National Archives of Ireland, 1911 Census; Commonwealth War Graves Commission.
26. Unpublished copy of a letter to the Marchioness of Waterford from 36-year-old Archibald Goodchild, a valet in service at Curraghmore House. Archibald had been in France since 11 September 1915 with A Squadron. He was fortunate enough to be sent back to the Cavalry Depot and was therefore not transferred to 7th Royal Irish. He was transferred to the Labour Corps in May 1918 and survived the war.

Chapter 8

1. National Archives Kew, WO363, Army Service Records, 1914–1920, Soldiers Records, Burnt Documents Series.
2. CC, 29 September 1915.
3. Shannon, 'Memories of the South Irish Horse', *Newsletter, XVIIIth Royal Irish Regiment and South Irish Horse OCA*, November/December 1977.
4. National Archives Kew, Army Service Records, WO363, op. cit.
5. Ibid.
6. *Southern Star*, 29 August 1914.
7. *The Irish Times*, 12 June 1915, p.5.
8. National Archives Kew, WO213, Judge Advocate General's Office: Field General Courts Martial and Military Courts, Registers; op. cit.
9. *The Irish Times*, 11 November 1914.
10. British Red Cross Society report and balance sheet in *The Irish Times*, 13 February 1915, p.6.
11. *The Irish Times*, 27 March 1915.
12. *Irish Independent*, 12 June 1915.
13. *The Irish Times*, 12 June 1915, p.5.

14. *Nationalist and Leinster Times*, 31 July 1915, p. 4.
15. Ibid., 26 December 1915, p.6.
16. Ibid.,.17 July 1915, p.5.
17. Ibid., 10 July 1915, 2.
18. *The Irish Times*, 13 December 1915, p. 9.
19. *Nationalist and Leinster Times*, January 1916, p. 8.
20. Herlihy, *The Royal Irish Constabulary*, p.100.
21. Buckley, *Cahir – Glimpses of the Past*.
22. *The King's County Independent*, April 1916.
23. *The Cork Examiner*, 3 November 1916, p.2.
24. National Archives of Ireland, PLIC1-1442.
25. Bureau of Military History, WS889, p.62.
26. *The Cork Examiner*, 9 October 1916, p. 3.
27. Private Letter to Major McDonald, courtesy Sally Finn-Kelcey.
28. National Archives Kew, WO 213, Judge Advocate General's Office: Field General Courts Martial and Military Courts, Registers, op. cit.
29. National Archives Kew, WO363, op. cit.
30. National Archives Kew, WO372, op. cit.
31. Sheffield and Bourne, op. cit., p.390.
32. National Archives Kew, Medal Card index and Rolls.
33. National Archives Kew, WO 213, Judge Advocate General's Office: Field General Courts Martial and Military Courts, Registers, op. cit.
34. Commonwealth War Graves Commission.
35. www.rmsleinster.com.

Chapter 9

1. National Archives Kew, WO95/1979/2, war diary 7th (South Irish Horse) Bn Royal Irish Regiment unless otherwise indicated.
2. Unpublished notes, Lady Dawnay from letters to her mother, from Lt Col Burns-Lindow 5 January 1935.
3. Casey, Cullen and Duignan, *Irish Doctors in the First World War*.
4. *The Kerryman*, 9 June 2000, p. 20.
5. National Archives Kew, WO95/1979/2, op. cit.
6. Ibid., WO95/1976, war diary 49 Brigade 16th (Irish Division).
7. *De Ruvigny's Roll of Honour*, Vol., 4, p.183.
8. National Archives of Ireland, 1911 Census; Commonwealth War Graves Commission
9. *De Ruvigny's Roll of Honour*, op. cit.
10. National Archives Kew, WO95/1956/1-5, war diary 16th (Irish) Division.
11. Ibid.
12. Fielding, *War Letters to a Wife*.
13. Honner, op. cit.
14. This shelling was also mentioned by Rowland Fielding. He recounts that it was two, not one 'casual' shell causing the damage in *War Letters to a Wife*, p.244.
15. Short letter to Thomas' sister Harriet dated 17 December 1917. He also recounts meeting Tom Johnston, James Allardyce's stepbrother, in the Field and together with Ned Thomas' brother, spent an hour or two reminiscing about the 'old times'. Allardyce was a friend of both Harriet and the Fletcher brothers and lived in the same locality as the Fletcher family at Emo, County Laois. Thomas signed off his letter with the phrase

'Please excuse this whizz-bang as the candle is nearly nap-poo' [Whizz-bang = a short letter: Nap-poo = finished or useless.] By kind permission of Bryan Love.
16. Commonwealth War Graves Commission.
17. *Cork Examiner*, 25 February 1918, p.3.
18. National Archives Kew, WO95/1976/6, op. cit. Major F. Call's account of the battle on 21 March 1918 was written upon his release at the end of the war in March 1919.
19. Ibid., WO95/1976/6, op. cit.
20. Ibid., Major F. Call's account.
21. Unpublished letter to his Mother from Lindburg PoW Camp dated 6 October 1918. By kind permission Ken Tucker.
22. *London Gazette*, 30 January 1920.
23. Ibid.
24. Ibid.
25. National Archives Kew, WO95/1976/6, op cit.
26. Ibid.
27. Hastings, *The Oxford Book of Military Anecdotes*, pp.371–2.
28. National Archives Kew, WO95/1956/1-5, op. cit.
29. Commonwealth War Graves Commission.
30. National Archives Kew, WO95/1976/6, op. cit.
31. Bowman, *Irish Regiments in the Great War – Discipline and Morale*, passim.
32. National Archives Kew, WO 213, Judge Advocate General's Office, op. cit.
33. *The Birmingham Mail*, 25 November 1918 p.3.
34. Unpublished letter Richard Tucker 6 October 1918 Limburg PoW Camp. By kind permission Mr Tucker.
35. National Archives Kew, WO95/1976/6, op. cit.
36. Geoghegan, *The Campaigns and History of the Royal Irish Regiment Vol II From 1900–1922* pp.118–26.
37. Commonwealth War Graves Commission.
38. Second Lieutenant Stanton was awarded the Military Cross for his attempts to join up various platoons of B Company, stranded along the line.
39. National Archives Kew, WO95/1979/2, op. cit.
40. Geoghegan, op. cit.
41. National Archives Kew, WO95/1979/2, op. cit.
42. Geoghegan, op. cit.
43. Robert Switzer had been in the South of Ireland Imperial Yeomanry and South Irish Horse since 1904. He was a cattle dealer at the time, and was born in County Mayo and lived just outside Roscrea, County Tipperary, but subsequently moved to Dublin. At the beginning of the war he was a sergeant in C Troop S Squadron and travelled to France on 17 August 1914. He was awarded the Meritorious Service Medal on 17 October 1916 and commissioned in the Royal Irish Regiment on 25 June 1918
44. National Archives Kew, WO95/1979/2, op. cit.
45. Ibid.
46. Geoghegan, op. cit., p.126.
47. Commonwealth War Graves Commission.
48. Ibid.
49. Ibid.

Chapter 10
1. The National Archives Kew, WO 213, op. cit.
2. Buckley, *Cahir. Glimpses of the Past.*

3. Ibid.
4. Bureau of Military History 1913–1921, Document WS 1324, Joseph Barrett, Brigade Operations Officer, Mid–Clare Brigade 1908–1921.
5. Bureau of Military History 1913–21, WS 1023.
6. Bureau of Military History.
7. *Freeman's Journal*, 14 July 1921, p. 6.
8. www.cairogang.com.
9. *The Irish Times*, 18 April 1921.

Chapter 11
1. 'The Geddes Committee and the Formulation of Public Expenditure Policy, 1921–1922', McDonald, *The Historical Journal*, Vol. 32, No. 3 (September 1989), pp.643–74.
2. Geoghegan, op. cit., p.134.
3. Ibid.
4. *The Irish Times*, 9 June 1922, p. 4.
5. Ibid., 21 June 1922, p. 5.
6. Ibid., 10 November 1928, p. 7.
7. Ibid., 5 June 1928, p. 4.
8. Ibid., 18 March 1930, p. 6.
9. Office of Public Works.
10. *The Irish Times*, 27 June 1946, p. 3.
11. Ibid., 1 September 1915, p. 6.
12. French, *1914*, p.294.
13. Tardif, op. cit., p. 76.
14. Johnstone, op. cit., p.388.
15. *London Gazette*, 10 September 1918, p.10743.
16. Ibid., 11 March 1920, p.3029.
17. Ibid., 27 August 1918, p.10113.
18. Ibid., p.10117.
19. Ibid.
20. Ibid., 11 March 1919, p. 3246.
21. Ibid., 13 May 1919, p. 6026.

Appendix I
1. 1906 Muster, *South of Ireland Yeomanry Club Gazette.*

Bibliography

Anglesey, Marquess of, *A History of the British Cavalry 1816 to 1919, Volume 7: The Curragh Incident and The Western Front 1914* (Pen and Sword Books, Barnsley, 2013).

Babington, Arthur, *The Devil To Pay: The Mutiny of the Connaught Rangers, India, 1920* (Pen and Sword Books, Barnsley, 1991).

Badsey, Stephen, *Doctrine and Reform in the British Cavalry 1880–1918* (Ashgate Publishing Aldershot, 2008).

Banks, Arthur, *A Military Atlas of the First World War* (Reprint Pen and Sword Military, Barnsley, 2013).

Baxter, Biddy (Selected and Introduced by) *Dear Blue Peter* (Short Books, London, 2008).

Bowman, Timothy, *Irish Regiments in the Great War – Discipline and Morale* (Manchester University Press, 2003).

Buckley, Paul, *Cahir, Glimpses of the Past* (Kilkenny People Printing, 2008).

Burnell, Tom, and Seamus, *The Wicklow War Dead* (Nonsuch Publishing, Dublin, 2009).

Burnell, Tom, Gilbert, Margaret, *The Wexford War Dead* (Nonsuch Publishing, Dublin, 2009).

Burnell, Tom, *Irishmen in the Great War – Reports from the Front 1914* (Pen and Sword Military Books, Barnsley, 2014).

Casey, P.J., Cullen K.T., Duignan J.P., *Irish Doctors in the First World War* (Merrion Press, Sallins Co. Kildare, 2015).

Conan Doyle, Arthur, *The British Campaign in France and Flanders 1914* (Hodder and Stoughton Third Ed. London, 1916).

Denman, Terence, *Ireland's Unknown Soldiers – The 16th (Irish) Division in the Great War* (Irish Academic Press, Blackrock, Co. Dublin, 1992).

Dennehy, John, *In a Time of War – Tipperary 1914–1918* (Irish Academic Press, Dublin, 2013).

Fielding, Rowland, *War Letters to a Wife* (Reprint, Naval and Military Press).

French, John, Viscount of Ypres, KP OM, *1914, London Constable and Company Ltd, 1919.*

Geoghegan, Brigadier General Stannus CB, *The Campaigns and History of the Royal Irish Regiment Volume II From 1900 to 1922* (Reprint Schull Books, Co. Cork. 1997).

Gould, Robert W., *Locations of Cavalry, Infantry and Machine Gun Units 1914–1924* (Heraldene Ltd, South Woodford, 1977).

Hastings, Max (ed) *The Oxford Book of Military Anecdotes* (Oxford University Press, 1985).

Hayden, Mark *Forgetting to Remember* (Privately Published, 2015).

Haythornthaite, Philip J., *The World War I Source Book* (4th Edition, Brockhampton Press, 1998).

Herlihy, Jim *A Short History and Genealogical Guide – The Royal Irish Constabulary* (Four Courts Press, Dublin, 1997).

Holmes, Richard, *Riding the Retreat: Mons to Marne 1914 Revisited* (Second Edition, Pimlico, London, 2007).

Horne, John, (Ed) *Our War – Ireland and the Great War* (The 2008 Thomas Davis Lecture Series, Royal Irish Academy, Dublin, 2008).

Hill, Carol *Tickhill Discover its Past* (Tickhill and District Local History Society, Northend Creative Print Solutions, 2014).

Johnstone, Tom, *Orange Green and Khaki – The Story of the Irish Regiments in the Great War 1914–18* (Gill and Macmillan Dublin 1992.

Kenny, Brian and Mary, *News from the Front: Gorey and the Great War* (C and R Print, Enniscorthy, 2014).

Kenyon, David, *Horsemen in No-Man's Land: British Cavalry and Trench Warfare 1914–1918* (Pen and Sword Military, Barnsley, 2011).

Mileham, Patrick, *The Yeomanry Regiments: Over 200 years of Tradition* (Third Edition, Spellmount Limited, Staplehurst, 2003).

Moore, Lucinda, *Images of War: Animals in the Great War – Rare Photographs From Wartime Archives* (Pen and Sword Military, Barnsley, 2017).

Murland, Jerry, *Retreat and Rearguard 1914, The BEF's Actions from Mons to the Marne* (Pen and Sword Military Books, Barnsley, 2011).

——, *Battleground Europe Retreat of I Corps 1914* (Pen and Sword Military Books, Barnsley, 2014).

——, *Departed Warriors, The Story of a Family in War* (Matador, Leicester, 2008).

——, *Retreat and Rearguard Somme 1918, The Fifth Army Retreat* (Pen and Sword Military Books, Barnsley, 2014).

Orpen, William, *An Onlooker in France 1917–1919* (Williams and Norgate, London, 1924).

Parnell Kerr, S., *'What the Irish Regiments Have Done'* (Third Impression, Unwin Ltd, London, 1916).

Prendergast, Jean, *Cork Voices of WW1* (2015, Kindle Edition).

Putkowski, Julian, Dunning, Mark, *Murderous Tommies* (Pen and Sword Military Books, Barnsley, 2012).

Richardson, Neil, *A Coward If I Return, A Hero If I Fall: Stories of Irishmen in World War I* (The O'Brien Press, Dublin, 2010.

Ryan, Eugene P. (ed) *Haig's Medical Officer – The Papers of Colonel 'Micky' Ryan CMG DSO RAMC* (Pen and Sword Military Books, Barnsley 2013).

Sheffield, Gary, *The Chief: Douglas Haig and the British Army* (Aurum Press, London, 2011).

—— (ed), & Bourne, John, *Douglas Haig War Diaries and Letters 1914–1918* (BCA, 2005).

—— (ed), *War on the Western Front: In the Trenches of World War I* (Osprey Publishing, Oxford, 2008).

Spears, Edward, *Liaison 1914 A Narrative of the Great Retreat* (Cassell and Co., London, 2000).

Stern, Albert G., *Tanks 1914–1918 The Log book of a Pioneer* (Hodder and Stoughton, London).

Tardiff, Phillip, *The North Irish Horse in the Great War* (Pen and Sword Military Books, Barnsley, 2015).

UK National Archives, Kew

WO95: First World War and Army of Occupation War Diaries PART I: France, Belgium and Germany.

WO 372: Service Medal and Award Rolls Index, First World War (through Ancestry.co.uk).

Judge Advocate General's Office: Field General Courts Martial and Military Courts, Registers; Series: WO 213 (through Ancestry.co.uk).

Pension and Service Records, Part of the Burnt Documents Series (through Ancestry.co.uk).

The National Archives British Trench Map Atlas: The Western Front 1914–18 1:10,000 regular series – DVD Rom, The Naval and Military Press Ltd 2008.

National Museum of Ireland
The Wicklow Papers, MS 38,626/8.
Tipperary County Museum.

Online Sources
Ancestry.co.uk www.ancestry.co.uk.
Find My Past www.findmypast.co.uk.
Irish National Archives: Census of Ireland 1911 www.census.nationalarchives.ie.
Forces War Records: Military War and History Records www.forces-war-records.co.uk.
Commonwealth War Graves Commission www.cwgc.org.
The Long Long Trail www.longlongtrail.co.uk.
Irish Defence Forces Military Archives www.militaryarchives.ie.
Bureau of Military History www.bureauofmilitaryhistory.ie.

Newspapers, Journals and Periodicals
London Gazette.
Irish Times.
Irish Independent.
Cork Examiner.
Evening Herald.
Leinster and Nationalist Times.
Birmingham Mail.
The Freeman's Journal.
Southern Star.
Dover Express and East Kent News.
Yorkshire Telegraph and Star.
New York Times.
Evening Express.
Nenagh Guardian.
King's County Independent.
The Irish Sword.

Privately Published
South of Ireland Imperial Yeomanry Club Gazette.
18th Royal Irish Regiment and South Irish Horse Old Comrades' Association Newsletter.

Index